TWAYNE'S WORLD AUTHORS SERIES

A Survey of the World's Literature

Sylvia E. Bowman, Indiana University

GENERAL EDITOR

CHINA

William Schultz, University of Arizona

EDITOR

D0087447

Li Po-yuan

TWAS 607

中國近代小說家李伯元君

Mr. Lee Pah Yuen.

The Great Chinese Novelish, Poet and Jouinalist.

(b. 1867—d 1906)

Li Po-yuan

LI PO-YUAN

BY DOUGLAS LANCASHIRE

University of Auckland

TWAYNE PUBLISHERS

A DIVISION OF G.K. HALL & CO., BOSTON

First Printing

Library of Congress Cataloging in Publication Data

Lancashire, Douglas, 1926–
Li Po-yuan.

(Twayne's world authors series: China; TWAS 607)
Bibliography: p. 181–86
Includes index.
1.   Li, Pao-chia, 1867–1906—Criticism and interpretation.
PL2718.I2Z77   895.1'34   80–39733
ISBN 0–8057–6449–6

To Auriel, Terence, and Gail

Contents

About the Author

Professor Lancashire was born in Tientsin, North China, in 1926 of missionary parents. His home was, for some years, in Tatung, Shansi, but he attended the Tientsin Grammar School.

His family returned to England at the end of 1938. In 1944 he joined the Royal Air Force and in 1945 was made Instructor in Chinese at the School of Oriental and African Studies, London University. Following demobilization in 1947 he continued Chinese studies until 1950 when he attended King's College, London University, and studied Theology.

From 1952 till 1960 Prof. Lancashire represented the British, American, and Scottish Bible Societies in Hong Kong and lectured from time to time on the Philosophy of Religion at Chung Chi College (now part of the Chinese University of Hong Kong).

In 1960–61 he was Tutor in Theology at the Union Theological College, Hong Kong, and in 1961–62 was Visiting Lecturer in Chinese and the History of Chinese Thought at the University of Michigan, Ann Arbor.

In 1962 he was appointed Senior Lecturer in Chinese at the University of Melbourne, Australia, and in 1965 Foundation Professor of Chinese and Head of the Department of Asian Languages and Literatures at the University of Auckland, New Zealand.

Apart from articles on Chinese thought and literature published in a variety of journals, Prof. Lancashire has completed a study of the novelist Li Po-yuan (Li Pao-chia) for Twayne Publications; translations of Li Po-yuan's novel *Wen-ming hsiao-shih* and of Matteo Ricci's *T'ien-chu shih-i* are currently being considered for publication. A work entitled *Chinese Essays on Religion and Faith* will be published shortly.

Preface

If the imitation of another artist's work is an indication of the popularity of that work, then Li Po-yuan's fiction, and particularly his novel *The Bureaucracy Exposed*, must indeed have been popular in the first decade of this century, for it has been estimated by the young scholar, Lin Jui-ming, that between 1905 and 1911 some twenty-seven works of fiction were written in imitation of it. However, despite this popularity, and in spite of the importance of Li Po-yuan's novels (and of almost all fiction of this decade) as forerunners of modern Chinese fiction, it is remarkable that the study of his work (and of late-Ch'ing fiction generally), has been largely neglected in the West until the 1970s. Perhaps one of the reasons for this was the low opinion in which Li Po-yuan's and other late Ch'ing writers' works were held by such eminent scholars as Hu Shih. Another reason, however, has undoubtedly been the dearth of source materials outside China; a circumstance which has been remedied to a considerable extent through the valiant efforts of A Ying to rescue as many of these materials as possible and to have them published and made accessible to the scholarly world at large, and through the republication in recent years of some of the most representative fiction of the period.

It remains true, however, that direct access to original sources stored in China is impossible for most scholars in the West, and this writer, for one, is deeply conscious of the problems this raises when one is attempting to provide a comprehensive picture of the life and work of an author such as Li Po-yuan. A survey of the titles of writings attributed to him alone suggests that there was probably much more to Li Po-yuan's character than is visible to the reader of a mere handful of his novels.

Another matter of importance which must be mentioned here, and one which has played a great part in the shaping of this book, is the lack of any published English translation of any of Li Po-yuan's novels. A study of the work of Dickens, Trollope, or Hardy can be written on the safe assumption that the reader of it will also have read their novels, or at least have ready access to them, and therefore be able to relate the views of the critic to the novels themselves without much difficulty. Since no English version of any of Li Po-yuan's novels is yet available to the reader (though an English rendering of the first five chapters of *A Brief History of Enlightenment* has appeared in the journal *Renditions*), and lengthy comment divorced from the object of that comment can be of little use to anyone, we have deliberately included fairly lengthy excerpts from the novels surveyed, and hope that, in doing so, a fair balance has been struck between these two elements. The aim, then, has been to provide fact and comment on the one hand, and a sufficient sampling of the narratives of the various novels treated on the other.

A number of persons deserve my special thanks for the interest they have taken in my study of Li Po-yuan and, in particular, in my translation of his novel *A Brief History of Enlightenment*. These persons are Professor Cyril Birch, Professor C. T. Hsia, and Miss Han Ti-hou. Although their comments have been limited to the translation, they have, naturally, also had a bearing on this more general study. I would also like here to express my appreciation to Samuel Chang, librarian in charge of the Asian collection in the University of Auckland, for the great lengths to which he has gone to locate material for me, and to Jane Johnstone for her devotion to excellence in the typing of manuscripts. One other person to whom I am deeply indebted is my wife, who has not only borne patiently with my commitment to this task, but has read through the text and made numerous suggestions for its improvement. Needless to say, faults in the work are due entirely to my own shortcomings.

Douglas Lancashire

University of Auckland

Chronology

1867   Li Po-yuan born, probably in Wu-chin, Kiangsu province.

1896   Having tried several times, without success, to pass the triennial examinations for the *chu-jen* degree, Li Po-yuan goes to Shanghai and establishes the *Chih-nan pao* (*Guide*).

1897   Establishes the *Yu-hsi pao* (*Fun*).

1901   Declines opportunity to enter government service and begins to write *Keng-tzu kuo-pien t'an-tz'u* (*Ballad of the Rebellion of the Year Keng-tzu*) and *Kuan-ch'ang hsien-hsing chi* (*The Bureaucracy Exposed*). The latter was serialized in *Yu-hsi pao*.

1902   *Keng-tzu kuo-pien t'an-tz'u* completed and published.

1903   Establishment of the magazine *Hsiu-hsiang hsiao-shuo* (*Illustrated Stories*) and launching of first episodes of *Wen-ming hsiao-shih* (*A Brief History of Enlightenment*) and *Huo-ti-yü* (*Living Hell*). First three parts (36 chapters) of *Kuan-ch'ang hsien-hsing chi* completed. Li becomes editor of the *Shih-chieh fan-hua pao* (*Shanghai Sights*) and remaining chapters of the novel appear in this magazine.

1905   *Wen-ming hsiao-shih* completed.

1906   Li Po-yuan dies, having completed 48 chapters of the *Kuan-ch'ang hsien-hsing chi*. Ou-yang Chu-yuan (Mao-yuan Hsi-ch'iu Sheng) writes part 5 and completes the sixty-chapter novel.

CHAPTER 1

The Setting

THE commencement of the process of reform and modernization in China is commonly associated, in the mind of the layman, with the overthrow of the monarchy in 1911 and with the subsequent establishment of republican government. In reality, however, these events represented parts of the outcome of the process rather than its initiators, and its origins have, when investigated, to be pushed at least as far back as the 1860s. Our reason for fastening on the 1860s is because it was during these years of internal unrest and growing experience of the power of Western nations that the Chinese began seriously to consider the need to take remedial action, both to stabilize the nation politically and to strengthen it economically.[1] From the 1860s onward, various enterprises were supported and promoted by government and individuals, and this thrust in the direction of modernization, together with increasing dissatisfaction over the social, political, and economic circumstances of the time, came to stimulate a movement for overall reform at the center of which were such talented men as K'ang Yu-wei (1858–1927), T'an Ssu-t'ung (1865–1909), Liang Ch'i-ch'ao (1873–1929), Chang Chih-tung (1837–1909), and Huang Tsun-hsien (1848–1905).[2]

In spite of the political setback which these leaders were to experience following the debacle of the "Hundred Days of Reform" in 1898, the process of modernization gained momentum, so that by the middle of the first decade of the twentieth century noticeable developments had taken place in the fields of communications, industry, education, publishing, military organization, and the like.[3] The truth of the matter, then, is that although China was clearly in a state of political and economic decline during the latter years of Manchu rule, the decline was, nonetheless, accompanied by an ever-accelerating rate of change, and the signs were there, for those who could discern them, that the slide would be arrested in the long run,

13

and that a new nation was in the making which would write a fresh page in China's long history.

I   Growth and Importance of a Popular Press

One of the most important vehicles for the dissemination of modern ideas and knowledge was the press.[4] A semiofficial publication known as the *Ching pao* (*Peking Gazette*) had long been issued with court support in Peking, but this journal limited itself to the publication of official documents, decrees, memorials, etc., and although frequently reprinted in full or in abridged form for popular consumption, was, by its nature, of little use to the person eager for knowledge of the world exterior to that of the Chinese civil service.

Modern journalism was first introduced into China from Hong Kong and the "treaty ports" where, under foreign protection, the *China Mail* and the *Hong Kong Daily Press*, as well as other popular journals, were published for the benefit of the foreign community. However, commencing in 1858, and at the suggestion of the English-educated lawyer and future diplomat Wu T'ing-fang (1842–1922),[5] Chinese translations of the *Daily Press* were made and published under the title *Chung-wai hsin-pao* (*Sino-Foreign News*). This was followed by the *Chin-shih pien-lu* (*Hong Kong News*), which was a daily paper established by foreigners in 1864.[6]

Another pioneer of Chinese journalism was Wang T'ao (1828–?),[7] who had a close association with some of the most prominent Protestant missionaries of his day, and who is probably known outside China chiefly for his long cooperation with James Legge in the translation of the Chinese classics into English. He took over the editorship of the *Chin-shih pien-lu*, and then in 1873 or 1874 founded the *Hsun-huan jih-pao* (better known by its Cantonese name, *Tsun Wan Yat Pao*) with the help of Huang Sheng, one of the first three Chinese students to study in the United States, and Wu T'ing-fang. In 1872 the influential *Shen pao* (*Shanghai Daily News*) appeared in Shanghai, its publisher being a certain Frederick Major.[8] This was followed by the *Hu pao* (*Shanghai Press*) in 1882 which was connected to the *North-China Daily News and Herald*.[9] According to S. I. Woodbridge, there were only twelve daily newspapers in China in 1895. Ten years later, however, this number had multiplied many times, and popular publications were becoming more varied, many monthlies and weeklies appearing in addition to the dailies. As Woodbridge rightly concluded, it was through these papers that much of modern knowledge was popularized throughout the nation. They also contributed to the overthrow of the imperial government in 1911, not only through the dissemination of modern ideas, but also through their exposure of corruption in official circles.[10]

II *Fiction Allied to the Press*

But newspapers were not the only literary vehicle for change. Novels, too, were recruited as a means of communication to awaken the nation to the dangers confronting it both within and without. Already, as in the case of the eighteenth-century novel *Ju-lin wai-shih* (*Unofficial History of the Literati*), fiction had been used as a channel for criticism of the bureaucracy through the employment of satire;[11] but now, at this crucial stage in China's history, the novel was frequently turned into a weapon and was employed, not merely to lampoon the scholar-official, but to further the cause of reform and even revolution. The form of the novel at the turn of the century changed little from that of its traditional counterpart, but where it rejected the role of mere entertainer, and where it chose to reflect contemporary society rather than societies and events of the past, it stepped out in a new direction and became the forerunner of the modern novel. The novelist and the journalist found themselves allies in their concern for the future of Chinese society and the Chinese nation, and, in consequence, newspapers soon developed literary supplements to carry the new novels in serial form, and story magazines devoted to the novel and short story also flourished.[12]

Among the causes for the rapid growth of modern journalism and journalistic fiction were undoubtedly such innovations as the news and information pamphlets put out by the first Protestant missionaries working among the Chinese; the growth of a foreign language press in Hong Kong and other localities where there were concentrations of Europeans and Japanese; and the introduction of modern printing techniques which obviated the need to continue with the laborious task of carving wooden printing blocks. But what gave urgency to the process was increasing concern among the more radically minded of China's intelligentsia to enlist the Chinese people at large in the battle to save the nation from collapse and from dismemberment by the nations of the West and Japan, and an increasing awareness of the significant part that both the press and fiction could play in achieving this. Many Chinese in government service and in other walks of life, such as education and commerce, had been increasingly troubled over the direction which political events were forcing the nation to take, but the Sino-Japanese War of 1894, which culminated in the Treaty of Shimonoseki (April 1895), brought about such loss of territory, and laid such a burden of international debt on the shoulders of China, that the Chinese government no longer knew which way to turn to escape disaster. Solutions to the nation's dilemma were offered from a variety of quarters. In the autumn of 1895 Wen T'ing-shih, a metropolitan official, established a society which was called the Self-Strengthening Study Association. The words "self-strengthening" were rapidly taken up as a watchword by advocates of reform who believed that what was required was some form of constitutional parliamentary government. K'ang Yu-wei, the acknowledged leader of the educated elite who thought along these lines, soon took charge of the Association, while his close associate, Liang Ch'i-ch'ao, published the Association's daily newspaper. The journal was initially regarded with such favor that permission was given for it to be produced with the aid of the facilities of the *Peking Gazette* and to be circulated to the *Gazette*'s readers free of charge. [13]

As the alarm over recent political events gradually died down, however, K'ang came under increasing criticism for his unorthodox Confucian views, and he and his friends had eventually to leave the capital to seek for support among provincial officials who had a greater understanding of the issues and who were consequently more progressive in their views. Liang Ch'i-ch'ao moved to Shanghai where, in August 1896, he established the *Shih-wu pao* (*Current Events*) as the successor to his Peking journal. But the experience of the Sino-Japanese War and its aftermath and the growing eagerness of various government officials to effect reforms meant that there was finally a willingness on the part of many men in authority to discuss political, economic, and educational issues openly, and the government, which had so far refused to grant the public the right, legally, to read newspapers, came to regard the dissemination of information as one of its duties. Senior officials in various provinces put in blanket orders for newspapers which they then circulated to the officials beneath them. Chang Chih-tung, a supporter of K'ang, for example, while viceroy of Hupei, had a standing order for 288 copies of *Current Events* which he distributed to every *yamen* ("official residence"), college, and school under his jurisdiction, and similar action was taken by the governors of Chekiang and Hunan and by Yuan Shih-k'ai (1859–1916). [14]

III *Reform, Reaction, and the Press*

In 1897 a fresh crisis shook the government in Peking out of any complacency into which it might have been drifting. This was the murder of two German missionaries in November of that year and the subsequent insistence by Germany that China lease the Kiaochow Bay region to her and grant her railway, mining, and preferential rights in the province of Shantung.[15] Before long K'ang Yu-wei was in touch with the Chinese Foreign Office (Tsung-li Yamen) and, finally, with the emperor. Convinced that K'ang and his friends held the key to the resolution of China's difficulties, the emperor brought them into the government under his own sponsorship. Liang's newspaper, *Current Events*, now became an official journal and he was authorized to establish a college of translators.

Decrees reflecting the wishes of the reformers now appeared in rapid succession. They struck at the old educational system by calling for the modernization of existing schools, the abolition of traditional examinations, and the establishment of a university in Peking. They ordered the setting up of a national bank and government organizations and bureaus to administer agriculture, industry and commerce, railways, and mining. A budget system was to be introduced, the army was to be restructured, and the bureaucracy was to be reformed through, among other things, the abolition of the system which permitted the purchase of rank and office.[16]

The torrent of measures initiating reform lasted a hundred days and then was brought to a halt by the empress dowager who, as leader of a conservative reaction, reassumed power in September 1898, confining the emperor to his quarters where he remained a virtual prisoner, and putting six of the leaders of the reform party to death.[17] Fleeing the capital, K'ang Yu-wei, Liang Ch'i-ch'ao, and others of their colleagues made their way to Shanghai, Japan, Singapore, and Hong Kong where they carried on their campaign for change by seeking to broaden their support, particularly in urban areas. In the cities, and especially in a center like Shanghai, where the cultural and political life of the West was made known to the literate through the Western press and through a growing number of Chinese translations of Western books, awareness of the part the press and fiction could play as instruments of education and change was intensified, and increasing use came to be made of them to win support for the reformists' cause. As the conservatives strengthened their hold on the nation's affairs, the feeling that more radical solutions than had hitherto been tried were needed to save China became widespread, and the views of men like K'ang Yu-wei, who sought to preserve the monarchy, were increasingly eclipsed by the idea that the monarchy would have to go and that it and the whole governmental structure should be replaced with a republican system.

Among the measures taken to reverse the policies of the period of the "Hundred Days of Reform" was the issuance of an edict explicitly forbidding the opening of newspaper offices. The purpose behind this and other edicts was clearly to have the press shut down throughout the country. K'ang Yu-wei and Liang Ch'i-ch'ao were singled out for vilification and their publications banned. Even journals that were politically relatively harmless were to suffer.[18]

With constraints put on them throughout the nation many publishers had no alternative but to transfer their operations to the foreign settlements or to arrange for foreigners to appear as the proprietors of their papers. But there were compensations. The Chinese press was able to make free use of anything that interested them in the foreign press around them, and since the Chinese press at first had no telegraph agency of its own, a high percentage of its news items consisted of material translated from foreign journals and periodicals.[19]

Although reform-minded publishers were anxious, as we have seen, to attract as wide a readership as possible, it is probable that the majority of Chinese newspaper readers was made up of students. The Chinese authorities had laid down a general rule that students were to refrain from participation in journalistic enterprises and that any written work not related to the school curriculum and not required for reference purposes was not to be taken into a school.[20] But whatever success the government might have thought it had in implementing this rule in schools outside the foreign-controlled settlements and concessions, the aim behind the rule, namely, the insulation of youth from radical journalism, was everywhere thwarted. Further, large numbers of students, both state supported and private, were now studying in Japan where they were increasingly coming under the influence of radical reformists and revolutionaries. Inspired by Sun Yat-sen (1866–1925) as well as by Liang Ch'i-ch'ao, overseas students in Japan began to publish on a large scale, and the Chinese government was powerless to stop them. Thinking to stem their influence in China, the government ordered that none of these journals was to be read in school on pain of expulsion, and that school authorities were to be dismissed from their posts should they fail to report infringements of the rules. In practice, however, it proved impossible to police these regulations, and authorities frequently turned a blind eye to those who broke the law.[21] With the resumption of power by the empress dowager, provincial authorities quickly stepped into line and changed their policy from one of encouragement of the press to one of repression. Publications by Liang Ch'i-ch'ao such as his *Hsin hsiao-shuo (New Fiction)*, and the book *Ko-ming chün (Revolutionary Army)* by Tsou Jung (1885–1905), were strictly forbidden, and more than twenty other similar journals and publications were also listed by the government which, if read or sold, could result in dire consequences for the offenders.[22] However, the more the government sought to restrict these newspapers and periodicals, the more they increased their readership in China. This was especially true of revolutionary journals which promoted nationalism and demanded the overthrow of the Manchus.[23]

IV *The* Su pao *Episode*

Seeking to stem the tide, the government looked for ways to curtail the activities of certain newspapers in Shanghai. The most celebrated example of its efforts in this direction was a court case which it brought against the *Su pao*. First published in 1897, the contents of the paper remained fairly innocuous until 1900 when it was purchased by a certain Ch'en Fan of Heng-shan in Hunan. Ch'en had been a magistrate of Ch'ien-shan *hsien* in Kiangsi and had been dismissed from office because of a legal case which had involved the Christian church. Resentful and angry over his treatment and what he saw as the decadence and corruption of officialdom, he determined to influence public opinion against it by turning the *Su pao* into a vehicle for his views. He began by advocating reform under the monarchy, but later adopted a position in which he called for outright revolution. The intensity and virulence of his attacks increased as his thinking grew more radical. Inviting men of known extreme views to serve as his editors, he turned the *Su pao* into a platform and the publishing company into a center for the promotion of revolution.[24]

Unable to keep silent in the face of insults and incitements to revolution, the court secretly telegraphed the viceroy of the Kiangnan provinces in Nanking as well as the governor of Kiangsu ordering them to take action to have the paper closed down. A warrant was issued for the arrest of the revolutionaries associated with the *Su pao*.

Ignoring rumors that action was being brought against them, the editors of the *Su pao* continued to publish as before. Prior to the case against the publishers being heard in court a strong appeal was made to the diplomatic corps and to the Shanghai Municipal Council for the paper to be closed down. On 6 July the foreign authorities obliged. The court, however, wanted also to extradite the offenders in order to punish them, but the consular body would not agree to this. In consequence, a special court was convened and lawyers representing both sides argued the case in Shanghai. The court met four times during which the crown maintained that since the throne had been insulted, and since the two chief culprits, Chang Ping-lin (1868–1936) and Tsou Jung, had behaved in a treasonable manner, they were deserving of death. However, since the throne wanted to be magnanimous, said the representatives of the crown, they would only ask for life imprisonment. Because of strong feeling generated by the case among the populace, the consular body refused to acquiesce, and negotiations were therefore entered into in Peking. The court in Shanghai finally sentenced Tsou Jung to two years imprisonment and Chang Ping-lin to three years. Two other accused were released.

The crown appeared to have won the day, but in reality its position in the country had been severely weakened. Sure of protection and a fair deal as a result of this trial, more publishing companies than ever before began to make the International Settlement their center of operations. Shortly after the *Su pao* was closed down, a new newspaper, the *Kuo-min jih-jih pao* (*National Daily*), was established in Shanghai. The men behind it were the same as those who had formerly been involved with the *Su pao*, but a foreigner by the name of A. Gemell was listed as the paper's proprietor. Its aims were the same as those of the defunct paper, but it was organized on a much larger scale. Its supplement, *Hei-an shih-chieh* (*World of Darkness*), was nationalistic in outlook and directed its attacks on corruption in the civil service. Various attempts were made by Chinese officials to hinder the circulation of this newspaper, but their efforts proved on the whole unsuccessful.[25]

V *The Emergence of the Political Novel*

Awareness of the part the novel could play in society can be traced back to an article which appeared in the first issue of the *Kuo-wen pao* (*National News*) in Tientsin in 1897. In this article entitled "Our

Reasons for Printing Fiction" the important translator of Western scientific and sociological works, Yen Fu (1853–1921), and the writer and critic Hsia Sui-ch'ing (1865–1924), set out to elucidate the value of the novel. Their comments can be classified under the following three headings, (1) the value of traditional fiction, (2) the usefulness of fiction in their own day, and (3) the techniques which should be employed in the writing of contemporary fiction. The value of traditional fiction, they said, lay in its ability to bring past history to life. History as it was found in the twenty-four orthodox dynastic histories was dead for the bulk of the population, but this could not be said for history as it was treated in the great novels of the past. However, fiction, they said, also kept a different kind of history alive, for it often attached importance to heroes whom the orthodox histories killed off. Its usefulness (and by implication the usefulness of contemporary fiction), then, lay in the fact that it provided a counterweight to "orthodox" history—a method for ensuring that other points of view would also be heard.[26]

Writing of the techniques necessary to a successful piece of fiction, Yen Fu and Hsia made five points: (1) the language used had to be as close as possible to spoken Chinese; (2) the language had to be contemporary; (3) the language had to be ample in the sense that it had to avoid the economy of classical Chinese; (4) it had to deal with everyday life; and (5) it had to "give form to popular aspirations."[27]

In a subsequent article of his own, in which he shifted his stance and adopted a more radical view of what a work of fiction should set out to accomplish in his own day, Hsia stated that instead of drawing on the heroes and historical events of the past, or merely inventing incidents, the novel should now reflect life as it was, depicting everyday events and portraying poverty and petty villainy. The author should draw on his own experience and refrain from comment. Fiction's other task, he held, was to "inculcate patriotism, democratic republicanism, a scientific outlook and national unity."[28]

Summing up his case for treating fiction as an important branch of literature, Hsia said: "There have always been two schools of thought and taste in China, that of scholars and gentry, and that of women and illiterates. Hence China's fiction also falls into two schools, one for scholars and gentry, the other for women and illiterates. . . . With the frontiers of knowledge expanding and scholars and gentry never idle, there is no need to further task their eyes with fiction. For women and illiterates, however, there are no books to read, yet they hunger for education; fiction is the only way."[29]

It is evident from the foregoing that some Chinese, no doubt as a result of increasing knowledge of the importance attached to the novel in the West, were now prepared to upgrade the status of fiction in China. However, it was not until Liang Ch'i-ch'ao added the weight of his authority as a leader of the reform movement to the elevation of this branch of literature by establishing a journal devoted to fiction, which he called *Hsin hsiao-shuo (New Fiction)*, in 1902, that late Ch'ing fiction, with its distinctive features, was truly launched.

Liang Ch'i-ch'ao, as a politically minded young scholar, had long recognized the important role the novel could play in the transformation of China into a modern state, and in 1898 had coined the term "political novel." In an article to which he gave the title "The Translation and Printing of Political Novels" he had asserted that progress in the political worlds of Western nations and Japan was directly related to the part the novel played in heightening political awareness. Unlike Yen Fu and Hsia Sui-ch'ing in their first article, however, Liang held the traditional Chinese novel in low regard, maintaining that works like *Dream of the Red Chamber* and *Water Margin* "were nothing but persuasion to lust and banditry." [30] Also, unlike Hsia, who had called for the simple recording of contemporary life with no comment, Liang saw the novel serving a didactic function among the common people similar to that served by the Confucian classics among the educated elite. "Few people who can barely read will read the classics," he said, "but they will all read fiction. Since they can't be taught by means of the Six Classics, fiction should be used. . . ." [31] But if the traditional novel exercized a bad influence on its readers, it was clear that "new fiction" had to be written to displace it. In the first issue of his magazine *New Fiction*, therefore, Liang stated: "To renew the people of a nation it is imperative to renew the fiction of that nation. Thus, to renew morality one must renew the novel; to renew religion one must renew the novel; to renew politics one must renew the novel; to renew customs one must renew the novel; to renew learning and the arts one must renew the novel; and if one wishes to renew the human mind and the human personality, then one must renew the novel." [32]

Liang argued that the novel wielded such incalculable power that it could control men's minds and was capable of transforming society. All the great writings of philosophers and sages, he said, had proved incapable of instructing the masses, whereas only one or two novels could more than corrupt them. On the other hand, one or two good novels could influence society for the better more than a thousand works of high-flown philosophy. Thus the novel had to be regarded as the highest form of literature. If one wished to bring about improvements in government, one had to begin by bringing about a revolution in the world of fiction, and if one wanted to renew the people, it was necessary to begin by reforming the novel.[33] In other words, the supreme importance of the novel lay not in its existence as a work of art, but in its power to educate and to influence the moral climate of a nation.

Although this article was followed by further articles on the novel by other writers, their views remained substantially the same as those put forward by Liang. The only person, says A Ying, to make any fresh contribution was T'ien-lu Sheng [34] who, in his article "An Historical Review of the Chinese Novel" published in the *Yueh-yueh hsiao-shuo* (*The All-Story Monthly*), stated that the motive for writing novels should be threefold: to express anger over government oppression, pain at the turbidity of society, and distress over the lack of freedom in marriage. T'ien-lu Sheng also made concrete suggestions regarding creative writing and translations. He advocated realism: the selection of facts which accorded with the circumstances of society and a format which the people of the nation would appreciate.[35]

Not everyone agreed with Liang in his evaluation of the traditional novel, but his comments did serve to encourage fresh assessments of its place in Chinese letters. Employing the goals of the political and social reformists as their yardstick, scholars and writers investigated such popular novels and plays as *Dream of the Red Chamber*, *Peach Blossom Fan*, and *Chin, P'ing, Mei*, and came down with fresh estimates of their worth as social documents. Disagreeing with Liang and approximating to the opinions expressed in the joint article by Yen Fu and Hsia Sui-ch'ing, they asserted that *Water Margin*, for example, advocated democracy and human rights, and that the *Liao-chai Fairy Tales* were to be classified as anti-Manchu tracts.[36]

Liang Ch'i-ch'ao's *New Fiction* was the earliest of the magazines devoted to fiction.[37] It first appeared in 1902 in Japan and ran to two volumes (*chuan*). It was followed in 1903 by Li Po-yuan's fortnightly *Hsiu-hsiang hsiao-shuo* (*Illustrated Stories*) which was published by the Commercial Press. This magazine continued through seventy-two issues and serialized two of Li's own novels: *Wen-ming hsiao-shih*

(*A Brief History of Enlightenment*) and *Huo ti-yü* (*Living Hell*), as well as the well-known *Lao Ts'an yu-chi* (*The Travels of Lao Ts'an*) by Liu E (1857–1909).[38]

The innovations of Liang Ch'i-ch'ao and Li Po-yuan, the new journalism, and the social and political climate of the times combined to encourage an unprecedented flow of publications, so much so, that it has been estimated that between 1902 and 1911 a dozen vernacular newspapers, at least thirty literary magazines, fifty titles of vernacular textbooks, and over 1,500 novels were published. Although about one thousand of the novels were later to appear in book form, almost all were first serialized in newspapers or in the magazines devoted to the encouragement of new fiction, and ninety percent of them can be said to have been inspired by the movement for reform.[39] Instead of merely seeking to entertain, novelists deliberately set out to reflect the circumstances then prevailing in government and society. So thoroughly did they do this that A Ying is able to classify the fiction of this period under the following headings: novels reflecting the social conditions of the last years of the Ch'ing dynasty; novels dealing with events during the Boxer Uprising of 1900; novels reflecting opposition to the treaty governing Chinese immigration into the United States; novels expressing the need to develop trade and industry in order to counter rising imports from abroad; novels in which the merits and demerits of constitutional government are aired; novels advocating revolution; novels concerned with the liberation of women; novels expressing opposition to superstition; novels devoted to the exposure of the lives of effete officials; and historical and court-case novels. In most of these novels writers intentionally attacked what they considered the evils then current in government and society. Internal rebellions, external aggression, the existence of treaty ports and concessions, the imposition of indemnities by foreign powers, etc., all served as further grist for the writer's mill.[40]

In his survey of late Ch'ing fiction A Ying sums up his assessment as to its worth by stating that although the novels of this period generally fall short of great literature, they do reveal new developments in the history of Chinese fiction.[41] They reflect the new interest in *all* levels of society, and by attempting to describe these various levels they react against the tendency to write only of "talented men and beautiful women." Apart from their entertainment value, they were also tracts for their times, probing beneath the surface respectabilities, satirizing the custodians of knowledge and power, and serving to inform the general public of the many new ideas, both scientific and

social, which were pouring into the country. Intentionally and unintentionally, the authors of this period contributed to the political and
social revolution which has marked the first half of the twentieth
century and, in the process, directed the Chinese novel along new
paths.[42]

VI   *The Life of Li Po-yuan*

In histories of Chinese literature the novelists usually mentioned
as representative of the late Ch'ing period are Li Po-yuan, Wu
Chien-jen (1867–1910), Liu E, and Tseng Meng-p'u (1871–1935).
Their works are mentioned for their literary merit, but also because
they, more than any others, are felt accurately to reflect late Ch'ing
society.

Li Po-yuan, with whom this study is concerned, lived out his short
life against the background of the declining power of the Chinese
government, the constant humiliation of the nation at the hands of
foreign powers, and rapid social change. Li's childhood years witnessed the grim aftermath of the T'ai-p'ing (1850–1864) and Nien-fei
(1853–1868) rebellions, and throughout his life he was to see the
successive loss of Chinese territory to foreign nations, the establishment of an increasing number of foreign concessions on Chinese soil,
and the Boxer Rebellion of 1900, which was followed by demands
from foreign powers for the payment of a crippling indemnity. He
was also, however, and particularly as a resident of Shanghai, to
become increasingly aware of the modern world outside China, of the
aims and aspirations of the reformists and revolutionaries, and of the
subtle changes which were already coming about in some areas of
Chinese society as a result of the intellectual ferment in the major
cities of the nation.

Sources of information for the life of Li Po-yuan are very meager
indeed, and those that are available provide us with only the briefest
of details. Undoubtedly the most important of these sources is an
obituary written by the novelist Wu Chien-jen who was a close friend
of Li. His style of writing has much in common with Li's, and he is
believed to have completed one of Li's unfinished novels following
his death.

The obituary, which was printed along with a photograph of Li
shortly after his death, appeared in number 3 of the *Yueh-yueh
hsiao-shuo*[43] of which Wu was the editor. According to Wu, Li was
born on the eighteenth of the fourth month of the year *ting-mao*

(1867) in the reign of the Emperor T'ung-chih (1862–1874). His personal name was Pao-chia and his style Po-yuan, and he was a native of Wu-chin (formerly called Ch'ang-chou) in Kiangsu province. He had a number of assumed names, but the one by which he was best known was Nan-t'ing t'ing-chang ("Keeper of the Southern Pavilion"). Wu tells us that Li was "no ordinary man" and that he "had the talent to rescue [his country]." However, continues Wu, "deeming it shameful to be a parasite and to cling to high-ranking officials," he remained in relative obscurity. Employing his pen to lament and to bewail [the times] he wrote literature which poked fun at, but which also castigated [the men of his day]."

Turning to his journalistic activities, Wu tells us that Li established (1897) the *Yu-hsi pao (Fun)*, the earliest of the Shanghai tabloids, and that he thereby created a whole new format in Chinese journalism. Quickly imitated by possibly more than ten other publishers, Li took great delight in finding ways to keep ahead of his competitors. Selling *Fun*, he established another tabloid called the *Fan-hua pao (Shanghai Sights)* which the eminent Chinese scholar, Hu Shih (1891–1962), later claimed was still being published in 1904 when he visited Shanghai.

In 1901 the court was seeking for scholars with administrative abilities. Wu tells us that Vice-President of a Board, Tseng Mu-t'ao of Hsiang-hsiang in Hunan, recommended Li for selection, but that Li declined the opportunity to enter government service with the words, "This is not the time for me to serve as an official."

Wu next asserts that jealousy of Li led certain officials to try to impeach him, but that Li's reaction was simply to laugh and say, "These people certainly know me!" Li then began to devote himself to the writing of fiction, his principal aims being to improve people's understanding of the rapidly changing world and to reprove those who were failing in their public duties. Concerned, says Wu, "over the dreams, hopes, and aspirations of men, women, and children and at their lack of understanding of current events, [Li] wrote his *Keng-tzu kuo-pien t'an-tz'u [Ballad of the Rebellion of the Year Keng-tzu (1900)]*." Hated and pursued by certain corrupt officials, Li next composed the *Kuan-ch'ang hsien-hsing chi (The Bureaucracy Exposed)*. "Lamenting that society should go with the stream and have no knowledge of progress," says Wu, Li "wrote the novels *Chung-kuo hsien-tsai chi [China Today]*; *Wen-ming hsiao-shih [A Brief History of Enlightenment]*, and *Huo ti-yü (Living Hell)*." Each novel seems to have been well received by the public, and so successful was he, says Wu, "that others wrote novels which they published under his name—a clear indication of the importance society attached to him."

Wu's final comment is that "If Heaven had allowed him more years [Li's] output would not have been limited to these few books. Because he was disaffected with society, however, he only lived to the age of forty. Alas that his talents should have been known to posterity only through fiction. Li's misfortune, however, was the world of fiction's good fortune."

Our second major source of information is an article by Hu Shih which is to be found in *Hu Shih wen-ts'un* (*Collected Writings of Hu Shih*). Hu Shih states in this article, which is essentially a critical study of *The Bureaucracy Exposed*, that few had any information concerning Li and that he had based the biographical section of his essay chiefly on Lu Hsün's *A Brief History of Chinese Fiction*, the information in which had been partly derived from a work entitled *Hsin-an pi-chi san* (*Jottings from Hsin-an*) by a certain Chou Kuei-sheng and partly from a long letter originally written to Hu Shih by Li's nephew, Li Tsu-chieh.[44] Much of the information Hu provides is similar to that detailed by Wu. He says, however, that Li hailed from Shang-yüan (rather than Wu-chin) in Kiangsu and that in his youth he studied the "eight-legged essay" as well as poetry and *fu* ("poetic essays"). He came first in the *hsiu-ts'ai* ("baccalaureate") examination and later attempted, on several occasions, to pass the triennial provincial examination for the *chu-jen* ("second") degree, but without success. Later he moved to Shanghai where he managed the *Chih-nan pao* (*Guide*), and on its closure established *Fun*.

As we have already seen, both this latter paper and *Shanghai Sights* were tabloids, a format pioneered by Li. According to Hu Shih, the Shanghai tabloids, of which there was soon a considerable number, were devoted to publishing information on the daily lives of prostitutes and visitors to brothels, and on the lives of actors and the like. Among these tabloids, says Hu, "*Shanghai Sights* stood out for the quality and charm of its writing." [45]

Li, says Hu, was a man of great talent and artistry and his poems, lyrics, and essays are to be found scattered among each of the tabloids of the time. He was also skilled at carving seals, and a treatise on seals by him entitled *Yü-hsiang yin-p'u* (*A Treatise on Seals*) was in circulation for some time.[46]

Hu states that when Li died at the age of forty he had no son and was very lonely. He had a good friend, however, in the person of Sun

Chu-hsien, an actor famous at the time in the Southern Theater, who arranged and paid for his funeral.[47]

VII   *Li Po-yuan's Novels*

Corroborating Wu Chien-jen's statements, Hu asserts that Li's long novels come from the period following the Boxer Uprising in 1900. He tells us that Li began *The Bureaucracy Exposed*, his longest novel, in 1901 and completed the first three sections of it in 1903, each section containing twelve chapters (*hui*). Another section was completed between 1904 and 1905, and since Li died in the following year, 1906, he believed that the fifth and final section was perhaps completed by another person who carried the novel through to its sixtieth chapter. When he died *Shanghai Sights* was serializing another of Li's novels which was concerned with life in the brothels of Shanghai. Hu tells us he had forgotten the name of this work at the time of writing, but that he had heard that a friend of Li with the surname Ou-yang continued the novel, though he had no idea what eventually became of it. The only novel Li actually completed, according to Hu, was *A Brief History of Enlightenment* which first appeared in serial form in *Hsiu-hsiang hsiao-shuo* (*Illustrated Stories*), the biweekly magazine devoted to fiction which was published by the Commercial Press and of which Li was the editor; only later was it published as a complete work.[48]

That there appears to be some uncertainty regarding the number of novels and other works actually written by Li Po-yuan is confirmed, not only by the obituary composed by Wu Chien-jen in which, as we have seen, Wu asserted that other writers had passed their work off as Li's, but also by Chao Ching-shen's preface to the edition of *Living Hell* published in Shanghai in April 1956. In this preface Chao states that apart from the four novels commonly attributed to Li: *Ballad of the Rebellion of the Year Keng-tzu (1900)*, *The Bureaucracy Exposed*, *A Brief History of Enlightenment*, and *Living Hell*, he also wrote *Hai-t'ien hung-hsüeh chi* (*Boundless Snow*)—an incomplete novel of twenty chapters in the Shanghai dialect which portrays the world of prostitution in Shanghai and which is probably the novel the title of which Hu Shih could not recall—and, according to Chou Kuei-sheng's *Jottings*, two works entitled *Li Lien-ying* (the name of the empress dowager's favorite eunuch) and *Fan-hua meng* (*Extravagant Dreams*). Chao also remarks that according to a book list put out by the Liu-i shu-chu (Six Arts Publishing Company), four further works are to be attributed to Li: the titles of these, with possible English equivalents, are *I-yuan ts'ung-hua* (*Comments on the Arts*), *Hua-chi ts'ung-hua* (*Humorous Comments*), *Ch'en-hai miao-p'in* (*Masterpieces of the World*), and *Ch'i-shu k'uai-tu* (*Glimpses of Unusual Writings*). Two other works commonly associated with Li are the *Nan-t'ing pi-chi* (*Jottings from the Southern Pavilion*) and *Nan-t'ing ssu-hua* (*Four Kinds of Comment from the Southern Pavilion*).

Unfortunately, with the exception of *Four Kinds of Comment from the Southern Pavilion*, none of the foregoing additional works listed by Chao Ching-shen seems to be available outside China, and it is therefore impossible to make any meaningful comment on them beyond stating that if the majority are similar in character to *Four Kinds of Comment*, they will be largely collections of anecdotes and brief comments on a variety of topics.

One other work needs to be mentioned before we conclude these remarks on writings attributable to Li Po-yuan. In his *Hsiao-shuo hsien-t'an* (*Leisure Chats on Fiction*) A Ying devotes a chapter to the authorship of the incomplete novel *Hsing-shih yuan* (*A Call to Wakefulness*) the twenty chapters of which were published in *Illustrated Stories*. On the basis of the themes treated by the author—attacks on superstition, foot-binding, and inherited wealth—and as a result of an analysis of the language and style of the text of the work, he concludes that we have here another novel in the making by Li.[49]

VIII *Major Themes of Li Po-yuan's Novels*

Even a cursory reading of the four major novels which are the subject of this study makes it clear that Li Po-yuan was a political novelist and a reformist who, though concerned to entertain and to amuse his readers, was even more interested, in the broadest sense, in educating them. To achieve this end he fashioned his novels around certain specific topics which were recurrent themes in the press and which his readers might more readily understand, and take an interest in, if dealt with in fictional form and written about in language which approximated common speech. Thus, *Ballad of the Rebellion of the Year Keng-tzu* is an account of the Boxer Uprising which adheres closely to newspaper reports, but which seeks in ballad, and therefore dramatic, form to apprise the "illiterate" (i.e., women and children, though Li would undoubtedly have had other "deprived" groups in mind) of the course of the rebellion in order to keep the events fresh in their minds, and to make them aware of the lessons which Li believed they should learn from them. In *Living Hell* Li turned from civil disorder to the penal system, and in a collection of separate incidents and stories drew attention to the iniquities practiced within the system and to the need for change. *A Brief History of Enlightenment* seeks to deal with the topic of modernization and the manner of its implementation, but more particularly to reflect the personalities caught up in the process.

In prerepublican Chinese society, where most educated men regarded the civil service as the most important outlet for their abilities, it was inevitable that bureaucrats and aspirants to office should appear to be the chief actors in any major attempt to transform society. That such was the case did not, however, guarantee uniformity of opinion among them, although it did make them, as a class, vulnerable to public criticism. In *A Brief History of Enlightenment*, then, the reader is presented with a whole cross section of opinions and attitudes current among scholars and bureaucrats during and immediately following the Reform Movement; and, insofar as his temperament and sense of humor allowed him to, Li looks on the efforts of the reformers with a degree of benevolence. In *The Bureaucracy Exposed*, however, Li sought to take the lid off the civil service and to reveal the decadence rampant at its every level. That this has been the most popular of Li's novels over the years, and for the majority of Chinese readers today the only work by which Li is remembered, suggests that it possesses enduring artistic qualities, and also that the Chinese public has continued to see in Li one of their champions in the unceasing struggle between the man in the street and the man in government service.

CHAPTER 2

Ballad of the Rebellion of the Year Keng-tzu (1900)

THE Boxer Uprising of 1900 provided the occasion for the last major attempt on the part of conservative leaders in China to rid the country of foreigners, to turn their backs on the outside world, and to seek to stem the tide of reform and modernization. The uprising itself, however, began, not among the ruling classes, but at the level of the peasantry in the countryside. It was a movement which was seized upon by conservative men in high places as a vehicle for attaining their ends, not, we can assume, exclusively in a mood of cynicism, although the usefulness of such a movement in their search for personal power and for control over the state was quick to suggest itself to them, but because they undoubtedly felt a certain sympathy with the current popular feeling which had brought the movement into existence, and because many were sufficiently superstitious to be impressed, and even overawed, by the religious elements which provided supernatural sanctions for the movement's activities.

I Causes of the Boxer Uprising

The causes of the Boxer Uprising are to be found in the general state of social unrest which marked the second half of the nineteenth century in China. In the mind of the ordinary person his feelings of discontent, together with the tensions he experienced in the society in which he found himself, were due, ultimately, to two major irritants: the Christian church and Western and Japanese intrusions in the political and economic spheres.[1] The church, which in its Roman Catholic form had maintained a presence in China since the late sixteenth century, had been officially proscribed, and the ban on its activities had remained until 1842. In 1860, however, the French secured by treaty far-reaching benefits for Christian missions. According to it, missionaries were granted the right to reside in the interior of China and to enjoy the protection of the Chinese authorities.[2] Although these new conditions were designed to benefit the Roman Catholic Church, in practice they favored all denominations, and encouraged missionary societies to redouble their efforts to expand their activities in China.

Apart from the annoyances which were bound to result from the physical presence of foreigners whose religious and social activities were frequently open to misunderstanding, there was the added friction often caused by Chinese converts to Christianity who found themselves in an advantageous position vis-à-vis the Chinese authorities and, in consequence, vis-à-vis their neighbors. As members of a foreign organization the protection of which was guaranteed by treaty, missionaries could be called upon in a legal dispute to represent their converts, and in a situation in which the Western powers were militarily dominant, magistrates' judgments more often than not favored the Christians.[3] But despite the protection already won for the Roman Catholic Church by the French government, the acquisition of a status which they felt commensurate with their position in society was not won by the bishops of the church until 1899. Through representations made by the French legation, the Chinese Foreign Office submitted to the throne a "Memorial as to Official Intercourse between Chinese Local Authorities and Roman Catholic Missionaries." According to this document Roman Catholic bishops were to be granted the right to wear mandarin buttons, to be transported from one place to another in sedan chairs in the manner of officials, and to rank officially with the governors-general and governors, and clergy lower down in the hierarchy were to be paired with other officials of appropriate rank in the civil service.[4] Clergy of other denominations were quick to declare their concern at the "interference of French and other Roman Catholic priests with the provincial and local government of China," [5] but the damage had long since been done, and to most Chinese the churches—Roman Catholic, Anglican, and Protestant—could be separated only with difficulty from the political and economic designs of the nations from which they came, and all were to suffer at the hands of the Boxers.

A Protestant missionary fleeing from the Boxers remarked that "The enmity of people and officials alike seemed to be chiefly directed against two classes—Roman Catholics and mining and railroad engineers—and we had all along the road to prove that we were neither the one nor the other." [6] Western merchants tended to confine their activities to the treaty ports and the foreign concessions. Railway builders and officials and mining engineers, however, because of the nature of their work, had, like the missionaries, to spend much time in the interior. It is no wonder, therefore, that popular reaction to Western economic intrusion into China should express itself in action against railways and mines. Both were attacked on the grounds that they disturbed the graves of the dead and adversely affected the harmonies which geomancers professed to divine in the landscape and which were believed to be necessary if the well-being of individuals and communities was to be maintained. [7] But on a more strictly economic level, those engaged in traditional modes of transportation could not but view the advent of the train as a threat to their livelihoods and the removal of minerals from their soil as in some way depriving them of potential sources of wealth. When to these and other innovations, such as telegraph lines, was added rough treatment at the hands of foreign overseers and the results of an increasing general economic malaise, it is not surprising that suspicions were fed and feelings of unease and resentment fostered. [8]

II   *Origins of the Boxers*

The origins of the Boxers as a movement are somewhat obscure. It is generally traced back to an organization formed in the 1890s in the province of Shantung and known as the "Plum Blossom Fists," although a sect bearing its later name *I-ho* ("Righteous Harmony") appears to have existed as early as the late eighteenth century. The Plum Blossom Fists, as a society, was undoubtedly anti-Christian and devoted to the removal of the foreigner from Chinese soil. [9] Some time later the name was changed to "Fists of Righteous Harmony," and possibly through the sympathetic attitude of the Shantung governors, Li Ping-heng and Yü-hsien, the Boxers came to adopt a prodynastic stand. [10] It was from the name "Fists of Righteous Harmony" and from the gymnastic exercises undertaken by members of the organization that the name "Boxers" came to be applied to the movement in Western circles. [11]

Morale among the Boxers was sustained by belief that its members enjoyed supernatural powers which would protect them from death when fired at and which would make them invisible in the face of foreign military might. [12] Unlike the Taiping rebels forty years earlier who sought to overthrow the dynasty, the Boxers, as we have seen, claimed to uphold it. Their slogan was "Support the Ch'ing dynasty and annihilate the foreigner." In very little time the movement spread from Shantung to Chihli (the present Hopei) and no serious attempt was made to suppress it. Prince Tuan, who was appointed head of the Chinese Foreign Office on 10 June 1900, was violently opposed to all foreigners and had given his support to the Boxers long before taking up his position in Peking.[13] There is much evidence also to suggest that the empress dowager, who was in effective control of the state, supported his attitude. She had, for instance, chosen his son, P'u-chun (Ta A-ko), to replace the Kuang-hsu emperor on the throne once the latter had been deposed; a plan which was not carried out because of disapproval expressed by the foreign powers and a number of provincial governors.[14] Publicly, of course, the empress dowager undertook to protect the foreign legations in Peking.

III Events of 1900

During the first six months of 1900 Westerners were attacked and, in some cases, killed, but the Boxers directed most of their hatred and violence toward Chinese Christians. Understandably uneasy, foreign ambassadors in Peking requested their governments to strengthen the forces which served as legation guards. By early June 1900 the unrest had increased to the point where rail and telegraph communications were cut off between Peking and Tientsin. The Fengtai railway station and locomotive sheds were set on fire on 28 May and the telegraph line was cut as foreign allied forces sought to advance on Peking from Tientsin. Rioting, the burning of churches, and the pillaging of homes of Chinese said to have good relations with foreigners was rife in both cities. The Boxers appeared to want to prevent reinforcements reaching the foreign communities in Peking and Tientsin and, when they had isolated them, to destroy them.[15]

As the situation grew increasingly desperate, British, French, Japanese, and German warships anchored off Taku, and on 10 June a small international body of troops was dispatched from Tientsin under a British admiral to protect the legations in Peking. It was soon attacked by the Boxers and forced to retreat, however. The allies now (17 June) attacked and seized the Taku forts and the Chinese authorities, regarding this as a deliberate act of war, retaliated by attacking the foreign concessions in Tientsin and by ordering all foreign diplomatic personnel to leave Peking within twenty-four hours. Seeking to find some solution to the impasse, baron von Ketteler, the German minister, was sent by the diplomatic corps to the Foreign Office to discuss the situation. He was shot by a Chinese solider en route.

On the same day, 20 June, a Chinese attack was launched on the foreign legations in Peking. At a council meeting of princes and ministers held on the day of the attack the more enlightened among them advised the empress dowager and Prince Tuan against taking such severe measures. Although not present at the meeting, evidence suggests that Jung-lu, commander of the army, was in agreement with them and that together they warned the empress that if China persisted in this line of action it could lead to the collapse of the dynasty. Ignoring their advice, the empress allowed the bombardment to continue. The legation community consisting of 470 civilians, 3,000 Chinese Christians who had taken refuge in the quarter, and 450 guards fought back. On 17 July the empress dowager, no doubt alarmed at news of the fall of Tientsin on 14 July and at reports of increasing anger among the nations of the West and Japan, ordered hostilities to cease, apologized for the deaths of Japanese and German officials, and, on 20 July, ordered fruit and vegetables, rice and flour to be delivered to the legations. Shortly afterward the bombardment was resumed, however, and continued through the end of July and into August.

Despite her power, the empress dowager was unable to carry the majority of the provincial governors with her in her patronage of the Boxers. Whereas the Boxers were supported by the provincial administrations in Chihli and Shansi and in certain areas of Manchuria and Inner Mongolia, elsewhere attempts were made to suppress them.[16]

On 14 July an allied force of 12,000 men captured Tientsin, the allies losing about 745 men and the Chinese about 15,000. Following the arrival of reinforcements, the army set out for Peking on 4 August. On 14 August, finding herself in desperate straits, the empress dowager summoned the council of state to a conference in the Palace of Peaceful Longevity. While the conference was in session news reached its members that the allies had entered Peking. It was decided that the court should flee the city, and early the following morning the royal party left the palace, dressed as peasants and riding in carts. Peking was pillaged by the invading troops. The Germans who occupied the imperial palace removed many of its priceless objects and shipped them back to Germany. The Japanese took three million taels of pure silver from the government treasury as well as seizing the rice and silk stores, and the troops and officials of the other nations made off with whatever they could lay their hands on.[17]

Whatever their political standpoint or sympathies, Chinese who lived through the events of 1900 believed the Boxer Uprising, the subsequent occupation of Peking by the allied forces of eight nations, and the flight of the royal family to be one of the greatest calamities ever to befall China in her long history, since it resulted in a treaty which seemed to impose greater shame and disgrace on China than she had ever before experienced, and subjected her to further control by the major powers of the West and Japan. On the other hand, the events and their outcome brought it home to those who understood the situation that the government, as constituted, was no longer capable of governing and that changes were needed.

IV   *Effect of Uprising on Chinese Literature*

The effects of the Boxer Uprising on Chinese literature cannot be said to be great if one merely looks for a quantitative response among works which grow specifically out of it. But if one looks at the manner in which fiction, for example, with a strong reformist, and even revolutionary, content comes into its own in the years following 1900, one must conclude that the events of that year did much to stimulate concern among writers to make greater use of the novel as a vehicle for change. A Ying in his preface to the 1935 edition of the book we are examining lists half a dozen works of fiction which sought to reflect the events of 1900, among the authors of which are the well-known Lin Shu (1852–1924) and Wu Chien-jen, and draws attention to the fact that poems and songs inspired by these events are to be found scattered in various collections of this type of writing as well as in the press. A Ying seemed to feel that had other conditions been right, the literary world could have expected immediately a whole flood of creative writing to have emerged from this traumatic experience. Whatever the validity of this judgment, he was undoubtedly right in concluding that circumstances prior to 1903 were not yet conducive to a major literary response. He gives as his reasons for the paucity of material, first, that novelists still had insufficient understanding of the "relationship of the novel to the government of the masses," even as expounded by Liang Ch'i-ch'ao; second, that the journals which were to carry the bulk of late Ch'ing fiction did not appear till several years after the Boxer Uprising; and third, that by

the time the journals were ready and writers had begun to understand the importance of the novel, other weighty matters commanded their and their readers' attention. To these reasons we must
surely add the fact that writers living outside the confines of foreign
concessions and enclaves—and therefore beyond the protection such
places afforded—stood in constant danger of being arrested for sedi-
tion—particularly if characters they wanted to include in their works
were to be little more than thinly disguised portrayals of well-known
officials and personalities.

V   *The* Ballad: *The Politics of the Uprising*

Nonetheless, however much others may have hesitated to capital-
ize on the events of 1900 by putting them into a work of fiction, Li
Po-yuan plunged almost immediately into just such an enterprise.
He commenced writing, so we are told, on the day the protocol came
into force in 1901 and completed the book just over a year later. It
appeared initially in serial form in the *Fan-hua pao* (*Shanghai
Sights*), and was then published in book form during the winter of
1902 by the Fan-hua Publishing Company.[18]
As in all but one of his major novels available to us, Li gave his
reasons for writing this work in an introduction. In it he says:

Several hundred years have gone by since the T'ang and Ming dynasties, yet
even writings concerning small and unimportant events of those times have
an inexhaustible and lingering capacity to stir the emotions of men of a later
period. How much more should this be so when the whole of China is
suddenly swallowed up and the capital is reduced to ashes in the space of
three months. It is inconceivable that loyal officials can remain unmoved
after reading about these sad and disastrous events, now gathered into one
book, and yet cherish the ambition of ruling the people of the nation.
. . . Since peace has been achieved popular feelings have suddenly changed.
Arrogance, extravagance, and licentious and idle habits have again entered
the hearts and minds of people, and the winds of negligence and perfunctori-
ness blow across the whole nation. . . . The author has therefore written this
Ballad of the National Upheaval of 1900 and, in tracing the activities of the
loyal and traitorous, the good and the artful, and in apportioning merit and
guilt and deciding between right and wrong, he has refused to submit to
anyone else's views or to prevaricate in his account of events.[19]

It is clear from these remarks that Li's primary purpose in compil-
ing this book was to keep the memory of the Boxer Uprising, with all

the shame, disgrace, and madness which had attended it, fresh in the minds of the people who were tending to put it behind them, like a bad dream to be forgotten, and who were returning to habits of mind inimical to the development of a responsible and progressive citizenry such as he felt was needed in China. But it is also obvious that he wanted chiefly to condemn those in high places who, in their lust for power, had jeopardized the welfare and security of the nation, and that he was determined to place the blame for the uprising where he believed it should lie, i.e., on the shoulders of Prince Tuan and his like-minded colleagues and subordinates in government. Li makes further reference in chapter one to the tendency of the Chinese people to put unpleasant experiences behind them and to his wish to keep fresh their memories of the recent disasters. He says: ". . . the minds of the Chinese are such that once today has dawned they forget yesterday; and when they are in possession of the comforts of today they forget the suffering of yesterday. Therefore, I wish to recount below the circumstances of the trouble caused by the Boxer bandits. . . . I have employed a metrical style (irregular verse) and common speech so that the masses will find it easy to understand, and so that both women and children will know what is said from a single reading." Similar sentiments are expressed in chapter fifteen.

The Ballad of the Rebellion of the Year 1900 in its present form consists of forty chapters. It sets out, as Li Po-yuan has clearly indicated, to trace the whole history of the Boxer Uprising in dramatic form, and therefore begins with an account of its origins. The rebellion began, so Li tells us, with a clash between an overbearing Roman Catholic family in Ch'ing-p'ing *hsien* by the name of Tso and a graduate of the military examination system called Chang who was a minor leader in the White Lotus Society, a secret organization which had been revived during the Ch'ing dynasty but which originated during the Yuan dynasty, and which combined within itself both supernatural claims and political goals. Having been beaten up by Tso, Chang lodged a complaint with the local magistrate. Aware that the Tso family belonged to the church the magistrate thought it advisable not to pursue the matter and persuaded Chang to drop his charge. Pressing its advantage, the Tso family prevailed upon the magistrate to teach Chang a lesson. Afraid to refuse their demands, the magistrate had the "military graduate" brought to court and beaten.

Unable to forget the wrong done to him, Chang's anger smoldered and grew and he determined to take some kind of action which would allow him both to avenge the wrong and to appear a hero in the eyes of the people. He therefore summoned more than five hundred of his followers in the White Lotus Society. Filled with indignation over the treatment meted out to their leader, Chang's followers covenanted among themselves in blood, burned incense, worshipped and made vows, and then, with drums beating and with the crashing of gongs, marched on the Tso family, wiping it out in a dawn raid. Alarmed at this and other atrocities, the magistrate submitted a report to his superiors; but when he set out to arrest the murderers he found that Chang and his followers had fled.

News of the massacre and of the spoils gained from the raid spread rapidly among members of the White Lotus Society and Chang soon had a huge following, among which was an expert on Taoist magic called Chu Hung-teng (Red Lantern Chu). Chu claimed that Heaven had commanded him to rid the world of Christianity and to support the emperor and the ruling dynasty. The hated foreigner, he said, was to be destroyed.

A key figure during the period of the Boxer Uprising and the person whom many held directly responsible for swinging the government behind the movement was the official Yü-hsien. This official was also to win notoriety in both China and the West as the Boxers' most merciless supporter. Li Po-yuan goes to some length, therefore, to trace the way in which Yü-hsien became involved with the movement and to provide the reasons for his pathological hatred of foreigners.

As Li points out, Yü-hsien, a Manchu, was the governor of Shantung to whom the magistrate of Ch'ing-p'ing *hsien* reported the original outbreak of trouble, and that at this juncture he was not overtly antiforeign. He had been promoted to the governorship of Shantung, so Li tells us, because of his successful handling of an outbreak of banditry during his period as prefect of Ts'ao-chou and because of the favorable impression he had made on Chang Yueh (Chang Ju-mei), the governor at the time, who, delighted with his abilities as a strong and decisive administrator, recommended him to the throne.

As soon as Yü-hsien heard of the fresh outbreak of trouble in Ch'ing-p'ing he sent two officials to the town to carry out investigations. The two officials were Lu Ch'ang-i, prefect of Tsinan *fu*, who was to make a secret investigation, and Yuan Shih-tun, the commander of his bodyguard. Yuan reported to Yü-hsien that the trouble was due to a case involving Chu Hung-teng (Red Lantern) in Ch'ing-p'ing *hsien*. Telling Yuan that he could not allow such happenings, Yü-hsien ordered Yuan to march on Ch'ing-p'ing with his troops to quell the troublemakers.

Yuan set off the same night with men and horses and, by dawn, had traveled a hundred *li*. Unfortunately, however, a fog suddenly came down so that Yuan could not see where he was going. Informed by a scout that he had found a village from which came sounds of drums and gongs, that this was clearly the Boxers' lair, and that the fog had undoubtedly been called down by the Boxers employing supernatural means, Yuan ordered his troops to attack, only to discover, when the village walls had been breached and the villagers killed, that he had made a mistake. He had stumbled on a village where preparations were being made to put on an opera in honor of the god Kuan Ti (the God of War), and the noise his scout had heard had come from the orchestra.

Fearful of the consequences, Yuan reported what he had done to Prefect Lu who agreed to accompany Yuan to the provincial capital and to help him explain his mistake to Governor Yü-hsien. Not unnaturally, Yü-hsien was furious over the way his subordinates had bungled matters. He ordered Yuan to be put to death, but relented somewhat following pleas from other officials. In the end Yuan was instructed to return to his barracks where he had his scout beheaded. Prefect Lu had three major demerits attached to his name and was allowed to retire to his home.[20]

Nothing further might have happened had not another difficulty involving Christians arisen in Yin-chou. Because the Boxers proved too strong to be put down by government troops, missionaries who escaped to Peking from regions in which they were active laid complaints with their ambassadors who, in turn, complained to the Tsung-li Yamen, the Chinese Foreign Office. Yü-hsien, in particular, was singled out for blame, and the Foreign Office was told that unless Yü-hsien were removed from his post foreign nationals would no longer be able to continue with their missionary work in Shantung, and that this could result in strained relations between China and their countries. The court thus had little alternative but to recall Yü-hsien to Peking and to keep him there until a position fell vacant elsewhere.

Not surprisingly, Yü-hsien was most angry over the way in which he had been treated. Annoyed that he was being used as a scapegoat, he felt resentful toward Commander Yuan for failing to rid the province of the Boxers and bitterness toward the missionaries for having appealed over his head to the capital, thereby bringing about his recall. Increasingly exasperated and melancholy over events, Yü-hsien sought, at first in vain, someone in government circles who would come to his rescue and help him to vindicate his name.

In the foregoing events Li provides the factors which, in his view, were so to affect Yü-hsien's mind that he was later, as governor of Shansi, to indulge in the orgy of killing described in chapters 13 and 14 of the *Ballad*.

The commitment of government support to the Boxers was also, so Li maintains, due to the activities and suggestions of Yü-hsien; although he does, of course, lay the chief blame for what eventuated at the door of those leading officials who embraced his proposals in order to further their own ends and employed them as a means whereby they could indulge their xenophobia. The person, says Li, who came to Yü-hsien's rescue was President of the Board of Revenue and Population, Kang-i, who had been promoted to the rank of associate grand secretary. Kang-i was uncompromisingly opposed to reform and the presence of the foreigner and had, moreover, strengthened his position at court by allying himself to Prince Tuan whose son (Ta A-ko) had been declared heir to the throne.

As Li tells the story, Yü-hsien had at one time befriended Kang-i, and he therefore now wrote a letter to him seeking help and dispatched it together with a gift of two thousand ounces of silver. When Yü-hsien was finally ushered into Kang-i's presence, Kang-i opened the conversation by saying that he understood Yü-hsien had left his post feeling resentful and that foreigners must indeed be powerful when they could cheat and humiliate a man of Yü-hsien's rank. It was necessary, said he, to plan some kind of revenge, and that only so could he wipe out the grievance. Kang-i then informed Yü-hsien that he had that day run into Prince Tuan in the palace, and that he had mentioned his name to Tuan. He said that Yü-hsien was to go to the prince's residence himself the following day, and that with the prince's backing everything was possible.

Yü-hsien visited the prince as instructed, was told by the prince that Kang-i had mentioned Yü-hsien to him, and was then informed that he, the prince, now wished to put Yü-hsien to the test. The prince said that his chief aim was to find a way whereby he and his son could take over the reins of government at the earliest possible moment and made it clear that Yü-hsien would be handsomely rewarded should he be able to contribute to the fulfillment of this aim. Yü-hsien thereupon announced that he had a plan. If, he said,

Tuan would back the Boxers, who were active everywhere in Shantung and Chihli and who claimed to support the throne, and would
support them in their campaign to rid the nation of the foreigner,
then, should they prove successful, he would have established the
greatest of merit and all power would be concentrated in his hands.
Prince Tuan, Li says, indicated his approval of the plan and acknowledged that if the foreigner could indeed be destroyed, he would
naturally win the throne. At court the following day Prince Tuan
declared his strong support for Yü-hsien and won for him the governorship of the province of Shansi.

VI *Religious Practices of the Boxers*

Having thus traced the origin of the Boxer movement, and having
established the causes for its adoption by certain officials and leading
figures at court, Li Po-yuan sets out to give an account of some of the
religious practices of the Boxers which appealed to the uneducated
peasantry, but which also proved attractive to those in high places
who were deeply conservative in outlook and who, in matters of
religion, remained superstitious.[21]
Shortly after Yü-hsien's recall Yuan Shih-k'ai, who was later to
become the first president of the republic and who had already won a
reputation for himself as a military leader of considerable ability in
Korea, was appointed to the vacant governorship of Shantung with
orders to pacify the Boxers. So successful was he that the Boxers were
forced to transfer most of their activities to the neighboring province
of Chihli where they engaged in plunder and slaughter. With the
support of Prince Tuan, Kang-i, and other princes and officials who
were becoming increasingly influential and powerful at court, the
Boxers were soon to be found everywhere in the region of Peking and
Tientsin propagating their brand of Taoist beliefs and practices.
These beliefs and practices did not stem solely from one religious
center, however. Li describes two or three "revelations" which
occurred through different persons in different places. Certain of the
persons who claimed to be the vehicles of revelation, and therefore
repositories of supernatural powers, came to exercise more influence
than others.
The first center Li refers to is a temple located near a village several
miles from T'ang-i *hsien* in Shantung.[22] According to the Boxers, an
old man reputed to be eight hundred years old who lived in the

temple had a dream in which Hung-chun Lao-tsu, a Taoist god,[23] approached him and taught him the essentials of the art of boxing as well as the correct interpretation of the Eight Diagrams, specified in the *Book of Changes*, which had been imparted to Taoist Immortals.

At first news of this revelation spread slowly, but later many ignorant country folk came to accept it and to believe in it. Altars were set up everywhere and sacrifices and gifts were offered with requests that Hung-chun Lao-tsu would draw near to his suppliants. Devotees were informed that they need have no fear of bullets or shells and that their leader bore the title of senior adept.

Li asserts that although the teachings of the Boxers were not entirely uniform, the doctrine of the descent of a spirit on his worshipper was central to all of them. When the spirit had taken possession of them, so they held, their martial arts were at their best and they could not be killed with bullets. The descent of the spirits was related to the Eight Diagrams, as were the worshippers themselves. Those whose diagram was *ch'ien* ("heaven"), for example, would prostrate themselves before the altar after entering the sanctuary. The senior adept, their leader, would then step forward and burn charms and chant spells on their behalf, inviting the spirit to descend. The devotees would then be told to clench their teeth and then to breathe in and out with their mouths open until froth appeared. When this happened the leader would say in a loud voice: "The Old Ancestor [Lao-tsu] has descended. Everyone kowtow and worship." The leader would then hand weapons to the devotees who would dance as if they were flying. The followers classified under the other diagrams went through much the same kind of ritual performance, except that those listed under the diagram *tui* ("exchange") were taught to box as if spirit-possessed. They all wore red turbans and red sashes round their waists.

Two other colorful characters who exercise much influence over the Boxers in this book are Chang Te-ch'eng [24] (known as divine master and elder brother Chang) and his consort Hung-teng Chao (Red Lantern Light). To give readers as much as possible of the flavor of the original text in which these characters appear, a translation of the whole passage follows. It should be noted that the narrator here is not satisfied merely to give an account of events. As we have already seen, the author had a serious purpose in view in writing this book, and part of that purpose, as the first and later lines of the quotation make clear, was to undermine superstitious belief and, thereby, to discredit the Boxers.

(Sung): From the times of P'an-ku [the Chinese Methusela] to the present there has never been a practitioner of the black arts who could cause the spirits to descend. But people say whatever comes into their heads and for more than four thousand years this strange claim has been made.

Chief among those who have made this assertion was a certain man by the name of Chang Te-ch'eng, a man of thirty or forty years of age who punted boats for a living and was quite unknown. Because he was well versed in boxing and in the use of the cudgel, however, he fearlessly traversed the rivers and lakes and was afraid of no man.

One day he arrived by chance at the township of Tu-liu and was giving a performance of his skills on the main street when he came across two boys who were either boxing or kicking (it was unclear which) at the end of the street. Master Chang walked over to look at them and laughed out loud two or three times saying:

(Said): "There's nothing remarkable about this kind of boxing. I could immobilize you with just one finger."

At first those two young lads refused to believe him, but when they put him to the test, it turned out that he was right. Quite by chance two stalwart fellows dressed in strange clothes and wearing red turbans and sashes strode up unheralded and, on seeing Chang Te-ch'eng, bowed their heads in salutation without uttering a single word.

Chang Te-ch'eng bowed his head repeatedly in return and quickly asked the two men their names and the name of their hometown. Scrambling hurriedly to their feet and detaining him, the two men asked, without giving their names: "Are you not, sir, the founder of the sect, the shrine of which stands before us?" Chang Te-ch'eng had always been quicker on the uptake than other men, and on hearing these words he realized the implications of what was taking place. He therefore replied: "I am indeed."

The two stalwart men said: "It is the great good fortune of our humble village that you, divine master, have today favored us by descending among us. We therefore invite you, divine master, to dwell in our shrine so that your disciples may receive instruction from you morning and evening."

(Sung): The three men strode speedily to the shrine and passed through its gates. Candles were lit and incense was burned with much decorum, and the temple bell was struck and the drum beaten to summon the villagers together. The whole village was stirred up and many people from neighboring hamlets gathered before the shrine to attend upon its visitor; and the "founder" promptly gave an account of himself and his aims.

(Said): Chang Te-ch'eng immediately said:

(Sung): "I was wandering aimlessly like a cloud when I chanced upon your esteemed place and was fortunate enough to be honored by you gentlemen who have pressed me into entering this shrine to become your leader. My every command must now be obeyed. Bring forth your wealth and possessions with all speed and offer them at this shrine for our use. You must harbor no niggardliness of mind. When your riches have been gathered together and provisions for our army are sufficient, I guarantee that we shall be able to destroy the Christian Church and restore stability to heaven and earth. If, Gentlemen, you do not believe me lift your heads and regard the clouds in the sky.

(Said): "I ask you to watch carefully, for when a hermit gives vent to his pent up feelings, you will see city walls rising up on four sides within the clouds. This is the hermit summoning the hosts of heaven to provide protection for your villages so that no matter how great the capabilities of foreign troops and guns, they will not be able to advance a single step against you."

(Sung): When all had heard these words they believed them, and together moved to the area before the shrine, where they rubbed their eyes and watched for a long time; but they saw nothing. They then fell to arguing among themselves. Te-ch'eng quickly asked them the nature of their arguments, and was given conflicting replies by the crowd. Some said that the clouds lacked any distinctive feature, whereas others claimed that, though indistinct, walls were discernible. Who could have known that they were all engaged in self-deception, and that these uneducated people had been so taken in as to regard [all this] as true.

(Said): From this time onward everyone in the township spread the news from one to another and were amazed, regarding the whole event as a wondrous mystery. When Chang Te-ch'eng saw that he had won over the minds of the people, he secretly arranged for the Boxers to be notified and summoned. The Boxers came and were received by Chang in audience, the event being dignified with the words: "An attendance at the imperial court by men of all nations."

Chang Te-ch'eng also issued instructions for two large banners to be flown on either side of the entrance to the shrine. On one were the words "Support the Ch'ing dynasty and destroy the foreigner." On the other, "The divine fists of righteous harmony."

Once the Boxer bandits from every quarter had received this designation they acted in accordance with it and openly and shamelessly burned down churches, and murdered missionaries in total disregard of the law. . . .

Their method for putting men to death was as follows: Whenever they seized someone they would take him to the shrine and ask the grand master and elder brother to burn some incense and report the matter to the spirit. The rise or fall of the ashes of the burned report was said to express the will of the deity and determined whether the prisoner should live or die. . . .

What was ludicrous was that apart from Hung-chun Lao-tsu the deities in the shrine to whom offerings were made . . . were Wang-ch'an Lao-tsu, Erh-lang Shen, Yen P'ing-chung, Kuan Sheng-ti chün, Sakyamuni, Chiu-t'ien Hsuan-nu, Sun Wu-k'ung, and Li-shan Lao-tsu etc. . . .[25]

When churches and homes were to be burned down spirits and kerosene were first poured secretly around them and a fuse laid. The grand master and elder brother would then lead his men to the spot, recite some verse facing the sky, and then as he raised his sword and [drew on the ground] with it fire leaped up. When people saw fire coming from his sword they were amazed and believed him to have great supernatural powers. . . .[26]

Li informs his readers that Yü-lu,[27] the viceroy of Chihli, unlike Yuan Shih-k'ai in Shantung, tried to ingratiate himself with Prince Tuan and therefore sought to rid his province of foreigners by drawing on the Boxers for help. He soon found himself controlled by the Boxers, however, and unable to make important decisions without first consulting Chang Te-ch'eng. Li describes in some detail a visit made "reluctantly" by Chang to the official residence of Yü-lu during the period when Tientsin was under attack from the allies.

At first Chang Te-ch'eng refused steadfastly to visit the viceroy, but after much pleading on the part of the officials who had come to fetch him he rose up and made his way to the residence in a palanquin.

(Sung): A palanquin with eight bearers received the immortal one and with shouting and the beating of gongs a path was cleared for him. A scout returned to the residence ahead of the palanquin to report Chang's imminent arrival and the governor, in ceremonial robes, stepped out to greet him. . . .

When the palanquin arrived at the entrance of the residence the governor knelt before it, but the master of the black arts remained seated, boldly pretending he had not seen the governor.

(Said): Chang Te-ch'eng made straight for the reception room before alighting from the palanquin and taking a seat in the center of the room.

Yü-lu led his subordinates into the reception room after Chang and then burned incense and bowed himself to the ground before him. After he had bowed his head to the ground Yü-lu said to him, still kneeling, "I am a mere mortal who, by the grace of my Lord, has been put in charge of this place, Chihli province. What is most detestable is the fact that the foreigner has talked his way into promulgating his religion [in this region] and has thereby deceived and misled the uneducated. I hope that you, divine master, with your great inspiration, will come to my aid. Such aid will never be forgotten throughout all ages."[28]

Needless to say, Chang promises to use his powers to aid Yü-lu, but he insists that his consort Red Lantern Light,[29] who cultivates the Taoist arts with him, must join him at the viceroy's residence. The viceroy accordingly arranges for her to be fetched. When his officers locate the woman they find her in a matting shed dressed from head to foot in red and receiving the veneration of a large assembly of people. She refuses to leave her worshippers immediately, but promises to go to the official residence when she is ready.

When she finally moves to the residence she has changed into yellow robes and is accompanied by fifty or sixty female attendants all of whom are dressed in red. She and her cortage are met by the viceroy and his officials on their knees and trembling with fear. She addresses the viceroy and, much to his relief, promises to come to his aid.

The emptiness of the promises made by Chang and his consort, and the farcical nature of this grand charade, are made all too apparent as events in and around Tientsin approach their tragic climax. Li recounts that as Yü-lu was made increasingly aware of the danger in which he and his army stood he went to consult Chang, putting a number of questions to him. What arts, he asked, could the Boxer leader employ which would cause the foreigners to withdraw? When would the armies of heaven appear to lend him their supernatural support? What use were the supernatural arts of the Boxers when bullets continued to kill people? Supplies of food were dwindling, he said, and the army had no way of escape.

Chang replied that the heavenly armies had gone overseas to kill devils and that consequently they had not been able to give their attention to local events. Chang then performed certain ritual acts to have the heavenly hosts transferred back to China, following which he stepped forward with sword in hand and assured everyone that he was about to rout the foreign armies. Claiming divine protection, Chang refused to be accompanied by Chinese troops, stating that this would only anger the gods. The viceroy consequently sent him on his way with great ceremony. No sooner had the divine master left the city, than he changed his clothes and made his getaway. Learning of his escape, Yü-lu went in great distress to look for Chang's consort only to find that she, too, had vanished.

Before recounting the story of the battle for Tientsin, precipitated by the arrival of the navies and troops of eight nations to protect their nationals resident in China, Li describes in detail the growth of Boxer power and Boxer activities in the cities of Peking and Tientsin. In chapter 5 he gives an account of the destruction of railway and telegraph lines, the looting of the foreign stationmaster's quarters at Feng-tai, and the attacks by the Boxers on anyone wearing foreign clothes. He also reveals the dilemma in which military commanders found themselves when faced with Boxer bands who regarded anyone who defended modern installations as traitors.

Li next describes (chapter 7) the manner in which Prince Tuan appointed officials favorable to the Boxers to key positions in the government and the army, and in chapters 8 and 9 tells of the cold-blooded murder of the chancellor of the Japanese legation and the subsequent killing of the German minister.[30] He points out that such actions stirred up public opinion in both Europe and Japan and led ultimately to the storming of the Taku forts by the allies and their attack on Tientsin.

VII *The Battle for Tientsin*

Although in his account of the Boxer Uprising Li lays the blame for the calamity which befell China as a result of it fairly and squarely on the shoulders of the backward-looking, xenophobic conservatives who employed the ignorant Boxers to achieve their own ends, and although he time and again goes out of his way to suggest that the nations of the West would not have acted in the way they did unless they had been provoked, there seems to be little doubt that he was shocked by reports that the allies had used gas in their final assault on Tientsin. The reader senses Li's feelings of patriotism and solidarity with the sufferings of his own people as the story is made to unfold. Much, no doubt, could be made of his comment that the use of gas was against international law, but that the allies defended their action in this instance by insisting that they were firing on savages. Could this remark be meant as an attack on the allies and a suggestion that they only attached importance to integrity and to the upholding of the principle of the rule of law when it suited them, or was it designed as a further attack on the conservatives of his nation who, in their refusal to become a part of the modern world had forfeited their right to be considered a part of the international community and had, consequently, to be treated in a manner which only "savages" could understand? Whichever interpretation is correct, and the two are not necessarily mutually exclusive, the passage describing this attack on Tientsin is one of the more noteworthy in the book.

(Said): Following Nieh Shih-ch'eng's[31] death Governor-General Yü issued instructions that attention be focused on precautions against a blocade. A large cannon was mounted atop the city wall and shells were fired unceasingly several *li* in the direction of the foreign concessions. . . .

The consuls of each nation wrote a joint letter to Governor-General Yü in which they said that if he persisted in firing his cannon at the concessions they would have to bombard the city of Tientsin with shells.

When Governor-General Yü received this letter he hurriedly wrote a reply, stating that since matters had reached such a pass the only course now open to them was to submit to the will of Heaven. Each side must itself decide what action to take and cease to concern itself with [expressions] of friendship, etc. When the officers of the allied armies read this communication they were, every one of them, exceedingly angry and attacked Tientsin with all the strength at their command.

(Sung): Western troops struck at Tientsin with all their might; they brought over two guns newly arrived from England. These were the famous chlorine-gas guns which, in the attack on the city that brought [the allies] victory, proved extraordinarily fierce. People only had to inhale the gas to die where they stood; they had no need to be in the vicinity of those cruel shells when they landed. International law had all along forbidden their use; [the allies] asserted they had reserved them for attacks on savages.

(Said): On the evening of the day on which they received Governor-General Yü's reply, more than eight thousand troops of the German, Russian, and Japanese contingents were divided up to attack from two directions.

(Sung): It was the middle of the sixth month. There had been several fine nights and the moon was full. The Western troops of the allied armies advanced on the same day, and the poison-filled shells were fired repeatedly on Tientsin.

When day finally dawned five hundred big guns opened up together, and shells flew in destroying every trace of life. Concluding, finally, that he could no longer resist, the commander in chief decided he would have to throw open the gates and withdraw his troops. Leading his decimated soldiers northward he yielded Tientsin to the enemy, proffering it with both hands!

(Said): At this point there was no longer any trace of Chinese troops either within or outside the city. Corpses lay strewn everywhere inside the walls; all houses were destroyed, and, because the foreign troops had fired chlorine-gas shells, no wounds were to be found on the dead who had fallen to the ground. Such was the effect of the gas that, three hours after the city had fallen, foreign troops saw large numbers of Chinese soldiers standing against the walls with rifles in their hands and eyes glaring, as if about to open fire. It was not until [the foreigners] drew near to them that they became aware that they were already dead from gas poisoning, and that it was only because they were leaning against the walls that they had not fallen to the ground. Within the city, from the East Gate to the Drum Tower, not a tile was dislodged. Few also had suffered any harm in the vicinity of the South and North Gates. But, outside the West Gate corpses were piled mountain high and no more than ten or twenty percent of the buildings remained intact.[32]

VIII   *Yü-hsien Takes His Revenge*

If one of Li's aims in describing the manner of the allies' onslaught on Tientsin was to emphasize the illegality, and even immorality, of the allies' actions, then the account of the rounding up and systematic slaughter of Westerners by Governor Yü-hsien and his fellow officials in Shansi was clearly intended as an indictment, not only of Yü-hsien, but of all those conservatives who refused to believe, or who found it inconvenient to admit, that the West had anything of value to offer China. Li brands Yü-hsien as being totally inhumane—the most severe moral judgment that could be leveled at anyone in traditional China—and, quite deliberately, puts into the mouths of two of the missionaries who are about to be killed speeches which are designed to show that China, indeed, had benefited from the Westerner's presence. Since the section describing Yü-hsien's wholesale slaughter of Westerners in Shansi has also been acknowledged as one of the more memorable in the book, we add the following translation from it as well.

(Said): Now from the time Yü-hsien had been ordered back to Peking from the post of governor of the province of Shantung, he had been fortunate enough to be able to beat a path to the door of Prince Tuan and had, in consequence, been appointed governor of Shansi. It was only with this appointment that he came fully to understand the aims and objectives of the gentlemen who held the reins of government. He therefore left the capital with all speed and headed for Taiyuan to take up office.

(Sung): Eager for glory and honor [Yü-hsien] could hardly be expected to disobey Prince Tuan's orders.

From the moment he reached Taiyuan and accepted his seal of office, he determined, with singleness of mind, to slaughter foreigners; first, in order to send in a good report to his highness, the traitorous prince, and second, because of the profound hatred he had formed for certain enemies of his in Shantung.

Concerned both with public policy and private grudges he carried out his orders with alacrity.

(Said): Yü-hsien had barely accepted his seal of office when he received news from Peking to the effect that the legations had been attacked and that the Boxers were now acting without any restraint. He therefore devoted his whole attention to the carrying out of Prince Tuan's orders. . . .[33]

Yü-hsien informs his senior colleagues of his intentions and finds that whereas some disagree with him, others support him. Shortly thereafter a communique reaches Yü-hsien from the court in Peking in which the foreigners are accused of commencing hostilities against China and Chinese officials are urged, in consequence, to show them no mercy. The Boxers, it claimed, were eradicating foreigners and thereby loyally supporting the dynasty.

When his subordinates have read the communique Yü-hsien uses it to legitimize his proposed course of action. He issues orders to the officials in charge of every prefecture, county, and district within his jurisdiction, commanding them to round up all foreigners. Fearful lest some might escape his net, however, he decides to couch his orders in terms which suggest that he is concerned to offer the foreigners protection. He wants them all, he says, to gather together in the provincial capital. To ensure their compliance he informs the foreigners that the Boxers are wicked men, and that they are roaming the province, unrestrained, and killing Christians wherever they find them. He assures them that in persuading them to shelter in his capital, he has no other motive than to provide protection for foreigners.

(Said): After deceiving all the missionaries in his province and persuading them to come to the provincial capital, Yü-hsien, the governor of Shansi, forced them to live together in one alley under the pretext that it was for their protection. Shortly thereafter he instructed someone to visit them to inquire after their well-being, though in reality he was secretly to investigate whether anyone had escaped from the net. To ensure that not a single foreigner had failed to come to the capital he checked with every prefect and district and county magistrate; then he thought to himself: "The foreigners can be as sharp and as shrewd as they like; but this time they've fallen into my trap!" . . .

When Yü-hsien saw that the foreigners had all been inveigled into coming, he issued secret orders to the commandant of the governor's brigade to come to his official residence and then to command his troops to seal off the two entrances to the lane in order to prevent any foreigner from either leaving or entering it. He said his reason for doing this was that there were many Boxers abroad in the city and that if foreigners left the lane he could not protect them.

(Sung): His face was full of compassion but he harbored treachery within his heart. The commandant posted guards without delay, and from this time on the foreigners were as good as imprisoned. It was virtually impossible for them to escape even had they wished to do so.

On this day it was just past noon when the governor suddenly issued an order. Officers and men mustered to their standards, knives and swords, spears and lances glistening.

A command was given that they should march outside the city walls to display their might, but midway they were suddenly brought to a halt and, before the lane, the troops dismounted.

(Said): The governor got down from his horse; stood at the entrance to the street, and gave an order to the commandant who immediately entered the lane and escorted all the foreigners to the governor's official residence for execution. Not one was allowed to escape.

(Sung): The commander in chief was so awesome and fierce that even ghosts and spirits were startled when he issued an order. Officers and men all shouted their compliance and hurried toward the lane to seize their captives.

The missionaries, startled by this bolt from the blue, became only now aware of the treacherous plan and regretted their decision to enter the provincial capital.

(Said): . . . Each missionary knew there was nowhere he could flee and therefore addressed the officers in the following manner: "We came here to propagate our religion, and we came by imperial command; moreover, we have committed no crime. But, since his excellency the governor now wishes to harm us, and we are few and cannot resist so large a number, and we are weak and cannot resist the strong, therefore, we have no choice but to die. But, for us, trustworthiness is of supreme importance, and since you wish us to die we shall make no attempt whatever to escape. We will lead our elderly and our young and proceed to the governor's official residence where we will wait with craned necks for our execution."

(Sung): When the foreigners had finished speaking they wept freely so that even men of stone or iron were moved at the sight. They had to walk out together on to the main street.

Leading the procession was the commandant and his troops who moved smoothly along, their knives, two-pronged spears, and banners sparkling. The governor himself brought up the rear, the plume of rank and red tassel on his hat marking him out.

In the middle were the missionaries, not one of whom was missing; men and women together numbered more than a hundred persons. Husbands and wives appeared walking side by side. . . . They put their heads together and kissed as an expression of their love for each other and led their children by the hand. There were many persons in each family and they, having spent their lives together, would now die together. No one could but feel very sad at the sight. . . .

Yü-hsien galloped ahead on his horse to his office, and Taiyuan became a city where death was to ensue from injustice.

(Said): Yü-hsien passed through the gate of his residence and, when he reached the Grand Hall of Justice and had dismounted, he took his judicial seat, struck the wooden block used to maintain order in court, and ordered the "devils," both old and young, to be brought before him. The officers and men lined up on either side responded together with a "Yes, sir."

(Sung): When he had seated himself in the Grand Hall of Justice he pointed to the foreigners, stared at them with the fearsome eyes of a tiger which threaten death, and talked wildly at them.

An officer ticked off their names one by one as they stood, completely surrounded, in the Grand Hall. There were twenty or thirty Catholics and more than a hundred Protestant missionaries. When the roll had been called they vacated the court and the governor, wielding his knife himself, began to put the prisoners to death. One can only wonder at the nature of the grudge he bore that his hatred should run so deep!

Where his steel knife fell heads rolled and spurting fresh blood spattered [the ground]. No distinction was now made between old and young. Poor people; their lives, without exception, returned to the underworld!

(Said): In due course it was the turn of an old man to die.

(Sung): An old man with white hair and beard, at about the venerable age of seventy, who spoke Chinese with ease and fluency, said: "I have lived in China forty springs. I have always sought to persuade people to do good, courteously preaching my religion and transforming the recalcitrant. Further, when there was famine in successive years I gave aid to tens of thousands of the distressed.

"Over the years I have solicited incalculable sums of money in the form of contributions, and for this alone you ought to grant me my life. Although I have committed no crime you are now about to execute me. The 'officials and people of the three states forming Chin' are too hardhearted."

When he had finished speaking he repeatedly bowed his head to the ground. One felt heartbroken as one listened to his words; but Governor Yü was poisoned with hate and his ears were deaf as if blocked. He rushed forward and his knife fell, and immediately body and head were parted.

(Said): The next victims were a husband and wife.

(Sung): Two persons knelt on the ground weeping and spoke of the matters which lay on their hearts: "Since coming to Shansi to propagate our religion," they said, "we have frequently employed our medical skills to save the people, handing out medicines and prolonging people's lives. In Shansi we have cured many people and for us to lay down our lives together at this time is far from being the mind of God who loves life."

When the governor had heard them out he broke into laughter and thought: "You can wail as much as you like but I won't hear you." He then ordered them both to come forward to be decapitated so that their heads could be raised on poles. Then they were executed; first the man and then the woman.

(Said): With a single knife-blow he first executed the man; then he instructed the woman to stand below the Hall and bound her hands together. He selected a sharp knife and slit her open, beginning at the lower part of her body. Disemboweled, and with her heart pierced, she died.

(Sung): Licentious, violent, cruel, and totally lacking in humanity, the governor was not happy until he had taken the lives of every foreign woman. A detached bystander would not be able to bear to listen to an account of what took place. When the foreign men and women had all been slaughtered no harm could have resulted from the release of the extremely pitiable children in all their youthfulness. But, afraid lest the leaving of roots should end in eventual distress for the living, this cruel governor, whose mind was thoroughly poisoned, put the children to death one after the other.

(Said): Finally, one foreign child aged ten alone remained. She was plump, white, and adorable, and was still ignorant of what was meant by the word "kill." She was on the ground crying and weeping bitterly as she clung to the dead body of her mother. When Yü-hsien saw her he reached swiftly for his steel knife and was about to bring it down on the child.

(Sung): There was a sudden hubbub in the Grand Hall which so excited the attention of the crowd in the official residence that they all rushed to the entrance of the Hall to see what was happening. The mother of the governor had been startled in her private apartments behind the Grand Hall.

The governor's mother was a woman with a heart of compassion. In her youth she had studied the classics and she therefore had a clear understanding of morality. Because she heard someone say that missionaries were being put to death in the residence she began to feel somewhat uneasy. Later, when she heard her slaves report that more than a hundred foreigners had been put to death, the heart of this dowager grew deeply fearful and she trembled from head to foot.

She strode as fast as she could to the entrance of the Grand Hall where she was confronted with the sight of corpses strewn all over the ground, fresh blood flowing everywhere, limbs separated from their bodies, and bodies which had been disemboweled—a sight to bring anguish to any heart. So mutilated were they that it was impossible to distinguish between one foreigner and another; yet one child still remained alive. The governor rose up and was about to take the child's life.

(Said): . . . When the old lady saw this she hurriedly called on [Yü-hsien] to stay his hand.

(Sung): She said: "Your actions are lacking in any humanity; your only thought is to remove the roots along with the grass. But what royal law has this child broken that you should want to sever its head from its body? I absolutely cannot condone this action. What harm can there possibly be in sparing this one life?"

When the governor had heard his mother out he said: "I am carrying out the will of the ruler in putting this child to death. An imperial decree has stipulated that all children must be exterminated, so even though you command me as my mother [to do otherwise], I cannot obey you."

When he had finished speaking, he raised his steel knife and took the child's life, and although his mother repeatedly remonstrated with him, this heartless governor behaved as if he did not hear her.

(Said): The knife fell. When the old lady saw that he was determined to root out every foreigner, her whole body shook with rage and, pointing at Yü-hsien, she said: "There is no telling how a person such as you, who so violates the fundamental principles of morality, will eventually die." So saying, she sighed several times and, supported by her slave-girl returned to her apartment.

When Yü-hsien saw that every foreigner had been killed he was overjoyed and hurriedly instructed some men to carry the corpses outside the North Gate and to leave them there. That very night he set out for Peking to report and to pay his respects to his master.[34]

As one would expect in a book which sets out to give a full account of an historical event like the Boxer Uprising, much space is devoted to each incident considered important by the author as well as to the actions and intrigues of officials in high places. It is impossible within the limits of a study such as this to examine these in any detail; and, indeed, such an examination, apart from throwing light on the nature of Li's sources, would probably tell us little more than would a competent history of the period, since Li makes the point that he is out not so much to be inventive as to tell the facts of the uprising in a readable and memorable form. In the remainder of the book, then, he follows the fortunes of his leading characters; tells of the reaction of the German kaiser and the German people to the killing of the German minister; describes the allies' attack on and occupation of Peking; gives accounts of the siege of the legation quarter and of attacks on churches in the capital; tells of the execution of leading officials opposed to government cooperation with the Boxers; describes the flight of the empress dowager and the court westward to Sian; summarizes the negotiations for peace carried out between Li Hung-chang, the Chinese minister chosen to salvage what he could from the wreckage, and the allies; and ends with separate accounts of the fates (banishment and suicide) of the officials whose actions had brought China to her knees.

IX   A Sino-Russian Border Incident

Perhaps because he needed the material to fill out his novel, or perhaps because the event took place at the same time as the Boxer Uprising and he found within it further evidence of those Chinese attitudes which he considered harmful to China's well-being, Li suddenly leaves what may be regarded as the Boxer episode proper and in chapters 34–36 gives an account of a clash between Russia and China on the Sino-Russian border.

Varying accounts are given by historians as to what actually took place. According to H. B. Morse,[35] Russian steamers were fired on at Aigun on the Amur River on 14 July and the Russian town of Blagoveshchensk on the north bank was bombarded by Chinese artillery across the river on the fifteenth. In response the Russians slaughtered thousands of Chinese—men, women, and children—their bodies floating down the Amur.

In his narration of this incident Li Po-yuan asserts that a conflict arose between Chinese and Russian forces stationed on the Sino-Russian border when General Shou Shan, who was responsible for the defense of the border region in Manchuria, reacted with unnecessary abruptness and rudeness to a suggestion from the Russian commander that his troops be permitted to pass through Aigun to protect the railway in Manchuria.[36] Replying that Chinese troops were quite capable of looking after the railway themselves, General Shou asserted that should the Russians carry out their proposed move he would meet them with arms. Despite warnings from other commanders and officials that China was not in a position to sustain an attack on the Russians should they cross the border, Shou ordered his troops to open fire when five Russian warships and other boats, together with a thousand troops, sailed down the Amur River. Although General Shou sent a telegram to the Russians accusing them of commencing hostilities, Li takes the view that it was really Shou who was guilty of this when he ordered his troops to open fire. Shou, therefore, through his obstinacy, had to be held equally responsible with the Russians for the subsequent death of thousands of Chinese (Li says 6,000) when men, women, and children were driven out of their homes by Russian cavalry and herded together on the banks of the Amur. According to Li, the Russians had undertaken to evacuate the people by boat, but that when the promised vessel failed to arrive, they put them to the sword. Many, in an attempt to escape, jumped into the river and were drowned.

In Li's account of this border episode the real antagonists are General Shou Shan and a certain civilian official by the name of Wang Huan. Li admits that both men are loyal to the throne, but clearly believes that Wang is right and Shou is wrong. Wang insists that so long as China has to cope with the Boxer problem she cannot win a separate war with Russia. Rather than risk further humiliation, therefore, he counsels caution and negotiations. Shou accuses Wang of being a traitor and threatens to behead him. He does not carry out his threat, however. Instead, he sends Wang away; but Wang leaves a letter behind accusing Shou of commencing hostilities. Furious, Shou has Wang arrested and charges him with dereliction of duty. Wang replies that he cannot abide to be with a man who opens hostilities. Despite a slap across the face, Wang continues to hurl abuse at Shou. Shou is faced with the choice either of beheading him or reporting him to Peking. He decides in favor of execution when he considers the possible effects of Wang's account of events on the court.

The fighting between the Chinese and Russian troops intensifies with the result that Shou loses one of his best generals and his armies are forced to retreat. So, says Li, summing up, Shou, by his action, caused China to lose Aigun, brought about the death of a good general, and opened the way for banditry (i.e., Boxer activity) in the territory. When the Russians, following their victory, demanded to meet General Shou, Shou tried to commit suicide by taking poison. Failing in the attempt he commanded his son to end his life by shooting him.

Having brought this episode to a close, Li returns to the main events of the Boxer Uprising, drawing his story to an end with the return of the royal family to Peking and providing a list of names of those officials who were rewarded or promoted for their efforts in bringing the whole affair to a peaceful conclusion. An appendix gives the text of the protocol agreed to by China and the allies.

Before we draw this chapter to an end two questions require an answer: (1) Whom did Li Po-yuan hold finally responsible for the Boxer Uprising? and (2) Can this work be classified as a work of fiction?

X Who Was Finally Responsible for the Boxer Episode?

In his introduction to the 1935 edition of the book A Ying asserts that due to the circumstances in which Li lived he had no alternative but to employ subtle techniques in order to hint at the true culprit. It is, he maintains, especially in an episode in chapter 21, that the clue to Li's judgment is to be found and his political views revealed.

The episode in question commences with the entry of foreign troops into the palace in Peking. An officer is met by some of the old retainers and eunuchs who ask for a show of clemency and plead that the palace be left intact and not destroyed. After enquiring after the emperor, the foreign officer remarks that the emperor was held in high esteem by all foreigners and that it was a pity that the reforms sponsored by him in 1898 had not been carried through to completion. In answer to the officer's question as to what has happened to the emperor a eunuch replies that the emperor had retired into seclusion and took no further interest in government. The empress dowager, he says, once again participated in government and was confronted morning and night with all the worries attached thereto.

A Ying concludes from this passage that Li took the conventional view that the empress dowager, having taken over the reins of

government, was undoubtedly the person responsible for the decision to ally the Boxers to the court, and that Li must be praised not
only for recounting the events of the uprising but also for his courage
in pointing to the person finally responsible for the tragedy.

The difficulty with A Ying's judgment is that it does not square with
Li's portrayal of the dowager empress in the remainder of his book. In
the earlier portions of the work it is Prince Tuan and his colleagues
who conspire together to make use of the Boxers for their own ends,
and Li explicitly asserts that these men kept the royal family ignorant
of the true state of affairs. The sending of foodstuffs by the empress
dowager to the foreign community under siege in the legation quarters in Peking is a case in point. Generally interpreted by historians
as an attempt on the part of the empress to improve her relations with
the foreign powers because of the fall of Tientsin and the consequent
danger presented to the court both militarily and politically, Li
instead says: "At the time two who understood [the significance of the
gift] said: 'This act illustrates the common Chinese saying which runs:
One may hide the truth from one's superiors, but not from one's
inferiors.' Everyone asked the two how this saying was to be interpreted and they said: 'The attack on the legations is assuredly the
work of senior officials [ministers] of the crown who wish to oppose
us. They hide the truth from the empress dowager and the emperor
so that they are kept in ignorance and therefore know nothing of the
suffering we have had to undergo, and have even sent us melons to
help us cope with the summer heat.' When all had heard this explanation they suddenly realized the truth."

Addressing his readers, Li says: "Dear readers. You should know
that in her handling of the affairs of government our empress dowager
is concerned for the welfare of the empire, is conciliatory to those
who come from afar, and is compassionate and wise. How could she
execute foreign ambassadors indiscriminately and for no cause? It is
clear from this that the siege of the legations was carried out by the
traitors Tuan and Kang and their ilk."

Li's emphasis on the compassion of the empress dowager and on
the way she and the emperor were kept in ignorance of events by
Prince Tuan and Kang-i is repeated over and over again and is
displayed most clearly in those chapters which tell of the progress of
the royal family as it flees the capital westward. The question consequently arises as to whether these judgments genuinely reflect Li's
real views or whether A Ying has given a distorted interpretation of

his position. A more careful examination of the text which A Ying considers crucial and which has already been referred to makes it clear, in our view, that there is no conflict between Li's general portrayal of the empress as a woman of intelligence and compassion on the one hand, and his comment regarding her position in government in the passage in question on the other.

The first point we should notice is that in the eunuch's reply to the officer's opening remarks in the palace he states that following the Sino-Japanese war of 1894 China's army was severely defeated and that China suffered the humiliation of the loss of territory and the payment of reparations to the enemy. It was therefore decided to carry out reforms and to employ members of the reform movement in government. Unfortunately, says the eunuch, officials of mediocre ability plotted to undermine the movement for reform so that it was brought to a halt after only three months. Nowhere does Li suggest that the empress dowager was involved in the plot to bring an end to the movement. In fact, the eunuch is made to say, immediately preceding his comments on the Sino-Japanese war and the reform movement, that the empress dowager never rested and was "diligent in carrying out her official duties . . . kindly caring for the common people, she overflowed with benevolence." Li clearly attributes the abrupt ending of the reform movement to plotting officials, and places the empress, who has the welfare of the nation at heart, on a moral level above the plotters.

Second, although it is commonly stated that the emperor was held prisoner by the empress dowager following her assumption of power after the collapse of the reform movement, Li merely makes the eunuch say that he has withdrawn and takes no further part in government.

Third, when the officer laments the withdrawal of the emperor and then asks why Ta A-ko, the son of Prince Tuan, has been made heir apparent, the eunuch says it is all due to the fact that powerful traitors are in high places and that Prince Tuan got the idea that he himself would like to sit on the throne. His encouragement of the Boxers, says the eunuch, was also due to this. Li seems to be suggesting that rather than cooperating with the empress, Tuan was actually intriguing behind her back in order to replace her.

There is no denying that there is a degree of ambiguity in the section which A Ying uses to support his view, but it seems to us that, taken in conjunction with the passages elsewhere in this book which set out to apportion blame, Li, probably because of his respect for the royal house, or at least for the concept of monarchy, exonerates the empress dowager.[37]

XI   *Is the* Ballad *a Work of Fiction?*

In attempting to answer our second question, Can this book be called a work of fiction? we should note first what Li himself said about it. As stated earlier in this chapter, Li asserted that he wrote the book in order to keep people's memories of the Boxer Uprising alive. This means that he was concerned to preserve historical facts even if these had to be adjusted somewhat to fit in with the needs and techniques of the storyteller.

In a postscript to his preface which is dated the sixteenth day of the tenth month, 1902, Li Po-yuan gives his readers a fairly good idea as to the reliability of the contents of his work. Forty percent of the material in the book, he says, is drawn from accounts in the Chinese and foreign press, and 30–40 percent from information given him by friends. The remaining 10–20 percent, he says, he is himself responsible for. We may conclude from this that Li sought to provide as accurate an account of the Boxer Uprising as he could, based on press reports and on the accounts—no doubt in many instances eyewitness accounts—of what had taken place given him by people he would naturally meet in the course of his work as a journalist and writer. The 10–20 percent which he claims to have contributed himself can no doubt be regarded as covering speeches which he put into the mouths of some of his characters, his own comments and judgments, and those embellishments which an author must of necessity employ if he is to make his material readable and attractive for his audience.

So far we seem to have all the ingredients for a popular history rather than a work of fiction. What puts this work into the category of creative writing is its form, and we must therefore examine this briefly in order to see precisely how Li viewed his work.

The term *t'an-tz'u*,[38] which forms a part of the book's title and which we have translated "ballad," is a category of literature which was generally ignored among the educated and cultured, but which was popular in a number of the provinces of southern China among the uneducated part of the male population, and particularly among women. A type of folk literature, the characters which figured in it tended to be folk heroes rather than the conventional elite who appear in China's traditional orthodox literature.

The origin of the *t'an-tz'u* type of ballad can, like certain other branches of popular Chinese literature such as the *ku-tzu-tz'u*, be traced back to the efforts made by Buddhists to popularize and propagate their faith as early as the T'ang dynasty (618–906 A.D.). Like *pien-wen*, the term used for popularized Buddhist texts, the *t'an-tz'u* ballad contains long sections which are meant to be chanted and the lines of which are therefore of fixed lengths so as to produce an appropriate rhythm. The majority of the lines consist of seven characters (and therefore of seven beats), but these are interspersed at times with lines of three characters or three beats. These three-character lines are frequently, though by no means always, employed for introductory phrases or sentences such as "at this time" or "it is frequently said". The lines in a typical chanted passage may therefore be depicted in the following manner:

$$- - - - - - -, - - - - - - -,$$
$$- - - - - - -, - - - - - - -.$$
$$/ / /, - - - - - - -, - - - - - - -.$$

Chanted passages introduced with the word *ch'ang* (sing or chant) alternate with passages which are meant to be spoken only. These are headed *pai* (speak) and are made up of lines of indeterminate length. Although the spoken passages are occasionally used for no more than the introduction of a lengthy speech which is chanted, they more often than not carry the story forward, the succeeding chanted passage being employed to repeat at least part of what has been said in a more striking and emotionally heightened manner.

The *t'an-tz'u* ballad invariably uses the technique of the third person narrator and has traditionally been employed to provide popular accounts of historical events of current interest. As its form suggests, it was designed to be read and chanted aloud. Under the influence of traditional Chinese opera, which shares similar origins with the ballad, the ballad in the Shanghai region tended to provide for more than one narrator. This was not the case elsewhere, however, where one person both narrated and chanted the text as a whole. The chanted portions were accompanied by string instruments.

Uncertainty surrounds the emergence of the *t'an-tz'u* ballad as a distinct genre, but evidence suggests that it had already won a place for itself at the end of the Yuan dynasty (1277–1367 A.D.). Of the ballads which have survived to the present day, the majority appear to be composed in the dominant dialect of the country, but in the Shanghai region especially the use of the local dialect seems to have been common. No doubt conforming to the practice of the stage, the narrator and major characters speak in the national language whereas minor characters speak in the local dialect. It is said that the *t'an-tz'u* ballad became increasingly the preserve of women and that the more talented among them came to employ this genre as a vehicle of artistic expression. Not surprisingly, the *t'an-tz'u* composed by women tend to reflect the lot of women in traditional society.

In view of the history of the *t'an-tz'u* ballad outlined above, it is not surprising to find that Li Po-yuan states explicitly in a postscript to his preface that his book is to be regarded as suitable for women and children and not the highly educated. His aim, however, as we have already noted, was a serious one. He may, in a sense, have been writing down to his audience, but he was doing so using a genre which, as we can judge from his own preface, he held in high esteem, and with a strong belief that women and the uneducated were of sufficient importance to warrant being informed of events of vital significance both to the nation and to the international community.

Among the faults which have been attributed to this work are the following: (1) Li was so anxious to include everything that took place during the Boxer Uprising that he was not sufficiently selective, and the story is therefore at times confusing. (2) Written episodically for the press and not revised when printed as a book, the work tends, as one progresses through it, to be increasingly repetitive and to suffer from a looseness of organization. We may agree with these criticisms, although it is possible that the genre itself predisposes a writer to fall into such traps. Nonetheless, Li's attempt to use this genre as a vehicle for such a large and serious event as the Boxer Uprising, and thereby to elevate it to the level of a major popular art form and medium of communication, deserves recognition. Our last comment must be that the *t'an-tz'u* and allied ballad forms in China remind the student of literature of certain elements in European folk literature, and this would suggest that a comparative study of the two traditions might well prove of great interest.

Living Hell

*H*UO *ti-yü* (*Living Hell*) was the second of Li Po-yuan's novels to appear in serialized form in his magazine *Illustrated Stories*. Unlike the other one, *Modern Times*, however, it did not appear in book form until 1956 when it was published in Shanghai with a preface by Chao Ching-shen.

Despite its many faults *Living Hell* is a unique work in that it appears to be the first book written in China which sought to expose malpractice and corruption within the Chinese penal system and to describe in detail a variety of the techniques of torture employed to extract information from prisoners. As might be expected, in view of the nature of the subject matter of the novel, *Living Hell* cannot be said to make pleasant reading, and the reader might be forgiven if he concluded, after perusing it, that Li was out to increase the circulation of his magazine by appealing to his readers' taste for the sensational or to their sadistic or other neurotic impulses. But if the general pattern of his writing following the Boxer Uprising is anything to go by, it must, we believe, be conceded that higher motives were at work, and that Li's declared purpose in writing this book—as recorded in his introduction—needs to be taken seriously. Because this introduction tells us something about the nature of Chinese penal and judicial practices as well as about the author's aims, it is worth presenting it here almost in full.

Why do I wish to write this novel? It is because the thing that we Chinese have to suffer more than fire, flood, and warfare [and which is] in fact, several times harsher in its effects than fire, flood, and warfare . . . is nothing other than that tiny magistracy located in county or district town. Each magistracy has an official, and the fundamental purpose of the court [in appointing him] is that he should pass judgment and determine what is right and what is wrong on behalf of the citizenry, settling disputes on the basis of his findings. When there is some matter or other which others cannot comprehend or bring to a successful conclusion, one is supposed to have it resolved as soon as this official has been sought out. . . . Put in this way, an official is a good thing who exists to be a benefactor, and who should never inflict suffering on the man in the street. Yet, strange to relate, the facts are exactly the opposite! . . . Although every official may have a salary and every clerk a living allowance, and although the law may be good, as time has gone by official salaries have ceased to be sufficient to meet the cost of gifts for superiors, and the living allowances of clerks have found their way into the private purses of local officials. . . . Dear readers, put yourselves in their shoes and consider their position: every man in a government office is a hungry tiger and a famished eagle, and if you deny him the right to blackmail the man in the street, whom is he to blackmail? There is a common saying which goes: "Big fish eat little fish, and little fish eat shrimps." . . . But when we come to the clerks and servants we find they have a saying which goes: "He who lives by the mountainside feeds off the mountain, and he who lives by the rivers lives off the rivers." Nothing that passes through their hands is neglected. Alas! the court sets up government offices for the benefit of the people and, lo and behold, they end up providing a shortcut for officials to make money. Don't you think that's lamentable? Moreover, there is a common saying known to all of you which runs: "It is easy to have an audience with the king of Hades, and difficult to ward off little devils."

And who is the king of Hades? He is that official who sits in his court and who can have people beaten or confined in a cangue. Look, he strikes his gavel and startles everyone in his court. Before a word is spoken the man before him is fainting with fright.

And who are the little devils? There is a host of them in every government office. The first of the official underlings is the messenger of death. As soon as a warrant is issued and a prisoner enchained he is hauled off and, before being brought to trial, is deposited in a detention center. The wealthy merely have to spend a few coppers and members of the prisoner's family are permitted to enter it to visit him and to negotiate ways of looking after him. Those without any money may just as well give themselves up to sitting it out and waiting, vacantly, for events to take their course. Thus, this detention center has come to be nicknamed "The Tower of the Homesick."

A magistracy also possesses an archway dedicated to "Justice, Life, and Understanding," and every prisoner who is brought to trial has to pass beneath it. By the time this happens, however, what is clear above all else is that he will get neither justice nor understanding, and that he is simply being hauled off to that city which is the abode of the spirits of those who have died through injustice. At a trial in the Grand Hall of Justice, the magistrate is the king of Hades; the clerks and underlings are the judges who demand the death penalty; the runners and servants, all three ranks of them, are like the ox-headed and horse-faced demon messengers from purgatory, and the flat-bamboo canes and instruments of torture designed to squeeze the flesh of people are like the two-edged sword-leaf trees and the hill of sabres in Hell. Before the prisoner has been assigned to his quarters or incarcerated in prison he has suffered more than enough! Alas! Heaven is above us and Hell is below! Although I have never seen this Hell of "the judges of Hell," I am afraid there is nowhere where one will not find such a hell on earth. That is why I say that its harshness is several times greater than that of fire, flood, and warfare.

This, then, is my reason for writing this book and for describing in detail the circumstances contained therein. If the officials of this world would read through this book of mine carefully a couple of times, and if they would make some effort to do the best they can to fulfill their role as parents of the people, making their demands for money less severe and thinking of ways to remove one or two of these evils inflicted on people, then, not only would the man in the street be grateful to them, but they would also do themselves good by accumulating secret deeds of virtue. There is a common saying which goes as follows: "The right place to cultivate morality is in public office." When Hell is before one's eyes, why not perform immediate deeds of merit and leave a grand memorial to one's self in the eyes of the common people? The following words sum up what I wish to say:

> The murkiness of the world has turned to darkness;
> None knows the day when light will shed forth its rays.
> This scholar holds in his hands tears shed for the
>   moral decadence of the nation;
> He swears an oath to cleanse the universe with them
>   and to save all sentient beings!

Now that I, the author, have clearly indicated my purpose in writing this book . . . I wish to describe in detail for the benefit of my readers everything that I have heard or seen.[1]

I *Structure of* Living Hell

Although *Living Hell* appears at first sight to be a single novel in the manner of *The Bureaucracy Exposed* and *Modern Times*, we find on closer examination that in spite of its overarching theme, the episodes are so loosely put together that the work is better described as a collection of fifteen short stories spread over forty-three chapters. It would seem, too, that not all the stories are from Li's own hand. Li died when he had completed only thirty-nine chapters, and chapters 40–42 were added by his friend, the novelist Wu Chien-jen. Chapter 43 was written by Mao-yuan Hsi-ch'iu Sheng, the pen name, according to A Ying, of a certain Ou-yang Chü-yuan.[2]

As we have already indicated, the stories in *Living Hell* dwell on the practices of officials, both senior and subordinate, within China's penal system as operated at the level of county and district magistracies. The contents of the stories were deliberately designed to shock the reader and to inform him of the deception and villainy found, so Li would have us believe, in every corner of the system. Although the stories are not located in as wide a variety of settings as the episodes in his two major novels, the author can still be said to range over a considerable portion of the country. The stories vary in length from those of one chapter to one which extends over eight chapters. As one would expect, the longer the story the greater is the number of characters introduced and the more complex are the events described. The following are summaries of some of the best of the fifteen stories.

II *A Feud and Its Consequences*

The first story, which is told in chapters 1–8, begins by taking the reader to Yang-kao *hsien*, which falls within the jurisdiction of Ta-t'ung *fu* in the province of Shansi, and which is situated approximately 130 *li* northeast of that city.

The narrator of the story tells us that Shansi has suffered successive years of drought and that in consequence many people find themselves in debt. Wealthy families are still to be found in the interior of the province, however, and despite the smallness of a town like Yang-kao it is still capable of supporting several such families. It is the custom in this town, says the narrator, "to live simply and frugally and, since there is nothing on which to spend money, it grows through being hoarded."

The reader is next introduced to one such wealthy family by the name of Huang. The head of the family, we are told, has purchased an official title and is consequently addressed by everyone as Secretary Huang despite the fact that he has never actually held office. The family owns land, and one day one of Huang's tenant-farmers informs him that his ox has been led away by a tenant-farmer of the Wu family—another wealthy family in the locality with which the Huangs have feuded for generations. The farmer states that he has been to the Wu's to ask for the return of the ox, but that the Wu's refused to return it and had even given him a beating.

Unable to contain his anger, Secretary Huang summons his general manager, Huang Sheng, and instructs him to send for a Mr. Tiao Chan-kuei who is an expert in the art of drawing up legal petitions and in finding his way among officials concerned with the handling of litigation.

Huang Sheng quickly "returned in company with a man whose face was thin and yellow and who exuded the air of an opium smoker. He had a drooping moustache, a pair of projecting ears, and spectacles on his nose. On his head was a 'melon-peel' skullcap, and he wore a greasy, shiny, blue cotton gown over which was an old sky-blue woollen-cloth jacket."

Huang repeats to Tiao what his tenant-farmer has told him—though adding a little color of his own to the story—and askes Tiao to prepare a charge. Tiao interrogates the tenant-farmer, finds insufficient evidence, but is nevertheless instructed by Huang to proceed with the case. Tiao, therefore, smokes a little opium and writes up the charge, but informs Huang that everything else is up to him.

The case is taken to court. The magistrate can find no wounds on the body of the tenant-farmer to confirm his claim to have been beaten, and he is about to dismiss the case when one of his secretaries urges him to delay his decision. Later, and in private, the secretary tells the magistrate that since both parties are wealthy money can be made out of both of them. The plaintiff, he says, should be told that he can have his charge accepted if he will pay several thousand ounces of silver toward the setting up of a school, and the defendant should be informed that for a similar sum the charge will be dropped.

In chapter 2 the secretary, whose name is Chao, summons a mounted messenger whom he can trust. This man, called Shih Hsiang-ch'uan, advises Chao that they should demand 10,000 ounces of silver from each of the families and that of this sum 8,000 should go to the magistrate. When Chao asks Shih what he hopes to get out of the deal, Shih suddenly remembers a case which he would like Chao to resolve on his behalf by making representations to the magistrate. Chao reminds Shih that there are "rules" which govern the actions of senior officials and the way in which money is to be dispersed. When agreement is reached on the manner in which Shih's own case is to be handled, Chao reminds him of his responsibilities in the case concerning the Huang and Wu families. Shih pretends to be affronted at this oblique suggestion that he might be lacking in probity.

The essence of the plan concocted by Chao and Shih Hsiang-ch'uan is to play the Huang and Wu families off against each other. Needless to say, the implementation of the plan comes to involve other subordinates in the magistracy, and the intrigues in the chap-

ters which follow reach a degree of complexity which it would prove
too tedious to unravel here. Part of the purpose of the story, however, is to give a graphic account of what it is like to be detained in a
magistracy prison, and Li Po-yuan does this by having Huang Sheng,
Secretary Huang's relative and manager, the tenant-farmer, Wang
San, and, later, Huang Sheng's wife, taken into custody pending the
magistrate's final decision. In the following brief passage taken from
chapter 3 we have a description of Huang Sheng's initial experiences
following his arrest.

Chao San, Shih Hsiang-ch'uan's clerk, led Secretary Huang's relative and
manager Huang Sheng, together with the tenant-farmer, Wang Hsiao-san,
into the lockup which was located inside the main gate of the magistracy
below the Great Hall of Justice. It consisted of a low building with three
rooms and was situated on the west facing east. When one passed through the
door of the building one found that two of the rooms opened on to each other
and that running from north to south was a wooden fence. Outside was a
narrow alleyway which accommodated only one person at a time. Although
the area behind the fence was quite large, forty or fifty people were crowded
into it. Huddled together in one place, it was impossible to determine their
exact number. Some wore clothes which were in good repair whereas others
were dressed in garments so tattered as to be virtually unwearable. Some had
very long hair and some had cloth bound round their heads like turbans.
Some were cruel and evil-looking whereas others appeared benign; some
were weeping; some were singing; some were cursing; and some were
sighing. There were old people and young people, fat people and thin
people. Some were sitting while others were standing, and some were
sleeping while others were awake. Those who were asleep slept on the floor,
but in a sitting position with their backs against a wall. None could find room
to stretch himself out to his full length. Those who were seated had also to sit
on the floor since no one was likely to provide anyone with a stool.
    Although it was just on the threshold of the second month and the weather
was bitterly cold, the stench was unbearable even before one ventured
behind the fence. When Huang Sheng and Wang Hsiao-san were brought to
the prison building by Chao San, another government servant, an assistant
runner who was in charge of the lockup and whose name was Mo Shih-jen
came over to them to take charge of them. Holding the chains with which
they were fettered with one hand, he muttered to Chao San for some time.
Chao San could be overheard replying: "Clerk Mo, these gentlemen are from
the Huang household. Treat them well and don't allow them to suffer
unjustly." When he had finished speaking he departed.
    At first Mo Shih-jen refrained from putting his two men behind the fence
and led them instead to an area below a window on the south side of the

building where he wound their chains several times round a post within the fence. He said: "How is it that a gentleman of the Huang household now finds himself brought so low?"

Realizing, when he heard this remark, that he was obviously being ridiculed, Huang Sheng said nothing in reply in order to see how his jailer would react. Mo Shih-jen continued: "There are a lot of people in this place and it's incredibly filthy, so would you please squat outside for the time being. When someone arrives to act as your guarantor and to bail you out, you'll be able to leave. Should no one come to bail you out, it'll be soon enough to put you inside when night falls and it's time for you to sleep."

These two comments could give the impression that the jailer was being a little solicitous toward his prisoners. Huang Sheng was unable to guess what he had in mind and therefore remained silent.

When he had finished speaking, Mo Shih-jen fetched a stool for himself and stationed himself before the door. Huang Sheng and Wang Hsiao-san remained standing for a considerable time, but no one they knew came to see them. Their legs grew numb and painful from standing. They decided to squat on the ground but found that since the slack of the chain, one end of which was wound around their necks and the other end round a post, was too short, it would prove impossible to lower their bodies without hanging themselves. Their next thought was to ask Mo Shih-jen to lengthen the chain for them, but they reflected that their jailers were unlikely to make things easy for them and that they had best endure the numbness in their legs and be patient for the time being.

There was, however, one thing which was proving unbearable. When they had entered the prison their noses had been assailed by wave upon wave of foul air. At first they had no idea of the cause of the odors, but later, sounds reached them which indicated that behind the fence, and close to where they were standing, was a jar for urine, and all the prisoners made their way to it to urinate. At first they were able to put up with the smell, but later, when the day grew late and they were beginning to feel hungry, they found it increasingly difficult to bear the fumes.

In no time at all darkness fell and Mo Shih-jen stepped inside to light a lamp attached to the wall. Some of the prisoners behind the fence had food sent in to them by their families; some had money on their persons and bought what food they wanted from a food vendor brought in by Mo Shih-jen. Then there was a person who had been instructed by Mo Shih-jen to prepare things for certain individuals; but there were also those who had to remain hungry because there was nothing for them to eat.[3]

Among other things, the foregoing passage is designed to convey a certain ambiguity in the attitude of Mo Shih-jen to his new charges. Having created uncertainty and anxiety in the minds of his prisoners, he pushes his advantage and makes it clear to them that their future welfare will depend on the cooperation of members of the Huang family and on the amount of money forthcoming from that source.

Following a night in the lockup with the other prisoners, Huang Sheng is thoroughly dispirited and, hungry through lack of food, asks Mo to inform his master, Secretary Huang, of his plight and to ask him to send him some money. Mo, however, says to Huang Sheng that he will first tell his wife and children of his circumstances. As soon as they learn what has happened to him, Huang Sheng's wife and children rush over to the prison in tears. The wife has brought a little money with her and asks Mo to use it to care for her husband. Mo tells her the money is insufficient, but then prepares noodles for all the prisoners and tells them that they have been donated by Huang.

At this point the warder, a man called Kou, passes by and hears a woman's voice. Stepping out of the prison building, the woman, Huang Sheng's wife, walks straight into Kou who is bowled over by her good looks. Mistakenly thinking that she finds him attractive, Kou arranges with Mo to have her detained in prison as well. This is accomplished by Mo telling her to return that evening with more money and then having her arrested for being on prison premises after hours. After being seized, she is handed over to a wardress. This gives Li Po-yuan his opportunity to describe a detention center for women and to detail one way in which women thus held could be coerced into granting favors to male prison officers. The section in question is found in chapter 6 and runs as follows:

When Huang Sheng's wife (née Chou) was discovered in the lockup by Attendant Kou she was scolded and then ordered to be led away and detained by the wardress in charge of women prisoners. At this moment Mrs. Huang regretted she could not grow wings and fly away; she also regretted her refusal to obey her mother-in-law by venturing alone into a place not open to the general public. Now that she was detained in the house of the wardress in charge of women prisoners she was bound to experience more bad luck than good. When she had thought thus far she could not restrain herself from sobbing into the hands with which she covered her face.

The wardress said to her: "When things have reached such a pass, there is little advantage to be gained from weeping. Come with me. This old woman has spent her days in fasting and in invoking the Buddha, and if there is any way in which I can be of service to you I shall certainly be so." There was little Mrs. Huang could do but accompany the woman. They had barely turned a couple of corners when they reached a tiny courtyard which stood apart. In it was a simple building comprising three rooms. The room in the center had an oil lamp above it and two old crones could be seen guarding it. The room on the east side was silent and empty of people, whereas from the room on the west side came the barely audible sound of people snoring. Because it was late all the women prisoners had long been asleep.

The wardress led Mrs. Huang into the building; instructed an old serving woman to light the lamp in the room to the east, and then led Mrs. Huang into the room where she was made to sit down. When Mrs. Huang had stepped inside and looked about her, she found that although the room had no furniture to speak of, the coverlets on the bed were clean. The old serving woman poured out a cup of tea which she handed to her to slake her thirst. The wardress now lit a lamp herself and went off to examine each of the prisoners in the west room. Because each woman prisoner was fond of her sleep no one got out of bed to welcome her. She therefore took advantage of her position; adopted an awesome mien; laid hold of a bamboo broom and, without more ado, rained blows on every woman in the room as she shouted: "You foxes disguised as women are in my charge now that you're in this place. You must all bow your heads to me the moment you see me whether you're rotten prostitutes or the wives of officials."

Not one of the female prisoners thus beaten and abused dared to answer back. While the beating and cursing was going on Mrs. Huang could hear everything and, cringing, she shook with fright, fearing lest she too would be included in the punishment.

Shortly afterward she saw the wardress returning from the room which stood to the west. The wardress was still hurling abuse at the "stinking prostitutes" and "complete good-for-nothings." The moment Mrs. Huang saw her coming she jumped, terrified, to her feet to meet her; but to her surprise the wardress treated her in a most agreeable manner.

Now why was this? It was because prior to the detention of Mrs. Huang, Attendant Kou and Mo Shih-jen had explained the reason for it to the wardress. They asked her to serve as a go-between and, initially, to speak kindly to Mrs. Huang. If things were made perfectly clear to her there would be no need to say more and to put one's self to a lot of trouble. If she should prove unwilling, however, steps could be taken to ensure that she would comply; and should she prove unyielding she might be induced to show some willingness through being forced to taste a little unpleasantness.

The wardress's name was Sai Wang and she was gifted with eloquence. When she spoke her words were sweeter than honey, but her mind contained more poison than a snake. She was the third generation in her family from the time her grandmother was alive to hold this official post.

The moment the wardress received her orders from Attendant Kou and Mo Shih-jen she patted her chest as if accepting a challenge and said: "I can certainly render a service as small as this. I'll not deceive you, attendant; there is no married woman in the world, no matter what kind of person she is, who can escape my trap once she has fallen into my hands. I'll have some news for you after the third watch."

Attendant Kou was delighted.

After the wardress had taken Mrs. Huang to her room and the latter had turned several times in her sleep it was already past the second watch of the night. The wardress then walked over to Mrs. Huang and looked her over from head to toe without uttering a word. She thought to herself: "To judge from her appearance this is an honest and upright woman and not one of those saucy creatures. But a woman has a woman's temperament, and should she become stubborn and unwilling to cooperate, it'll be hard to find a way to bring her round. Beatings and abuse will prove useless. The best thing I can do is to give her an example of what she can expect and gradually wear down her resistance, thereby avoiding any waste of effort."

When she had decided what she would do she said to her women assistants: "The prostitute has been here three days now. I've treated her with kindness and have made every effort to be persuasive; but she is stubborn and refuses to do as we ask her: this is because she doesn't know when she's being well treated. It's not my fault if I've now got to make her taste a little suffering."

The two women assistants were in collusion with the wardress and were completely aware that she was employing the stratagem whereby one lets it be known that an attack is proposed from the east while the real advance is to be made on the west. Without mentioning any name, therefore, they turned to Mrs. Huang and said: "Can you imagine it! That there should be anyone in the world so ignorant of what's good for her! Every person who ends up in this place of ours is a criminal so you've only yourself to blame. Whether you're a wife and mistress in the household of a high official or merely a maiden and unmarried girl, once you've entered these gates you must submit to our control. The reason for this is that, as the saying goes, 'When the prince offends against the law the common people follow suit.' Since you must submit to our control you must obey our regulations. Whether you're the wife and mistress of a household or a maiden and young unmarried girl; no matter how much wealth is owned by your family or how much power it wields, you will be treated in exactly the same manner as the common people and will have to experience a little hardship and suffering. Since such is the royal law, where does the blame lie for breaking it but with yourself? Nevertheless, the law allows for differences and distinctions. We try to save genuine criminals by providing slightly better accommodation and somewhat better food; but, of course, we can never release them. As for you, you haven't really committed any crime to speak of. All that is required is that Attendant Kou should come over here, raise his noble hand, and order your release—a very easy thing indeed."

Mrs. Huang suddenly asked: "What does Attendant Kou do?" The women replied: "His sole responsibility is the charge of male and female prisoners. If he shows himself eager for your welfare, then you're in luck and you'll be able to leave this place this very night."

Mrs. Huang said: "What do I have to do to persuade the venerable gentleman to have my welfare at heart? Unfortunately, my husband has already been held two days in the magistracy and my mother-in-law at home is already a person of great age. Then I have a large number of children. If I don't get home what will become of them?" When she had finished speaking she began to weep; she then knelt down in front of the wardress and struck her forehead on the ground, beseeching her to put in a good word for her with Attendant Kou and to plead with him to act graciously toward her at the earliest possible moment.

The wardress heard her out in silence and then, after a long pause, said: "I can't take the initiative in this matter; you'll have to do what's required yourself."

Mrs. Huang said: "And what must I do?"

The wardress replied: "It would be a crime just to mention it; however, people who end up here are not in a position to use the word 'chastity.' "

Now although Mrs. Huang had been born into a lower-class family she was familiar with the broad principles of life and was not one of those who engaged in one love affair after another. The moment she heard these remarks of the wardress she felt her face turn scarlet and she slowly lowered her head and remained silent for a long time.

Having already discerned the way things stood, the "worthy" wardress said no more to Mrs. Huang but simply urged her two assistants: "Hurry up and ask that rotten prostitute whether she's changed her mind. If she hasn't, let her know that I've already waited a couple of days and that I'm not that patient."

The women left and, a few minutes later, returned from the west room leading a young woman of twenty or so years of age. Her hair was disheveled and her face dirty and she was sobbing with distress into her sleeve. Although it was impossible to see the beauty of the woman in the light of the lamp, it was possible to discern the slenderness of her figure and that the clothes she was wearing were still clean.

When Mrs. Huang caught sight of her she started and her pulse began to race. Suddenly she heard Wardress Sai Wang shout at the top of her voice: "Now that your time has come do you still stand there unmoving?" As she shouted she struck the woman three or four times across the face, driving her to her knees. The woman begged the wardress for mercy.

Wardress Sai Wang said: "Creatures like you are not worth a good turn. I've nothing more to say to you. We'll decide what's to be done after you've had an enjoyable night."

So saying the wardress instructed her two women assistants to lower a long, thick rope from the beam in the roof. She then had the young woman pressed down to the floor and her hands and feet trussed as one would truss a pig. The rope was now passed between her hands and feet and, when this was accomplished, it was firmly tied with a knot. Wardress Sai Wang and her two women assistants together pulled the other end of the hempen rope with all their might. In no time at all the young woman was suspended high above them. Wardress Sai Wang cursed unendingly as she sought for a bamboo cane with which to beat this cheap object who was "not worth a good turn." Suspended in midair, the woman had long since begun to experience dizziness and she simply groaned or cried out wildly. Mrs. Huang, on the other hand, hid herself away in the room on the east side, curled up into a terrified, trembling bundle. Having found a bamboo cane, Wardress Sai Wang was about to make use of it when she suddenly heard clanging sounds made by the iron ring which served as a door-knocker outside. Those who knocked on this door always used a secret code, so after listening carefully, Wardress Sai Wang knew that it was Attendant Kou who was knocking on the door. She hurriedly put her bamboo cane aside and went to open the door.

As soon as she had assured herself that it was indeed he, she said: "You've come here too early, sir. I still haven't completed the negotiations!"

Attendant Kou said: "I've been waiting outside this door for goodness knows how long. Hearing you beating someone just now I was afraid you had reached an impasse, and I therefore deliberately decided to let you know I was here."

"You may accuse me of being a stupid old woman," said Wardress Sai Wang, "but even if I am stupid, I'd hardly dare torture the woman on whom you've set your heart. The one I'm beating is the creature who's not worth a good turn; not the one who's only just come."

"Where is the one who arrived today?" asked Attendant Kou.

Wardress Sai Wang said: "In the room on the west side."

Attendant Kou pretended to be quite unconcerned, but stepped inside and took a look around.

Wardress Sai Wang said: "First go outside, sir, and wait until I've done what I have to do and send for you."

Attendant Kou said: "Don't talk nonsense! I've been ordered by my superiors to come and investigate the criminals." As he spoke he withdrew and the door was closed once more.

Wardress Sai Wang raised her cane and, allowing no time for words, applied it fully several hundred times to every portion of the woman's body suspended in midair. The woman sobbed and cried out and Wardress Sai Wang said, as she beat her: "You hussy, not worthy of a good turn! When you came inside this old woman treated you so well. I served you as if you were a noblewoman when it came to food and sleep, but thus far I've not succeeded in reforming your conscience. Since rotten prostitutes like you wish to establish memorials to your chastity you ought not go and break the law; but since you have broken the law and landed yourself here you must stop all this pretence to chastity!"

As she abused her in this fashion Wardress Sai Wang dealt the woman a further twenty or thirty strokes of the cane. The woman's whole body was covered in bloody weals but she uttered not a word, simply screaming with pain. The two women assistants on the floor pleaded with her saying: "Hurry up and promise to cooperate! Not only will you avoid all this agony but you'll even be given silver money." The woman remained silent and Wardress Sai Wang said: "There's no need for you to plead with her any more. It's obvious good fortune isn't the lot of this baggage. Even if we should lose this one we've got others!"

When she had finished speaking she went inside to talk with Mrs. Huang. She said: "Just think; there actually are people like this in the world who don't know what's good for them! Because this woman's husband is dead and because she's young, her parents-in-law wanted to sell her to a man from another city; however, the deal was barely two days old when, quite unexpectedly, she escaped and fled back to her home. She is being sued, and therefore the magistrate issued a warrant for her arrest and assigned her first to our charge. Luckily, she attracted the attention of our venerable Kou who is responsible for prisoners. As he liked her, he entrusted me with the task of go-between. Who'd have thought that such a strumpet would die rather than do as she's asked? In my view any woman consigned to this place is a lawbreaker, and how can anyone pretend to be chaste once she's broken the law! . . . the running of this place, at all levels, is in the hands of this venerable Kou. . . . Those who comply with his wishes—murderers apart— can rely on [him] to speak up for them before the magistrate, no matter how serious their offence; for example, those who ought to be detained for several months can be released immediately if they go along with him; and even if they're not released, those in my charge need experience no suffering. I would guess from the looks of you that you haven't committed any major crime. Only do what the venerable Kou wants when he comes here shortly and I'll guarantee that you'll have no difficulty in getting out today or tomorrow. All I ask of you in return for my advice is that you do not forget me when good fortune comes your way."

Mrs. Huang's face flushed and her heart beat fast in her breast as she listened to what this woman had to say, and she was at a loss to know how to reply for the best. As she remained there stunned, she heard someone knocking on the door. Wardress Sai Wang went to open the door while Mrs. Huang felt so terrified that she did not know which way to turn.

Should you wish to know who it was that entered the room, please read the following chapter.[4]

Li Po-yuan does not give the reader the satisfaction of seeing Mrs. Huang resolve her dilemma on her own. Instead, while she is still pondering the alternatives before her, he comes to her rescue by bringing about a speedy disbursement of funds among the various persons in the magistracy involved in the case and thereby effecting her, and everyone else's, release.

III *An Overzealous Magistrate*

The second story in this collection is contained in chapters 9–11. The reader is introduced to a new incumbent of the Yang-kao magistracy who, eager to show his gratitude to his superiors for his appointment as well as to display his administrative abilities, attends court daily and is determined to handle every item of business himself. He refuses to allow his clerks and assistants to take any decision of their own or to make any money out of legal transactions. So scrupulous is he, in fact, that he refuses to accept any money himself. Being overzealous about minor matters he quickly finds himself faced with a rise in the number of cases brought before his court. Later, however, as it becomes known that this magistrate also orders severe floggings for minor offences, the people become afraid to bring cases before him. Since no one dares to say he is anything but a good official, his reputation as a man who can uphold law and order reaches the ears of his superiors and, when the opportunity arises, he finds it relatively easy to have himself transferred to more pleasant pastures in Canton.

On arrival in Canton the magistrate, whose name is Yao, advocates the use of steel canes instead of the usual bamboo to deal with men detained following an outbreak of banditry. A Cantonese bandit called Liang Ya-keng is brought before Yao who interrogates his prisoner while eating his meal (to save time). Liang sidesteps the charge of aggravated robbery brought against him and instead complains that he was wrongfully arrested while working peacefully in his fields. He admits that he has confessed to the crime, but insists that the confession was extracted under torture and that he now wishes to withdraw it. Yao tells him he believes he is telling the truth, but says that some of his inexperienced colleagues demand that he be put to the test. Yao then instructs the court attendants to set up a rack in the shape of a cross. Liang is hoisted on to it, but when he shows himself able to bear this form of torture, other techniques are introduced. The following passage describing Liang's tortures appears in chapter 10.

The "Weighing Scales Rack" was in the form of a cross and the prisoner's arms were stretched out on either side of him by means of a wooden pole. His queue was tied to the shaft and he knelt, upright, on the ground. Liang Ya-keng, however, had an unexpected capacity for endurance and was able to bear the torture. By the time Magistrate Yao had completed his meal, wiped his face with a hot towel, rinsed his mouty, stepped across to another room to sit on a divan, and his servants had filled the bowl of his pipe more than ten times, fully three quarters of an hour had gone by; yet Liang Ya-keng refused even to groan.

Realizing that he was better than the average man, Magistrate Yao looked at him, and, smiling, said: "This is nothing. I should imagine you look on it as being of no more significance than a common meal at home." [Then, turning to his attendants, he said:] "Provide him with a couple of chains."

When he had finished speaking two attendants stepped forward. They rolled up the bottoms of Liang Ya-keng's trousers and coiled a couple of large thick chains on the ground where he had been kneeling; then they made him kneel on top of them. Liang did so for some considerable time but still managed to maintain silence.

Magistrate Yao said: "So he won't give in; he really is capable of endurance." He then issued instructions that incense be lit; he continued: "Though you may be able to withstand these various forms of torture you must be made to experience every single one of them. If one is unsuccessful, we must apply another; this is called 'moving from the shallow to the deep.' "

As he spoke, the attendants took two sticks of incense, each as thick as a finger, and, having lit them, fastened them to Liang Ya-keng's arms. From time to time they blew the ash off the incense lest Liang be burned by the ash alone and the results prove less painful.[5]

Despite the torture, Liang continues to refuse to swear an affidavit and, realizing his prisoner might faint, Magistrate Yao orders the torture to cease.

Yao now turns his attention to a murder case which has resulted from an adulterous affair. A woman by the name of Chang admits that she has committed adultery but denies the charge of murder to which she at first confessed. Asked why she has changed her plea, she says that she was unable to withstand the torture previously meted out to her. She is then stripped of her clothes and a flat-iron with nipples attached to it is filled with charcoal. The magistrate orders the woman held by her hair with arms outstretched as if she were on a rack. He then instructs the attendants to apply the heated nipples first to her left arm and then to her right. The author tells the reader that the woman screamed like a pig being slaughtered but refused to admit to any crime other than adultery. The iron is next heated until the nipples are red hot, but at this point the woman faints away. Finally, when she comes to and realizes that the torture will continue, she acknowledges guilt and pleads for mercy.

Of the remaining stories in this collection several are little more than further elaborations on the themes of corruption and torture. Artistically weak, they merit no more attention here. The stories contained in chapters 23–26 and 29–33, however, deserve to be noted for their artistic qualities.

IV *The Framers*

The first of these stories is set in a village of five hundred or so families in the province of Anhwei. The majority of the menfolk earn their livings as fishermen; but one young man, a twenty-one-year-old called Chu Chung, belongs to a relatively well-to-do family and has received several years of schooling. His parents die, however, and he runs through the family fortune in two years. A relative puts him to work in his shop in the city nearby, but unable to handle him and to persuade him to change his lazy ways, sends him off with ten strings of cash.

One day an opera troupe gives a performance at the temple of the city's guardian deity and Chu Chung goes to see it. He notices an elderly man in front of him in the audience who is wearing a pair of sunglasses. When the sun goes down the man removes them and puts them in his pocket. Chu Chung takes advantage of the movement around him, occasioned by someone squeezing his way into the audience, to steal the glasses. He has barely extricated himself from the crowd and put the glasses on his face, however, when someone comes up from behind him, taps him on the back, and asks: "Is business good?" Chu Chung does not know the man, but the man says: "You'll know me when we've had tea together."

Chu Chung and the stranger go to the foot of the city wall, where there are some matting booths, and sit down. The stranger asks Chu Chung where he got his glasses. Chu Chung replies that they are his and that where he got them is no business of the stranger. Chu Chung makes to leave but is immediately surrounded by two or three men who are told by the stranger that he has business elsewhere and that while he is away they are to teach Chu Chung his manners. One of the men then seizes Chu Chung by the queue, throws him to the ground, and binds him up. His cries for help are ignored and when he is tortured with chopsticks, which are inserted between the rope and the skin, his captors tell him that this is a form of initiation rite for thieves. The stranger returns and tells Chu Chung that he will accept him as an apprentice burglar and that the spoils from his activities will be shared between them in such a way that he will receive thirty percent of them. He is told what to do if he is captured, to remember the houses he raids, and to leave the gentry alone since officials take their side in a dispute.

While Chu Chung is wondering to himself whether he can get out of his predicament by confessing to officials his theft of the glasses, a man is brought into the room by one of the thieves. The thief says his master has been trying to press a case against a certain family but that he has so far been unable to proceed. He now wants his captive to provide evidence on his behalf. To terrorize him into compliance, the captive is tied up in matting and stood behind the door where he soon experiences disorientation.

Chu Chung is just thinking that it would be better to go to court and to confess his crime than to have to undergo this kind of treatment at the hands of the thieves when another man is brought in to make a confession. He is tied to a bench with his hands behind his back and an increasing number of bricks is inserted between his back and the benchtop until he finally gives in and promises to make the required confession. It turns out that the statements and confessions which the two captives finally undertake to make are in fact to be used on behalf of certain officials. The two men are therefore led off to make a court appearance. Clearly, the thieves are also unofficial minions of subordinate officials in the magistracy who use them to provide the kind of witnesses and evidence which will help them manipulate court cases so that they work out financially or otherwise favorably to themselves.

Chu Chung's initial theft of the sunglasses, his subsequent capture by the thieves, and the methods the villains employ to intimidate their victims, are all described with great skill. The story successfully evokes the atmosphere of a small country town with its occasional open-air opera performances, its lean-tos along the side of the city wall, and its dangerous and tricky ruffians whose sole motive is profit and who will work with corrupt government officials provided it serves their own ends.

The cases brought before the court and subsequent actions in the remainder of this episode are also most convincingly described; but, as we would expect, much emphasis is placed on detailing the beatings and tortures meted out to those from whom confessions are extracted. The financial intrigues which take place in the background are also given much play.

V *A Family Intrigue*

The second story, which has its setting in the village of Shih-chia ts'un, which is about fifty *li* from Ch'ung-sha *hsien* in the province of Hunan, is a most skillfully told tale of jealousy and family intrigue which involves impersonation, misrepresentation, accusations of adultery, and murderous intentions as well as legal chicanery. It is a story, the events of which take place at a level of society with which the author is obviously familiar, and which he is happiest at describing both here and in his other stories and novels. The dialogue and detail which he employs in episodes such as this bring his stories to life in a manner which is most convincing, and which contrasts rather sharply with the staginess and unreality with which some accounts of the lives and activities of senior bureaucrats are presented elsewhere.

The narrator tell us that although the majority of the people in Shih-chia ts'un bear the surname Shih, two men connected with the village who are distantly related to one another are called Min. One of these men, Min Shu-ch'un, is a dealer in gems and travels widely. As a gem merchant his home is really in the nearby city, but he lives in the country to avoid involvement in city affairs. His distant relative, Min Chung-hsing, however, has been a teacher in the village and has now decided to make it his home.

Although living in rather poor circumstances, Chung-hsing has reared two sons, both of whom are gifted. Shu-ch'un, on the other hand, has spent his youth cultivating casual female acquaintances, and has therefore failed to provide himself with an heir.

Deeply fond of one of his relative's sons, Shu-ch'un would dearly like to adopt him, but refrains from saying so. Chung-hsing is able to detect the lines along which Shu-ch'un is thinking, but Shu-ch'un's wife dislikes the idea of adoption because the boy would not be her own. She decides that if there is to be a legitimate son in the family, it would be better to acquire one through a concubine. She therefore makes inquiries and finally locates a young widow who, over a period of four years, had produced three sons. Having assured her husband that the woman is good at producing sons she pays the widow's mother-in-law more than a hundred dollars and takes the woman into her own home. Two months later she is found to be pregnant and eventually gives birth to a boy. Shu-ch'un is naturally delighted and throws a feast for his friends.

Shu-ch'un's distant relative, Chung-hsing, however, is far from happy since he believes he could have benefited financially from Shu-ch'un's adoption of his son. He therefore begins to consider ways whereby he can still achieve his ends. He contemplates killing the child and sending his own son to his relative to claim heirship. To prepare people's minds, he goes about telling them that sons fre-

quently die and that people are often left without an heir. He insists
that his relative is too old to beget a son, that the baby bears no
resemblance to him, and that trouble could result from someone of a
different family and bearing a different surname usurping the
heirship and thus committing a crime against the family's ancestors.

When Shu-ch'un's son reaches the age of nine, Shu-ch'un falls ill
and dies. On receiving news of the death, Chung-hsing gathers some
luggage together and hurries into the city where he sets himself up as
a teacher and acquires a few pupils. Fifteen months later Shu-ch'un's
wife also dies.

Although he is now living in the city, Chung-hsing follows his
relative's affairs closely and his son often brings him news of events in
the village. People in the village, however, are merely told that
Chung-hsing has gone away on business, and no one outside his
immediate family knows that he is residing in the city. Receiving a
letter from one of his sons and hearing of the demise of Shu-ch'un's
wife, Chung-hsing is delighted, and his seventeen or eighteen pupils
are startled when he enters the classroom, bangs his table, and tells
them they can have a holiday.

Returning to the Shih village, he takes the son for whom Shu-ch'un
has shown fondness to Shu-ch'un's home. Stepping inside he sees the
tablet erected to Shu-ch'un's spirit and pretends to weep with sor-
row. At this point Shu-ch'un's concubine appears, leading her son by
the hand. Chung-hsing pretends not to recognize her and asks someone who she and the child are. A servant replies that this is his
(Chung-hsing's) nephew. Chung-hsing tells the servant to stop joking
and goes on to say that Shu-ch'un had once told him that following his
death *his* son was to be regarded as Shu-ch'un's heir. Because Shu-
ch'un had no children, Chung-hsing says, the servants contrived to
cheat their master by presenting him with the child of a prostitute.
He then calls his own son over to him and tells him publicly that
because his uncle had no heir he, his father, had long ago
handed him over to his uncle to be his son. Now that the boy's aunt
has also died, he says, he must put on mourning before the spirit
tablet. At this, the son rips off his outer clothes to reveal a mourning
gown. He takes a hempen headdress from his sleeve, puts it on, and
pushes his way to the front of the mourners where he bows his head
before the tablet. Chung-hsing now states that his son is the legitimate heir and that the child of the concubine should be led away.

Close friends of the deceased who promised him to care for his
small son now step forward to refute Chung-hsing's claim, and a

tremendous argument ensues. Chung-hsing says that the matter is none of their business and that he simply wants to keep his family free of pollution by bastards. He announces he will take the matter to court and then withdraws. The concubine makes a plea on behalf of her child, but Chung-hsing's son remains seated in the chief mourner's position. The friends of the deceased, however, promise to come to the aid of the concubine should Chung-hsing create more trouble for her.

The following morning Chung-hsing sets out to find an advocate. He discovers a certain Wang Po-tan who specializes in offering advice. The amount of advice he gives, of course, depends on the amount of money forthcoming. He receives Chung-hsing's gifts and then leaves him for two hours to smoke some opium. When he hears what Chung-hsing wants, he remarks that he has been presented with a matter of much gravity, that if Chung-hsing wins the case he will be wealthy, and that there is a saying that "people should sweep the snow from their own front door and leave the frost on other's roofs alone." Why, asks the advocate, should he at his great age set out to commit so great a sin?

Chung-hsing replies that although there is little he can do at this stage, if the case should succeed, he will not forget the source of his good fortune. The advocate says he cannot take on a case such as this for less than five or six thousand ounces of silver. However, when Chung-hsing tells him he will send him three thousand, the advocate is delighted and promises to do his best.

The advocate now suggests that there are three ways to handle this case: first, the concubine's friends can be paid to stop taking an interest in her welfare. Should one of these friends stand by her, however, he can be accused of adultery with her. This plan, says the advocate, is called "clipping her wings." Second, the mother of the woman's first husband can be sent for. She can be given money and told to claim the woman's child as *her* grandson and to say that, whereas she had sold her daughter-in-law, she had not sold her grandson. The old lady would also be threatened with reprisals if she gave the game away. Third, a man could be hidden under the concubine's bed and discovered by men who would go to her room and accuse her of adultery.

Needless to say, all three of these plans are put into operation. Two of three friends of Shu-ch'un accept bribes and agree to refrain from meddling in the family's affairs. The third friend, angry over the behavior of the other two, asks: "Are we to sell a dead friend for a few ounces of silver?"

The loyal friend goes to warn the concubine and, two days later, is told by another friend that it is being rumored that the concubine is an immoral woman and that she has had an affair with him. The loyal friend is advised not to visit the concubine so frequently.

The concubine's first mother-in-law now appears and claims the woman's child as her grandson. The old woman says that because the concubine's new husband was old it was decided she would pretend to become pregnant by him, and that a baby she had had shortly before by her first husband would be smuggled in and passed off as the child of her new husband at the appropriate time. Household servants refute this story, however, and the old woman is trapped into giving the plan and herself away.

Chung-hsing now has no alternative but to put plan number three into operation. He goes to Shu-ch'un's house where, before the spirit tablet, he accuses the concubine of adultery and says he has brought a dozen men with him to search the premises. Although he has arranged for a man to hide under the concubine's bed, the plan goes awry and the men find no one there. Searching out the man who had agreed to hide under the bed, Chung-hsing is told by him that he had not been able to carry the plan through because he had not been feeling very well. Upset by Chung-hsing's refusal to accept his excuse, he steps outside and announces to everyone he meets what Chung-hsing had planned to do. Chung-hsing has to fly home to avoid the anger of the crowd that gathers.

Visiting his advocate once more, Chung-hsing is told by him that, having failed to carry through all three plans, he now has no alternative but to take the concubine to court. To meet the heavy expenses involved, Chung-hsing has to write out promissory notes and to sell off his land. Once he has raised sufficient money, however, the case goes forward.

In the meantime, aware that Chung-hsing will not give up, the concubine's loyal servant transfers the concubine's money elsewhere to give the impression that she has no reserves, and draws up false agreements which purport to show that her property has been sold and is no longer her own. Eventually, the servant is arrested and taken to the city to take part in the trial. When told that the concubine will lose the case now being brought against her, the servant makes the seemingly naive remark that the magistrate will surely endeavor to search out the truth. He is told, however, that the truth of the matter is that whoever pays the most money will win the case. The concubine and her mother-in-law are now also arrested.

When the two women are brought before the magistrate they kneel in front of him and the mother-in-law gives an account of the way the concubine was brought into the family. She says there is no truth in the allegations made against the concubine. The magistrate, however, rules in Chung-hsing's favor.

Chung-hsing now demands that the house and all other possessions of his deceased relative be handed over to him. But when he inspects the documents and account books presented to him, he finds that there is no money and that the house appears to have been sold. When he asks for explanations from the family's clerks, they simply tell him that they have none. Chung-hsing therefore has to look elsewhere to find the money he needs to meet the legal expenses he has incurred. The loyal servant now writes to all his old friends asking for their support in making an appeal to the courts. When Chung-hsing accuses him of making off with the inheritance, the loyal servant and his friends make lavish payments to appropriate individuals and thereby ensure a change of verdict.

VI *The Unconventional Scholar*

Since the last chapter of *Living Hell* was, as we have seen, added by another author following Li Po-yuan's death, and since it is regarded by the critic Chao Ching-shen as representing a more revolutionary outlook than Li's, and is based on an episode which actually took place in 1905,[6] it is worth presenting it here in full.

It is said that in North T'ung-chou there was a certain holder of the *hsiu-ts'ai* or bachelor's degree whose surname was Wang and whose given name was Kuo-chung. He was a man full of talent and learning and from childhood was given to pride. When he grew up he developed an even more eccentric temperament. Should anyone make the slightest mistake when speaking with him, he would glare at him and start shouting. Because of this, some people by-and-by refused to make friends with him. When he entered school and took his *hsiu-ts'ai* degree, his conceit became insufferable.

Although there were many educated people in North T'ung-chou there were few with any genuine understanding. They were all men who lived out their lives merely trying to preserve a few volumes of elegant essays or composing examination poems and "eight-legged essays." Graduate Wang proved to be the one exception for, although he gave the appearance of being obstinate and opinionated, he was modern in outlook and constantly entrusted people with the task of purchasing up-to-date books and newspapers which, when he was at leisure, he used to dispel depression and boredom. The more he read, the more interesting he found such writings.

At first he did no more than read the new books and journals published in Shanghai, but later he came to read the *New People's Magazine* published in Japan, Rousseau's *Social Contract*, and Adam Smith's *Inquiry into the nature and causes of the Wealth of Nations* and the like, and at this point began to understand the reasons for China's accumulated weaknesses and poverty. Sometimes, when he read something he found particularly interesting, he would seem [in his excitement] to "draw his sword and hack at the ground" or "grasp a wine-cup and make inquiries of Heaven." Gradually, in conversation with people, words like "freedom" and "equality" began to creep into his speech. The people of North T'ung-chou thought him a madman; a few with a little more understanding, however, said he was a revolutionary.

From the time that Graduate Wang acquired the name "revolutionary," some of his relatives and friends began to keep him at a distance, afraid lest they be implicated with him. From this time onward rumors spread from one to ten and from ten to a hundred, and some penetrated the ears of officials.

Now the officials could not distinguish between green and red, black and white. When anyone said anything, they accepted it at face value. Moreover, Graduate Wang had numerous enemies. Some of these invented stories about him saying, at one moment, that he was a disciple of K'ang Yu-wei, and at another, that he was one of Sun Yat-sen's operatives. Because the officials had no evidence, however, they found it inexpedient to arrest him and simply stored his name secretly away in their memories.

Now as fate would have it an assassin appeared on the Tientsin railway station in that very year. The assassin threw a bomb with which he hoped to kill an ambassador of the crown. The assassin had not been able to keep his plot secret, and when his plans leaked out, he found that "of the thirty-six moves in chess, flight was the best." He had therefore long since been worthy of felicitations.

Officialdom instituted a search to apprehend members of the gang, and snow-white dispatches were circulated to all prefectures and counties. Prefects and magistrates hurriedly deputed messengers to go daily to tea houses and wine shops to seek out the assassin and his band. Whenever these men ran into anyone whose face was not familiar to them, they hauled him off without a "by your leave," and it would not be until he had experienced several days of hardship and had cleared himself during interrogations that he would be allowed to obtain a guarantor and effect his release.

In the end the search was carried to North T'ung-chou. The people in that locality began to suspect Graduate Wang, asserting that there was cause to be suspicious of him. At the time of the trouble at the station Wang was away from home, having gone to Tientsin to visit relatives. He did not return home until after the attempt [on the ambassador's life] had failed and the assassin had escaped. People, therefore, grew increasingly suspicious of Wang, and when officials in the district magistracy got wind of this, they immediately issued a warrant for his arrest and seized Graduate Wang as an eagle grasps a swallow or sparrow in its talons. Because the case was one of assassination, no one dared to delay. The man was checked and delivered the same night to Tientsin. When the magistrate of Tientsin received a dispatch he verified the age and appearance of the prisoner and then ordered him to be put in irons and detained.

In the circumstances in which he now found himself, Graduate Wang was unable even to offer an explanation. Blunt and outspoken by nature, he could do little else but curse everyone for being sons of bitches. The official messenger took no notice of him but simply pushed and shoved him through the prison gates.

Suddenly all was darkness before Graduate Wang's eyes and he felt himself to be in another world. When he looked carefully around him he found himself in a place as black as a cave. The floor was extremely damp and the smell of mildew was overpowering. When he looked above him he saw a high wall built to be exceedingly strong so that even a bird would find it impossible to escape, let alone people. The wooden posts in the trellis door were as thick as a man's arm, and behind the first trellis was another. Within the enclosure a large number of murderers could be seen squatting on their haunches—they had ceased to resemble human beings—their hair was about an inch in length and their faces were unbearably filthy. Their garments were such as to cover them only partially. A chain was locked at their throats with a link the size of a walnut and both their hands and feet were shackled. The upper part of the chain was attached to an upright pole so that even if a prisoner should want to sit or sleep he could not.

The expressions on the faces of the prisoners were such as one would expect in these conditions; some hurled abuse and some sang songs. Graduate Wang felt as if he were gazing at a depiction of hell by the celebrated painter Wu Tao-tzu. A jailer in front of him who was wearing a worn-out hat askew on his head, a blue jacket, and a pair of straw shoes, led Graduate Wang like a monkey on a string to a certain place where he said: "Wang, my lad, rest here a while. We'll see each other again tomorrow. If there's any message you want passing on I'll have it sent round to your home and tell them to have some cash delivered to you."

Graduate Wang shouted angrily: "If I had some money, which I haven't, I wouldn't demean myself by awarding it to slaves such as you."

The jailer allowed a cold smile to cross his face and said: "It's easy enough to be abusive, but wait and see what happens when I get back!" Whereupon he took the chain round Graduate Wang's neck, attached it to a door in the fence and stalked off, shaking his sleeves.

Finding himself as he was, Graduate Wang could think of no solution to his dilemma and had no alternative but to squat on his haunches like his companions. On one side of him was an old prisoner whose hair was now completely white and who, seeing Graduate Wang get down on his haunches, glared fiercely at him and called: "Young Three, where are you?"

A young man some distance away shouted in reply: "I'm over here."

Young Three crawled over to him an inch at a time and the old prisoner signaled to him with his lips. Getting the message, Young Three crawled over to Graduate Wang and, deliberately twisting his body, fell across Graduate Wang. Graduate Wang found himself unable to shout and grew nervous and agitated. He could feel Young Three's head next to his own. Now, Young Three's head was a mass of lice, and as soon as the two heads of hair came into contact and the lice smelt the fragrance of Graduate Wang's flesh, they crawled, one by one, from Young Three's hair onto Graduate Wang's hair. The two men's hair became, as it were, a bridge for the lice which bit Graduate Wang until his skin both itched and felt painful. Later, his body grew numb as well and began to behave so stupidly that he could no longer squat on his haunches. The moment his feet crossed he started to tumble but, fastened as he was by the chain, he was unable to do so. Graduate Wang found himself virtually suspended in midair; and so he passed the night.

Early the next morning the jailer from the previous day led Graduate Wang away, holding an appointment card and saying that his case was about to be heard. When Graduate Wang appeared in court the Tientsin county magistrate interrogated him and sought to make him swear an affidavit. Graduate Wang repeated his former statement over and over again and the magistrate of Tientsin, who was no fool, came to the conclusion that a mistake had been made and ordered Graduate Wang's shackles removed and his transference to the lockup in the magistracy.

Although he now had a heap of rice stalks and a few deal planks [for a bed], so that his circumstances were vastly improved when compared with those he had encountered the previous day in jail, Graduate Wang was detained in this lockup for many days. Luckily, a schoolmate of his was a lecturer at the Pei-yang Military Academy. When he came to hear of what had transpired, he wrote a most detailed letter to the magistrate of Tientsin in which he stated that Graduate Wang was no more than an unconventional scholar and that he had never, in his whole lifetime, done anything notorious. The magistrate was advised not to listen to, and to be prejudiced in favor of, one side of the story, and thereby to brand his prisoner a criminal, etc. At this point the magistrate of Tientsin found someone to go surety for Graduate Wang and released him.

Graduate Wang returned home in such a fury that he cut off his queue, changed his style of dress, sold all his possessions, returned his wife to her home, and went overseas to study. When he was about to leave, he said: "Even when I die, I shall die in a foreign country. I don't wish to live any longer in this world where the sun has ceased to shine." Although these words were said in anger, they accurately describe the situation as it is today.

Graduate Wang boarded a steamer which took him to Shanghai and made inquiries about a ship sailing to Japan. It was sailing on a Sunday, so he went first to purchase a ticket and then waited for it on the San-ling Company's wharf. The ship sailed in the afternoon. It was called the "Kobe Maru" and carried five to six hundred passengers, the majority of whom were Chinese. Graduate Wang had no feelings of loneliness as he took in the sights along the ship's route.

One day he was pacing the deck with a pipe in his mouth. Another Chinese who had also changed his style of dress and whose face bore a most solemn air, was standing there looking first at the sea and then at the sun, totally absorbed. Graduate Wang walked up to him and the squeaking of his shoes startled the man out of his reverie. He turned his head and, seeing it was a Chinese who had newly changed his style of dress, nodded to him and said "hello." The two men asked each other their names and Graduate Wang discovered that the man was called Hsing Kuo-ming and that he came from the province of Chihli. The two men got into a conversation and found that they hailed from the same town. In no time at all they were the best of friends.

Graduate Wang asked Hsing Kuo-ming why he was going to Japan and he said: "I am the chief of the Police Bureau in Chihli and I'm on my way to Japan to investigate police methods."

Hsing Kuo-ming also asked Graduate Wang a few things about himself and Graduate Wang answered him in detail, saying how he had always been a law-abiding person, how he had been falsely accused of being a revolutionary, and how he had had to undergo suffering in prison. Now that it was clear that he had been wrongly accused, however, and because of the hatred he cherished, he had "burned his bridges" and was now on his way to Japan to further his studies.

Hsing Kuo-ming sighed, and then said: "The Chinese penal system is truly engulfed in darkness!" [7]

Despite Chao Ching-shen's claim to discern a more positive attitude to revolution in this final story[8] it seems to us that the sentiments expressed in it remain basically those of Li Po-yuan. Like other Communist critics, Chao asserts that Li was an enlightened member of the Ch'ing scholar-official class, that he hated the effete and corrupt officials of his day, and that he was a great patriot; but that because he favored the retention of the monarchy and refused to condone a revolutionary solution to the problems of his day, he could do no more than plead, as he does in his introduction, with "the officials of this world" to "read through this book . . . and . . . make some effort . . . to fulfill their role as parents of the people. . . ." [9]

But does the author of the final chapter really ask for anything more? Like Li in his stories, he wishes to draw the reader's attention

to the appalling conditions in Chinese prisons and centers of detention, and to those corrupt and evil practices in magistracies which
made a mockery of justice at the very point where the majority of the
population was expected to find it. The central character in the story,
Graduate Wang, is not a real revolutionary, but a young scholar who
finds Rousseau's *Social Contract* and other such works appealing and
who, in anger at being falsely accused and imprisoned, severs his ties
with his homeland. That he might join a revolutionary party in Japan
is, of course, a possibility, but the author says nothing of that, and
seems primarily to be concerned to show how a young person can be
pushed too far, and to be warning officials of the consequences of
their actions among the younger generation. Further, if the author
were really concerned to promote the revolutionary cause, it is
unlikely that he would have ended the episode with the chief of a
police bureau condemning the Chinese penal system while on his
way to Japan to investigate its police methods, presumably with the
aim of effecting reforms on his return to China. He certainly would
not have given the police chief the name Hsing Kuo-ming which, as
Chao himself asserts, is meant to stand for Hsin Kuo-min ("New
Citizen").[10] Surely what we have in the person of Hsing Kuo-ming is
an enlightened official who is responding to the appeal in Li's introduction cited above and who therefore provides a fitting conclusion
to the book.

VII   *Evaluation of* Living Hell

Evaluation of *Living Hell* as a single, unified work is exceedingly
difficult. If it is viewed merely as an attempt to catalog methods of
torture employed in Li Po-yuan's day in magistracies throughout the
country, or simply as an enumeration of the corrupt practices which
distorted government at its most fundamental level in Chinese society, then, all that can be said of it is that it is a work of importance for
the social historian. As the first exposé of its kind it must always
remain an invaluable source of information for the student of the
Chinese penal system in late Ch'ing times. The question that we
must ask, however, is whether the book has any artistic merit. Chao
Ching-shen, in his preface, agrees that part of the value of the work
lies in its social significance, but then proceeds to claim that it also
reflects artistic maturity. Every item and every event, he says, leaves
the reader with a bright and clear image. The quarreling and abuse
which goes on between officials, thieves, and robbers is pungent and

biting, and the characters are both lively and believable. If Li has weaknesses, he says, they are a tendency to exaggerate and, in consequence, to deprive his writing of some of the realism at which he was aiming, and a failure to plan his work as carefully as he might have and therefore to pay too little attention to structure or to the refinement and polishing of his writing.[11] A better judgment of this book is that it is artistically uneven.

There is no avoiding the fact that Li's overriding purpose was to attack the system, and that what we are presented with is, in a sense, a political pamphlet couched in a form guaranteed to win it a wide readership. But having said this, the very fact that the attack is embodied in a medium of artistic expression means that, if carried out with sufficient skill, the handling of the artistic medium may warrant attention in its own right.

The first thing to remember when seeking to pass judgment on the artistic merits of *Living Hell* is that it is essentially a collection of fifteen separate stories on a single theme. When this is fully appreciated and each story is evaluated separately, one is forced to conclude that some of them succeed artistically while others fail. In our judgment, those summarized and partially translated in this chapter are among the best.

CHAPTER 4

Modern Times

A S we noted in chapter 1, *A Brief History of Enlightenment* (or *Modern Times*, to use the title given this novel in its English translation) is the only novel, along with *Ballad of the Rebellion of the Year Keng-tzu*, which Li Po-yuan was able to complete himself. Li wrote it in order to provide a fictional account of the Reform movement, but he did so not so much to inform his readers of the events which took place in Peking during the period of the Hundred Days of Reform in 1898, as to enlighten them regarding the manner in which it affected official and civilian life in the provinces. This novel, then, is a study of the men and women in high and low places throughout the nation who found themselves caught up, willingly and unwillingly, in the early stages of the process of modernization in China; and since its author sought to place them in their social setting and to describe the interplay between them and the people with whom they were in daily contact, the novel serves as a valuable adjunct to histories of the period, recreating something of the atmosphere in which the major political and social changes of the time took place.

Although the reader of this novel may be forgiven for thinking that Li has little or no sympathy for any of the characters he portrays, whether conservative, revolutionary, or reformist, when his purpose in writing the novel, as this is spelled out in his introduction, is taken into consideration, it becomes clear that far from wishing merely to hurl abuse in all directions Li is, in reality, attempting to offer an accurate picture of the nation at every level of society at a particular stage in its development; and that, as a realist, he is willing, and even determined, to admit that the participants in this development are mostly flawed. Accordingly, in his introduction, Li says, ". . . irrespective of whether these people have succeeded or failed, been cast aside or are flourishing, been public spirited or selfish, proved genuine or false, they will eventually be regarded as men of merit in a civilized world." [1]

As we would expect of a work which seeks to portray social change in a period of transition, this is also a novel of conflict. In it conservatives argue vehemently in defense of the status quo while reformists struggle to implement new ideas in the fields of education, law, commerce, and industry. Students, not surprisingly, are the most radical element, organizing and attending meetings, seeking the experience of an overseas education, demanding revolution, engaging in assassination attempts, and defying their parents. Campaigns are launched against foot-binding; opium smoking is shown up as an evil; religion and superstition are depicted as enemies of science and as standing in the way of the diffusion of modern knowledge, etc. The unique character of this novel, however, is that there are no paragons of virtue even on the side of the virtuous; no exemplary models. Even the persons with whom Li is most clearly in sympathy have their Achilles's heels. Reformists are as often as not portrayed as men of shallow knowledge and shaky principles who are as subject to arrogance, greed, envy, and dishonesty as their opponents. However, they are clearly to be preferred to the revolutionaries, whose ideas and activities Li believed to be inimical to the well-being of the nation and to be likely to destroy it.

I Nature and Structure of the Novel

Although Modern Times has been less well known among Chinese readers than The Bureaucracy Exposed, there are good reasons for asserting that it is the better of the two novels. Despite the many features which they have in common, Modern Times is richer in the variety of persons, situations, and incidents it portrays, and it ranges geographically over a much larger area. It moves from Hunan to Hupei; from Hupei to Wukiang; from Wukiang to Soochow; from Soochow to Shanghai; and then from Shanghai to Chekiang, Peking, and Shantung. From Shantung Li takes his readers to Nanking, and from Nanking he moves to Anhwei, Hong Kong, Japan, and America, before returning once again to Nanking and Peking. In all these regions and places (apart from America and Japan) he deals with events during the period when the movement for reform was in the ascendancy.

As one would expect from the foregoing comments, Modern Times, like The Bureaucracy Exposed and many other novels of this period, has no central character or group of characters around whom a plot is developed. In spite of this, the reader does not feel a lack of unity in the novel since, although the characters change, their thoughts and feelings are related; there is a continuity of theme which binds the various episodes of the novel together. The political and social issues of the day take the place of central characters, and one is made to feel that one is eavesdropping on the whole nation as it discusses, reacts to, and attempts to find solutions to, these issues. There is no denying, of course, that because of his ideological commitment Li sometimes misinterprets facts, caricatures individuals, and is inaccurate and extravagant in some of his comments; but his character delineations, his accounts of the activities of ordinary people, his descriptions of the ways in which officials toady to foreigners, and his portrayals of the behavior of the gentry are all presented with such liveliness, and are so believable, that the positive aspects of the novel can confidently be said to outweigh its shortcomings. That almost every character is presented as in some way flawed could have resulted in a depressing work, but the flaws are mostly seen through the eye of humor and are described with tolerance and even compassion. Li's humor, however, can be sharply satirical, as is particularly clear in passages like the one which follows. It is taken from chapter 11 and brings to a close the first major episode (many Chinese critics would say the best episode) in the novel.[2]

II *Officials Lampooned*

A certain Prefect Fu, who was appointed to the prefecture of Yung-shun in Hunan because of his reputation for firmness, has brought down hatred on his head and stimulated a spirit of noncooperation among the people under his jurisdiction because of the harshness of his measures. Recalled to the provincial capital, the prefect is anxious to make the best of a bad situation by giving his superiors the impression that he is really liked and that the populace is anxious to accord him a farewell commensurate with the "good government" with which he has provided them. He therefore sets about ordering, at his own expense, those gifts customarily donated by the populace to good officials—farewell umbrellas and new boots, etc.—arranging for a shrine to be erected in his memory as well as other farewell ceremonies. Prefect Fu sends his secretary to discuss the possibility of appropriate ceremonies with the district magistrate, indicating that he would be perfectly prepared to meet the costs out of his own pocket. In his conversation with the magistrate the secretary eventually comes to the question of the shrine.

"As to the shrine," said the secretary, "my master has already indicated how to go about erecting it; there will be no need for a huge building. At the back of the library there's a courtyard, empty except for a disused three-roomed building. . . . All we have to do is to set up a tablet and altar of the type used for honoring great benefactors, and to hang up a horizontal tablet, duly inscribed, over the door, and we have a ready-made shrine! But on the day the farewell umbrellas are to be presented, there simply must be a few people, suitably dressed in hats and gowns, to make the presentation; the great problem is who!" "Well that's easy to arrange," said the district magistrate. "If no one turns up, the clerks in the magistracy can be formed into a deputation." [3]

Arrangements for a face-saving send-off are finally worked out by the secretary and the district magistrate and the time comes for the prefect to depart.

Determined to show himself off in all his regalia, Prefect Fu arranged for all his insignia of rank, including his palanquin, his farewell umbrellas, and tablets bearing witness to his virtuous administration, to be displayed along the street; and, once again, the cost was painfully met out of his own pocket. But at a critical moment such as this he had no alternative if he were not to lose face. . . .

He moved over to the entrance to the library where he saw the college director accompanied by several students waiting to take their leave of him.

Prefect Fu stepped down from his palanquin and entered the library where he exchanged a few comments about the weather with the deputation. The college director was determined to propose a toast. Prefect Fu would not accept it; but the students pleaded with him, bowing their heads to the ground.

Prefect Fu responded to these ceremonial bows, and then instructed his majrdomo to present each person with a white folding fan on which was written an eight-line poem with seven characters to a line embodying sentiments appropriate to a parting. The fans were accepted with both hands by each person.

This performance had been planned ahead by the prefect through his old tutor who had also written the poems. The prefect simply gave the impression during the ceremony that the whole thing was genuine.

Just as the courtesies were being performed a clamor was heard outside the door. The prefect was about to send someone out to investigate the noise, when a man entered the room to report that the tablet suspended over his shrine, together with the tablet and altar erected in his honor, had been smashed to pieces by a group of vagrants, who were also threatening to drop [an] inscribed stone monument into the public latrine. [4]

Angered at this affront to his dignity Prefect Fu indicates his intention to step outside to deal with the "vagrants." He is dissuaded from doing so, however, by the college director who warns him that his person is in danger.

Finally, the district magistrate arrived; but it was only with great difficulty that he managed to get the prefect safely out of the library and to the city gate via a small lane.

As the prefect waited to participate in the boot-removing ceremony, another crowd suddenly emerged and rushed willy-nilly toward him. Not only was he unable ceremonially to leave his boots behind, but he even had his hat knocked off in the press. He had just removed one boot, and had not yet been able to put on the new one, when everything was scattered by the milling crowd, and the prefect had to hobble his way through the mob with a boot on one foot and only a stocking on the other. Fortunately for him, the loss of his official hat meant that the crowd was unable to pick him out as the prefect, and he was spared a beating. Within a very short space of time, however, his palanquin was destroyed, his insignia scattered, his farewell umbrellas broken and lost, and the tablet proclaiming the virtues of his administration smashed to splinters.

With great difficulty Prefect Fu searched out one of his attendants who found a small cottage where he was able to hide for some considerable time. There he waited until the storm outside subsided before he dared to emerge. . . .

After searching for some time the [district magistrate and the garrison commander] were unable to find the prefect, and wondered whether the crowd had made off with him. The district magistrate became extremely anxious lest the crowd had put him to death. There would be no end of trouble if that had happened. He immediately ordered the local constables to lead a group of magistracy attendants in a house to house search. In the end, after much difficulty, they found the prefect in a simple cottage. The local constable knelt down and, striking his head on the ground, said: "Your honor, I've searched high and low for you! Please come outside since the district magistrate is waiting for you."

Prefect Fu believed the constable to be a rioter who was trying to trick him into going outside to receive a beating. He could not conjure up the courage to step outside, but simply remained where he was, shivering with fright. . . . It was not until Prefect Fu set eyes on the district magistrate that he finally relaxed and found the courage to emerge from his hiding place.

The district magistrate said: "Your honor has been given great cause for alarm!"

Prefect Fu ignored this comment, but accused his farewell deputations of playing him false because he had already handed over his office and no longer exercised power. He said that even if the crowd had beaten him to death they would have done nothing to rescue him. They were all shameless sons of bitches!

The district magistrate, hearing him curse in this fashion, felt there was nothing more that he could say. He simply ordered that the palanquin be prepared so that the prefect could take his seat. The commander deputed sixteen soldiers and a lieutenant to accompany the palanquin, and to provide protection until it had crossed the prefectural boundary.[5]

III *Reform Preferred to Revolution*

Although Li Po-yuan has been sufficiently in favor in China since the Communists came to power to have three of his novels—*The Bureaucracy Exposed, Modern Times*, and *Living Hell*—reprinted with introductions, Communist critics have taken him to task for advocating reform rather than revolution, and constitutional monarchy rather than a republican form of government. That Li was against revolution and held many revolutionaries to be guilty of endangering the state is abundantly clear from the manner in which he treats the advocates of revolution in *Modern Times*. So clearly does he spell out his position in one episode in chapter 59 that, although largely couched in obscure rhetoric and elaborate tongue-in-cheek reference to the divination symbols and exegesis of the *Book of Changes* (*I-ching*), the editors of the Communist edition of the novel felt it necessary to excise a speech opposing revolution which is several pages long.[6] Li does not, of course, deny that the best of the revolutionaries are patriots and are as eager to build a strong and prosperous state as anyone else. In his view, however, the means they have opted for to achieve this end are mistaken and self-defeating. Thus, in the excised speech, the speaker, Tsou Shao-yen, compares the state which is faced with revolution to a man with a wife and a concubine. He says:

Consider, will you, the situation in which a man has both a wife and a concubine and these two women are jealous of each other. Is this man's family likely to prosper? At first each woman will think only of how to appropriate the man as her husband alone, but when this doesn't work their determination to destroy each other will emerge. They will fight because of the love they have for their husband, and once they have begun to fight they will continue to do so despite the fact that they are fully aware that their strife will eventually injure their husband. Persistent strife will lead to the destruction of the husband's family and then to the ending of their own lives; but they will care nothing for this.

But if Li advocated reform rather than revolution, along what lines did he think it should proceed? It seems likely that his overall attitude is to be found in the words of an elderly teacher named Yao Shih-kang who appears in the first chapter. Yao is made to advise a prefect, who is about to go to his first post in the country, to take his responsibilities seriously and to exercise all his skill "when it comes to reforming the people and their customs." He states flatly that, whereas in the few seaports which are open to commerce with the outside world "it is comparatively easy to act as the times dictate," in the provinces "people hold stubbornly to mistaken views" and that in consequence an official "should not act in haste when introducing anything new or when getting rid of anything old." "To beat the grass and startle the snakes," he says, "will only produce ugly results." [7]

Gradual and patient reform, then, and a willingness to consider the effects of one's actions upon the populace even when it is wrong-headed, seems to have been the ideal which Li Po-yuan espoused in both politics and the modernization of the country. It should not surprise us, therefore, that Li ridicules, satirizes, and denounces both revolutionaries and conservatives whenever he is afforded the opportunity. Although poles apart, both ignore the hopes and aspirations of the people, forcing themselves upon them for their own commercial advantage or for reasons of ideology or power.

IV *Student Activists*

It is, perhaps, not surprising that Li Po-yuan should frequently exhibit an ambivalent attitude toward the students who appear in his book. He cannot denounce their ideals since many of these are his own. Their advocacy of modern education, their undoubted patriotism, and their stand against such social evils as opium smoking and foot-binding are positions which he himself obviously adopts. Further, many are not so much revolutionaries as reformists whose flaw is merely that they are subject to youthful impetuosity. Li's problem is clearly that, although he is in agreement with many of their stated aims, and is understanding of their impatience and youthful follies, he is also appalled by the arrogance and hypocrisy which they so frequently exhibit, and is convinced that the actions of the most radical among them lead only to a hardening of attitudes on the part of conservative officials and, frequently, to the silencing of dissent through imprisonment and execution. In this novel, then, Li both devotes much space to Chinese student activities in China and Japan, and makes a point of drawing attention to the weaknesses of students. Sometimes he describes their failings in a humorous and teasing way, as when he makes them go into raptures over the tiny bound feet of girls immediately following loud protests against the abuse of foot-binding, but at other times without attempting to cushion his strictures in the least. An excellent example of the manner in which Li sought to criticize students who thought of themselves as Chinese equivalents of Western progressives and who imagined they were adopting the mores of these progressives when they attempted to model themselves on characters in Western fiction, is found in chapter 23 in a speech made by a student called Ting-hui to his fellow students. Ting-hui, who is accompanying the young son of a provincial governor to Peking so that both may further their studies, arrives in Shanghai where he attends a party given by a group of students. Before long drinks are ordered and women are summoned to pour the drinks and to accompany the students around the tables. Since Ting-hui and his companion, Hua-fu, have no female friends in Shanghai the other students try to introduce women to them.

Ting-hui decided not to take the situation seriously and entered into the spirit of the occasion; but Hua-fu, finding himself in the midst of a world of seduction, went crazy and accepted the suggestion, made to him by the women who were serving him, to play host and call for a round of drinks. Ting-hui frowned in disapproval but his fellow students were all excitement and strongly urged the young man on.

It was by now twelve o'clock and Ting-hui therefore attempted to take leave of the group in order to return to the inn to get some sleep. His fellow students reacted by accusing him of being overly virtuous and not sufficiently enlightened. Ting-hui answered: "If this playing around were unpremeditated there wouldn't be any harm in it, but this infatuation with vice is not appropriate to students. People have a great respect for students, believing they understand self-discipline. Of what use will we of our generation be when in future years we have to take complete responsibility for important matters? This kind of misbehavior represents total corruption; what kind of responsibilities are we likely to be able to bear in future? I beg you all, gentlemen, to reform as soon as possible."

There were some in the party who listened to this plea with timorous respect and bore a look of shame on their faces. Two who were half intoxicated, however, refused to be cowed. One of these said: "We're not really debauched. We just wanted to gather a few of our fellow students together and we called for some women to lay the tables and pour out the wine. The petty scruples of some of our comrades are none of our concern. Besides, it is the heroic young men and women who are united in their passion for love. No civilized nation has ever been without it. If this were not so, how could the novel *La Dame aux Camelias* have been written? Our old fellow student here is much too conservative."

"Not at all," said Ting-hui. "The first part of what you say has some truth in it, but although it cannot be denied that civilized countries also have people who play around, can you say that our standards of learning are as high as theirs? If this were all we wished to learn from them, then what kind of supremacy are we striving for?" [8]

In chapter 42 Li incorporated a cautionary tale which was no doubt meant to warn students of the futility of radical action and of the risks they ran in espousing the revolutionary cause. At the same time, however, it shows, together with the larger episode into which it is set, the way in which government officials sought to control and prohibit the circulation of books and magazines which they considered subversive.

Li begins his story by informing his readers of the growth in popularity of overseas study and of the recent increase in numbers of Chinese students studying in Japan. "But once numbers have increased," he says, "it is difficult to avoid fish and dragons appearing in the same pool—to distinguish between the good and the foolish." Some, he says, go overseas merely to play around, hoping that their families will grant them a large allowance so that they can do exactly as they please. Many young men, he goes on, "when passions are not yet stabilized, follow whatever example is set before them; if they do not become volunteers in the revolutionary army, then they set themselves up as China's future masters. Fluctuating between emotional extremes, their true characters and attitudes even elude themselves. They are at odds with themselves over what they think constitutes freedom or equality; and they are nothing more than a huge joke."

Having provided this introduction, Li launches into his story which concerns an ill-educated and untalented lad called Liu Ch'i-li who, even after eighteen months of study in Japan, "had not correctly learned the few simple sentences of Japanese necessary for greeting people."

When his parents have spent more than a thousand dollars on his overseas education, Ch'i-li's father "began to regret the loss of his money and to look forward to the return of his beloved son." Since Ch'i-li has in any case grown weary of his stay in Japan and has himself been thinking of returning home, he welcomes his father's suggestion that he return to China and boards a ship for the return journey as soon as the summer vacation comes around. The story continues:

Although he had not completed his studies, his appearance had long since changed completely. He wore a foreign suit, a panama hat on his head, and leather shoes on his feet. When he saw his father he raised his hat and shook him by the hand, thus greeting him according to foreign custom. When his parents first saw him they refrained from criticizing him for his behavior; they simply raised their heads and looked hard at him. They saw that the hair on his head was only about half an inch long. Formerly, when he left home, he had had a queue that was both thick and long; now, however, it had gone, goodness knows where.

The young man's parents were hurt at what they saw and asked him why he had removed his queue. He replied that the cutting off of his queue would make things easier for him in the future when the revolution took place. Subsequently, a friend of his returned from Japan and put it around that this queue of his had been cut off with a pair of scissors by someone else, one day while he was sleeping. When his parents listened to his long and involved conversation and saw how he behaved, they deeply regretted the fact that their good and obedient son had been spoiled overseas; but, since things were as they were, there was nothing to be gained by talking about it. All they could do was to bear their disappointment uncomplainingly.

As to Liu Ch'i-li, after living in a foreign country for fully two years, he did nothing but regard everything with disdain as soon as he returned to China. If he did not say that houses were too small and lacking in ventilation, he was sure to assert that Chinese food was injurious to health, and was not as well made as it was in the large restaurants overseas.

At first his parents took no notice of him when he talked in this fashion, but later, when they had heard these comments repeated over and over again, his father said to him: "This is the way we do things in my home; if you can't get used to living here, then go back overseas. I'm Chinese, and I wouldn't dare have a foreigner like you as my son."

This comment made the young man angry, and he returned to his room where he put his personal belongings together, packed a large leather case, and departed, carrying his luggage on his back. As he walked out he said to himself: "Now I understand how even in a family there can be severe repression; but I'm not afraid. If we're now to have a revolution, it should begin in the home! " [9]

Liu Ch'i-li makes his way to the New Learning Bookshop, where he has a number of friends, and arranges to live on the premises for the time being. As its name implies, the bookshop is a center of radical opinion. When the official in charge of the police department, Prefect Huang, overhears Liu branding him "a robber of the people" as their respective pleasure boats pass each other on the Ch'in-huai River in Nanking, and catches Liu's subsequent remark, when both happen to be in adjoining rooms in the same brothel, that he would like to rob the prefect of his favorite girl, he orders his men to search the shop for incriminating evidence.

When they reached their destination they looked for the New Learning Bookshop. It was midnight and Liu Ch'i-li and his friends had already returned. Prefect Huang issued orders for his troops to secure both the front and rear entrances, and then, leading his men himself, beat on the door and entered the premises, seizing everyone in sight. He also went into the shop and carried out a thorough search. Although he was unable to find any seditious publication there, he did discover two copies of *Freedom Magazine* in Liu Ch'i-li's leather case. Prefect Huang read them and said: "The editor of this magazine is a great rebel; his publications have been banned by imperial decree. The fact that this fellow is in possession of these magazines is sufficient proof that he is secretly planning rebellion."

As he spoke he had the doors of the shop sealed and the arrested men bound up with cords and taken to police headquarters. . . .

When the prisoners were brought forward for interrogation Liu Ch'i-li refused to kneel and remained standing. When he was asked why he refused to kneel, he said he was a student in a foreign school and . . . had to keep the customs of his school; foreign countries did not have the practice of kneeling before officials.[10]

When the interrogation is over and a report is presented to the viceroy, the viceroy hands down his decision regarding what is to be done with Liu and his friends. He states that in view of the fact that Liu has changed into Western dress and secreted prohibited publications, he must be regarded as a malcontent. "It is essential," he says, "that he be incarcerated for several years to restrain his barbarous nature." Liu is finally given six years imprisonment. The bookshop is sealed up, and the owner of the shop is sentenced to a year's supervision for "harboring a criminal." The story is drawn to a conclusion in the following manner.

When Liu Ch'i-li was taken to the prison at Kiangning *hsien*, the magistrate there showed him a copy of the viceroy's findings after which he was going to clap him in irons. At this point, the young man began to weep and to beg to see his father. The magistrate of Kiangning agreed to his request and ordered someone to find the father and bring him to him.

Alas, after the young man had left home in a fit of pique and failed to return for several days, his father was beside himself with anxiety. He had known nothing of the escapades of his son and his friends, of the subsequent sealing up of the bookshop, and of the arrest of his son. On this particular day he was just thinking of going out to visit the bookshop to see how his son was getting on, when he saw the local constable together with a messenger from the magistrate. They informed him that his son was in the magistracy and was waiting to see him. They said he was about to be put in jail, and that he must hurry.

When the old man heard this report he was at first incapable of understanding what had happened and questioned the messenger further. The messenger gave him a detailed account of what had taken place, whereupon the old man was almost frightened to death.

Both anxious and pained, he stumbled after the messenger to the magistracy. When father and son saw each other they could not stop themselves weeping. One could hardly blame the father for feeling hurt when he saw that fetters had already been placed on the boy's hands and feet, and that his fine son who wore Western dress now looked exactly like a criminal.

It was too late for resentment and moralizing. He simply said: "This is all due to your playing with revolution day after day; you've involved yourself with it to the point where you've now almost revolutionized your own life out of existence. I really ought not to have allowed you to go to Japan. By doing so I've ruined your whole life!"

When he had finished speaking he burst into tears once again. His son's jailer, however, had already lost patience from waiting and hurriedly shooed the old man away. He led the boy back to jail, and the clanking of his chains could be heard every step of the way.

The old man could not help weeping once again as he looked toward the prison gates. As soon as he arrived home he gathered some silver together and delivered it to the jail as a bribe on behalf of his son to mitigate the young man's suffering during his incarceration. Nevertheless, no matter how much money the father spent while he was in jail, the only equality the young man was to know was the equality he shared with the other prisoners; and he would never again be allowed his liberty! [11]

V   Reactions of Conservatives to Reform

A. The Legal System

Just as Li Po-yuan sought to provide a faithful record of the views and actions of radicals and revolutionaries, though not without indicating his approval or disapproval either directly or indirectly, so also did he present the opinions of the conservatives at each point in the novel where change and innovation are adumbrated and where one would expect them to argue for the status quo. Thus, where suggestions for reform of the legal and education systems, for example, are made by scholars and officials of the reformist persuasion, their conservative colleagues are allowed every opportunity to express their opposition; and where arguments touching on the sensitive areas of religion, faith, and morals are brought forward, Li does everything within his power to grant all sides a fair hearing, though again, through comment or some other device, he leaves the reader in no doubt of his own preferences and commitments.

The question of bringing the Chinese legal system into line with legal systems in the West is introduced in chapter 29. In that chapter Li states that the question of reform of the legal system arose because China was experiencing losses on every hand in its dealings with foreign nations, and because, although foreigners seemed to be able to flout China's laws with impunity, Chinese who broke foreign laws found themselves at the mercy of the foreigners. The argument of the reformists, he says, was that if the Chinese legal system was made to correspond to legal systems in the West, the West would no longer have grounds for demanding special treatment for nationals of Western countries living in China who happened to run foul of Chinese law, and Chinese living in areas controlled by foreigners would feel themselves on firmer ground when pleading for justice and fair play.

The problem for China's conservatives, of course, was that the Chinese legal system had grown up as a means for protecting and preserving certain ideas and values which were held to be of fundamental importance to the well-being of the Chinese state, and they were therefore justified in asking whether changes to the legal code meant a rejection of the traditional principles it enshrined and supported. In a speech put into the mouth of one official concerned over the proposed changes, the official says: "These laws have been handed down to us from the emperors T'ai-tsu and T'ai-tsung; they have been transmitted from one sage to another, and have been added to, but never changed. If the whole corpus of the law is now to be cast aside and replaced with a code which ignores the relations between emperor and subject and between father and son, then such mischief, I fear, will transform China, which has always been as secure as a great rock, into a nation lacking in stability." [12]

The arguments over the merits of the existing legal system are carried over into chapter 30 where another conservative official, Imperial Superintendant of Instruction Huang, repeats the former argument, but adds to it his observations on Western systems of law which, he maintains, must be defective because political crimes are committed under them. He says:

Not only have the laws of China been handed down to the present over a period of several thousand years, but they've also been investigated by several sagely scholars during the present dynasty. So detailed and all-embracing are they that I fail to see what omissions can require remedying? Having listened to President of the Board Lu, the court now wants to copy foreign nations; but those foreign nations are not to be emulated for, without any justification, they execute their kings. Do you think that a good example to follow? An official at the university told me that when an American president was watching a performance at the theater he was shot and killed, and that the murderer was never dealt with. A Russian king was so afraid of being stabbed that he decided he no longer wanted to be king, and handed the throne to someone else. One hears even more frequently of military leaders being assassinated. All such disorder is due to imperfections in the legal code. Do we still hope to live in peace after learning from those people? I guarantee we'll have an extraordinary increase in the ranks of the rebels. It's alright for the emperor: he lives in the palace. Officials, however, may leave their homes to go for a walk unaware of any danger, only to encounter unexpected mishaps. So I say that even if everything else is changed, the law code must on no account be altered.[13]

B. *The Education System*

Not surprisingly, the examination system, and by extension the whole system of education, is defended by conservatives for reasons similar to those adduced by defenders of the legal system. The examination system and the type of education it perpetuated was based on the premise that the kind of educated man most valuable to the state, and especially to the civil service, was the one with a thorough grounding in the Confucian classics and the moral principles they were designed to promote, together with a mastery of Chinese literature and the techniques of literary composition, including calligraphy. Clearly, such a system meant that subjects such as mathematics, foreign languages, politics, law, medicine, and the like, even if available in educational institutions, would be neglected by Chinese looking for a career in the civil service. That the traditional examination system was not finally put aside until 1905 meant that the implications of doing so were perfectly obvious to everyone. Nowhere are these implications stated more straightforwardly in this novel than in the prelude to the remarks on the law made by the official, Huang, and which we have already noted. He is speaking, of course, of the situation during the Hundred Days of Reform in 1898.

China was in an excellent condition, but it has been so troubled and disturbed by that group of reformers that order can no longer be restored. Just think of it; the selection of scholars by means of the "eight-legged essay" examination was an excellent method worked out by the first emperor of the Ming dynasty. Those able to compose the "eight-legged essay" were invariably men of sincerity. The Emperor K'ang-hsi of our present dynasty thought of changing the system, but found that he couldn't, and had to continue with it! Fortunately, there's still an examination based on the classics, and it's not too different from the "eight-legged essay." This represents a delaying tactic, but it can't be maintained for long. What I dislike is that with the elimination of the "eight-legged essay," a number of men have emerged who have *reputations* for talent and ability and whose efforts on behalf of the country are *expected* to be particularly efficacious. But what has been the result? When they took over, there was no visible change for the better; in fact, if anything, they were an even greater disaster than the products of the "eight-legged essay." . . . the "eight-legged essay" has served as a vehicle for the teachings of sages and worthies and is inseparable from such terminology as "loyalty to the ruler," "patriotism," "filial piety," and "respect for one's elders" which daily transforms those who use it, and makes them unwilling to engage in rebellion.[14]

In this speech it is the avoidance of rebellion (i.e., the maintenance of the status quo) and the fostering of Confucian virtues which Huang sees as the prime function of the traditional examination and educational systems. In chapter 32 an official in Shantung is made to state not only his belief in the need to retain the traditional content of Chinese education, but also his dislike for the modern schools which were beginning to spring up in various parts of China. His comments are directed to a young man who goes by the name of Assistant Secretary Feng and who is trying to solicit funds to establish a school devoted to the teaching of commerce. The official, Censor Liu, is one of Feng's old mentors, so that Feng is more than a little disconcerted by his reaction to his request. The old official addresses him as follows:

Although you are a friend of mine, I have no respect for you at all in this matter. What I've always hated most is people setting up modern schools. When excellent pupils are sent to such a school they end up by not being able to read and write. They dress up in foreign clothes and wear a foreign hat on their heads; they put a pair of leather shoes on their feet, and their mouths are full of foreign languages with which they double-cross the ignorant. . . .

If you really want to run a school, you must follow my instructions and invite a few good men with masters' and bachelors' degrees to teach your students how to read the *Four Books* and *Five Classics*. You must purchase copies of Master Chu Hsi's *Minor Studies, Reflections on Things at Hand*,[15] and the like, and these must be expounded to your students so that later, when they reach maturity, they will understand the importance of venerating orthodoxy and dismissing heresy.

My dear younger brother, be done with error and delusion! [16]

VI *Shanghai: Haven of Progress, Knavery, and Vice*

Some of the most amusing parts of *Modern Times* are those in which our author pokes fun at that large number of persons who, because of their imperfect knowledge of the nature of modernization or who, out of a desire to show off in front of their friends, ape the foreigner in every conceivable way. Li depicts some of these characters as simple buffoons, some as snobs who regard their fellow Chinese with disdain, and some as confidence men who take advantage of the ignorance of their fellow countrymen to cheat them and to make money out of them. During the nineteenth century, and particularly in the wake of the T'ai-p'ing rebellion, [17] Shanghai rapidly became the focus of international trade and, before long, also the city where Chinese eager to know more of the world outside China increasingly congregated. Inevitably, however, it also gained a reputation as the Chinese city with the greatest concentration of evil and vice and as a haven for political intrigue from which youthful hotheads and the discontented could direct abuse at the establishment. From the point of view of the youthful provincial, Shanghai was a city which beckoned; but it was also a city the awesome reputation of which struck fear into the hearts of parents whose sons were determined to visit it, and, perhaps, to make a living or to study in it.

Li Po-yuan introduces his readers to Shanghai in an episode which begins in chapter 14 and ends in chapter 20, and takes this opportunity to describe some of the city's outlandish characters and their activities. The story begins in Wukiang, south of the Yangtze River, where three young brothers from a fairly well-to-do country family discover that their family tutor knows nothing of modern education and decide to make themselves the pupils of a man who has studied in Shanghai and who is rapidly gaining a reputation for his knowledge of the modern world. The three young men, the Chia brothers, are introduced by their new tutor to the newspapers and magazines published in Shanghai, and when he suggests that they accompany him to that city so that he can find a suitable boarding school for his son, they jump at the idea.

Ignoring their widowed mother's commands not to go to so dangerous a place, the Chia brothers join their tutor and sail by steamer down the river to Shanghai, their aim being, as they put it, to broaden their education by seeing with their own eyes the things about which they have read in the Shanghai press.

In chapters 16–18 Li uses the tutor as a guide to Shanghai. The Chia brothers are first introduced to the novel possibility of renting rather than buying newspapers, and are made to be suitably impressed over the fact that they can now read a newspaper on the day of its publication. Theater advertisements also capture their attention, and they decide to see a play that very evening. The opportunity is taken to comment on the high esteem in which actors are held in the West and on their sad treatment in China.

It is the people they see and encounter who prove most fascinating, however. Seated in a restaurant they witness the break-up of a de facto marriage which, it becomes clear, was entered into in a manner which was meant to emulate the modern mores of lovers in the West. This minor event ends with the police being called in to drag the quarreling lovers off to the police station. Before they leave the restaurant the Chia brothers see the arrival of a man dressed in foreign clothes who is greeted by a person already seated at a table and addressed as "generalissimo."

Noting the strange appearance of these two men, and thinking that perhaps they were friends of "modern knowledge" whom it was incumbent on them to meet, Master Yao [the tutor] and his companions remained seated and watched their actions carefully. They saw the man in Western clothes greet his friend with folded hands and heard him say: "Brother Huang Kuo-min, it's been many days since I last saw you. When did you get here?"

"Just over an hour ago," replied Huang Kuo-min.

"Brother Kuo-min," said the man in Western clothes, "I remember, when we accompanied each other to the city to take part in the crickets contest during the tenth month of last year and had tea in the Hu-hsin Pavilion of the city temple, that your head was clean shaven. It seems no time at all since then, and yet in those three months your hair has grown quite long. You'll have to have it shaved off again."

"Foreigners say that hair ought not to be shaved too frequently, since, after a haircut, the head is left bare and the wind can easily enter the empty pores, thereby damaging the brain. I've decided, therefore, to have my hair cut once every four or five months," said Huang Kuo-min.

Changing the conversation, Huang Kuo-min asked: "Generalissimo, have you had anything to eat?"

The man in Western clothes replied: "Ever since I decided to wear Western clothes I've completely adapted myself to foreign ways in the matter of eating and in the way I live; thus, I only take two meals a day: one at noon, and one at seven o'clock in the evening. I never touch food in between. But there is just one thing: I can copy everything the foreigners do except their practice of bathing and changing their clothes daily. This I cannot learn."

"When foreigners take a daily bath," said Huang Kuo-min, "they not only get rid of the dirt on their bodies but tone up their muscles and blood, so why don't you copy them?"

"I don't bathe for the same reason that you don't have your hair cut. I'm afraid of catching cold, for if I catch cold I get a cough, and if I get a cough I have to spit out my phlegm. Now, have you ever seen a foreigner spitting phlegm? It's one thing for us to chat about it, but you know as well as I do that if we really meet a foreigner and we have some phlegm in our throats, we have no alternative but to swallow it. I remember how, when I first changed into Western dress in the twelfth month of last year, I set out with singleness of mind to learn the Westerner's ways. I took a bath in cold water, and on this very first occasion was frozen stiff. The next day I found myself with a heavy cold and coughed till nightfall. A foreigner unexpectedly came to visit me. We talked together for a long time, and during the whole time I didn't dare spit once: I practically choked to death. So, you see, I've not dared to have a bath since then." [18]

From the restaurant the Chia brothers are taken by their tutor to see the bookshops where modern publications are widely and readily available and where they are introduced to the important business of the translating of foreign books. However, it is when their tutor is suddenly called home to be with his wife because of difficulties she is experiencing with her confinement that the Chia brothers and the tutor's son themselves become actors and not mere onlookers. Not surprisingly, perhaps, their first brush is with prostitutes on Foochow Road—the major thoroughfare devoted to the "trade." Li describes the scene which met the young men when they first stumbled into this quarter of Shanghai in the following words:

At this moment, on Foochow Road, there was music and singing all about them; the din of gongs and drums reverberated round the heavens and the palanquins of singsong girls "on call to parties" passed back and forth like weavers' shuttles. Having newly arrived in Shanghai the young men did not understand what was meant by the expression "on call to parties," and therefore thought that the women in the palanquins were all female dependents of prominent households. Amazed at the sight they cried: "What are all these ladies doing moving about the street in their palanquins?" Later, however, they noticed that inside each palanquin, and placed at the side of each occupant, was a *p'i-pa*, or balloon-guitar. Only now did they begin to have a glimmer of understanding as to what was taking place. They had heard, of course, that there was a great number of prostitutes in Shanghai, and they therefore drew the conclusion that the girls who were thus weaving their way in all directions were on their way to accompany men who were drinking in the surrounding houses. But these girls were seated in open palanquins and were not in the least bashful when they saw a man; they behaved as nicely as the modern young ladies described in books: trained in the ways of modern civilization! The significance of it all eluded the young men, however.

As they stood gazing at the scene in foolish amazement, they could hear a confused hubub coming from the First Pavilion. It all sounded very exciting, so much so that they decided to enter the building and climb to the upper stories.

Now it so happened that the "pheasant market" at the First Pavilion had already opened for business, and some "pheasants" who were without clients were striking all manner of unusual poses to solicit customers. The four young men were wearing outmoded clothes: their short jackets were two feet eight inches long, and their sleeves were seven or eight inches wide. When the girls saw that they were dressed in up-country styles, they decided to try to seduce them.

Chia Tzu-yu was in front of the rest, and the moment he ascended the stairs a "pheasant," heavily rouged, but with wrinkles betraying middle age, thrust out her hand and laid hold of him. Chia Tzu-yu struggled unsuccessfully to free himself while Chia P'ing-ch'uan, Chia Ko-min, and Yao Hsiao-t'ung, who were following him, all fell into the clutches of similar women. Their vision blurred, they were unable to distinguish between young and old; all they could feel was the violent beating of their hearts. But these four young men were not brave and, since they were new to Shanghai, were still thin-skinned. They struggled for some time, but the girls refused to let them go. Unable to bear it any longer Chia Ko-min grimaced and shouted: "You shameless creatures. If you don't let us go I'll call for help!"

When they saw that these young men were nitwits, the girls realized they would have difficulty doing business with them, and even if they were successful, the young men were not likely to spend much money on them. They therefore loosened their grasp, uttered a few impudent remarks, and allowed them to escape. The four young men reacted as though they had been given a reprieve and rushed headlong toward the exit.[19]

The young men have no sooner escaped the clutches of the prostitutes than they run into the "generalissimo" and some of his acquaintances. Recognizing them, the "generalissimo," whose name is Wei Pang-hsien, invites them over to his table and introduces them to his friends, one of whom is called Liu Hsueh-shen and is said to be a teacher recently returned from Japan. Although the conversation commences with discussion on the running of modern schools and the translating of books, the fact that they are all seated round a table in a restaurant frequented by singsong girls and prostitutes (popularly called "pheasants") means that they cannot long ignore the topic of prostitution and modern ideas on love and marriage. Li introduces the subjects in the following way:

Just as the conversation was becoming interesting, a "pheasant" strolled over and promptly patted Liu Hsueh-shen with her hand. The action of the girl completely electrified him, so that his spirit trembled and even his vision was distorted. He sat in his chair no longer master of his emotions.

"Brother Hsueh-shen," said Wei Pang-hsien turning to him in laughter, "I wonder how many past existences you've devoted to self-cultivation in order to have such luck with women?" Turning to his companions while pointing at Liu Hsueh-shen, he continued: "You should know that brother Hsueh-shen is twenty-seven years old this year and is still without a wife. He intends doing as the foreigners do, and insists that it's best for people to have the freedom to choose their own marriage partners. This year, after returning from Japan, he has not only made great progress in the field of learning, but he has advanced in other fields as well. He has a theory which I shall now pass on to you gentlemen, and which I am sure you gentlemen will all respect."

"Please tell us about it!" cried everyone.

"Well, brother Hsueh-shen claims that every change in society must start out as a change within the domestic sphere, and that absolutely no change can take place in a state, anywhere in the world, without that change first being effected."

"How very true, how very true!" said Chia Tzu-yu nodding his head in agreement.

"Brother Hsueh-shen also says," Wei Pang-hsien continued, "that the physician can serve as the perfect example for those wishing to govern a country. Governing a country is like curing an illness: when there is a crisis one must take appropriate measures and divest one's self of all bigotry; it is only by ceasing to be bigoted that one can begin to talk of freedom. When freedom has been won in every sphere of life, there will be no need for talk of change since change is integral to freedom. But no people who are bound and oppressed by others are at liberty to talk about change. Brother Hsueh-shen, therefore, had determinedly refused to return home to take a bride, despite numerous letters from his revered father and mother asking him to do so; he insists on remaining in Shanghai and on choosing a girl of his own liking. He says that there are four hundred million Chinese of which two hundred million are women; but that it is only the women of Shanghai who can be regarded as totally enlightened and educated. Because they are in deep accord with the principles of equality and freedom, they behave with complete confidence whenever they meet anyone, and are free of any trace of shyness. Hsueh-shen is therefore determined to select the woman he wants right here."

"That's all very fine," said Chia Ko-min, "but all these women are prostitutes."

Chia Ko-min was barely able to complete his sentence before Liu Hsueh-shen interrupted him and said: "You're a human being and prostitutes are human beings too. They may have been brought low by their profession, but they were no different from anyone else when Heaven and Earth first produced human beings. If we despise them we turn our backs on the principle of equality. Therefore, although they're prostitutes, I treat them exactly as I would treat other people. If I select one of them and find that we are happy together, I shall make her my wife. What could possibly be wrong with that?" [20]

The conversation turns next to the subject of foot-binding, and the Chia brothers are informed that the abolition of the practice is closely related to the question of the preservation of the Chinese race and the strengthening of the nation. They are also told that Wei Pang-hsien's wife has helped to organize an association devoted to the abolition of this age-old practice and that he is preparing a speech for her to deliver at a meeting of the association.

The holding of this meeting at which women make speeches and deliver lectures provides the Chia brothers with their first experience of public oratory, and our author with the opportunity both to inform his readers of the nature of public lectures as these are held in Shanghai, and to give a humorous account of how some of the less reliable of the reformists, and the less able, conduct these affairs.

Following the meeting of the Association for the Abolition of Foot-binding, Wei Pang-hsien states that he has been thinking of holding a public meeting in the garden of a well-known family, and that following it he would like to have all the speeches made sent to the press for publication. Since Wei is encouraged to proceed with his idea, arrangements are made for pamphlets advertising the time and place of the meeting to be printed, and a notice is put in the press. The entrance fee is fixed at fifty cents per person.

On the day of the meeting the Chia brothers and Liu Hsueh-shen make their way to the gardens where it is to be held.

The moment he noticed the four young men approaching the gate with Liu Hsueh-shen following behind them, Wei Pang-hsien exchanged greetings with them and then, with a wave of his hand, invited the five companions to pass through the gate.

After entering the garden they turned a couple of corners and came upon the Pavilion of the Grand Seal. . . . At this moment the four young men were in no mind to take in the sights and beauties of the garden: they were determined solely to listen to the speeches. They strode into the crowd and, after much difficulty, were able to find somewhere to sit. They immediately sat down together and began to listen to the speeches. Two or three people had already stepped forward to deliver their talks; and no more than a quarter of an hour later Wei Pang-hsien also appeared, having completed his duties. Chia Tzu-yu listened attentively, but no remarkable ideas were put forward by the speakers; in fact, the speeches differed very little from those made by the girl students a few days previously. He began to feel deeply disappointed.

In the midst of his reflections he noticed that the current speaker had just completed his talk and that no one was succeeding him. Wei Pang-hsien grew anxious and began pacing up and down shouting: "Who is the next gentleman to speak?" He shouted again, but still no one responded.

Wei Pang-hsien had no alternative but to step in front of the gathering himself where he lifted his hat in a salute to the crowd. The gesture was followed by a burst of applause from the audience and shouts to the effect that since no one else was willing to speak the "generalissimo" himself should ride out and do battle. Having greeted the audience, Wei Pang-hsien walked into the middle of the crowd and stood with both hands on the speakers' table; then, in a voice like a saw cutting its way through wood he said: "Gentlemen! gentlemen! We are in the midst of a great calamity, and are you, gentlemen, still ignorant of it?"

A shudder of alarm swept through the audience at these words, but Wei Pang-hsien continued: "China, today, is like me—one person—while the eighteen provinces are like my head, arms, and legs. The Japanese have occupied my head; the Germans have occupied my left shoulder; the French have occupied my right shoulder; the Russians have occupied my back, and the English my belly; then there is Italy which is riding my left leg and the Americans who are astride my right leg. Alas! Alas! As you can see, my body has been divided up and occupied by all these people: can I be expected to stand for it? Think, will you; how can I be expected to live?"

The audience again burst into applause. Wei Pang-hsien closed his eyes, calmed himself, took a couple of deep breaths, and continued: "Gentlemen, gentlemen! In such times as we experience today should we not think of organizing ourselves? If we were to organize ourselves into a body the Japanese wouldn't dare occupy my head; the Germans and French wouldn't be able to rob me of my shoulders; the Americans and Italians wouldn't be able to occupy my legs; the Russians wouldn't dare gouge out my back; and the English would be afraid to scrape a hole in my belly. If we organize ourselves there will be no cutting up of the melon; but if we don't organize ourselves, the melon will be carved up immediately. Consider, gentlemen, which is better, to organize ourselves or not to organize ourselves?"

A fresh burst of applause rang out as the audience assumed that Wei Pang-hsien had more to say, and that he would continue to argue his case with eloquence. The audience was somewhat surprised, therefore, when Wei Pang-hsien suddenly began to grope for words. His eyes searched the ground for some considerable time as if he had lost something: he searched and searched but could not find what he was looking for. Eventually his anxiety mounted to such a degree of intensity that beads of perspiration covered his head; but still he could not find the thing he was looking for. He scratched himself all over, but uttered not a word.

The crowd waited, growing increasingly impatient. Too embarrassed openly to urge him on, however, it resorted to clapping. When he saw the crowd clapping, Wei Pang-hsien felt he was being laughed at. His face turned scarlet and his muscles tensed. He stopped looking for whatever it was he seemed to have lost and, supporting himself with both his hands on the table, coughed twice, and then burst out with the words: "Gentlemen, gentlemen!" However, having uttered these words, he again fell silent. He coughed once more and was just descending into gloom over his inability to find anything to say, when he lifted his head and saw Liu Hsueh-shen walking toward the crowd from outside. He suddenly thought of a way out of his dilemma: he announced that Liu Hsueh-shen had originally intended to make a speech on this particular day, that he had finally arrived, and that he, Wei Pang-hsien, now wished to invite Mister Liu to come up to the front to deliver his talk. When he had finished making this announcement he raised his hat, bowed his head, and said that he would step down. The audience could make neither head nor tail of what was going on and resorted to another burst of applause. Taken aback by the way in which he had been introduced, Liu Hsueh-shen could do little else but step to the front. It was lucky for him that he was able, having recently visited Japan and having gained considerable experience there, to muddle his way through a few diplomatic sentences without losing the thread of what he was saying. When he had finished he was followed by two other speakers who had arrived after him. Having listened to these speeches the crowd again clapped, but nothing else took place which merits attention. When Wei Pang-hsien saw that it was already half past five he ordered the speech-making to end, whereupon the crowd dispersed.[21]

The Chia brothers are somewhat disappointed with the quality of the speeches they have been listening to, and when they overhear Wei Pang-hsien and Liu Hsueh-shen quarreling over their takings at the end of the day, they become thoroughly suspicious and begin to doubt the probity of the two men. Li Po-yuan takes advantage of this to draw the episode to a close and to transport the young companions back to their homes.

VII *An Ideal Reformer*

It is a mark of the authenticity of the picture Li gives us of the people of his day that so few of his characters are unfailingly loyal to the principles of reform even when presented as reformists. Over and over again persons who are at first introduced as being firmly in the reformist camp eventually display sides to their characters which reveal that their knowledge of the significance of the course on which China has embarked is shallow, and that the degree of their enthusiasm for change is often in direct ratio to the effect it has on their financial and social circumstances. The narrator in the novel is made repeatedly to assert that in the management of their affairs Chinese have the "head of a tiger and the tail of a snake," i.e., that they show promise at the beginning but prove disappointing in the end. Afflicted as the nation was with the commercialization of rank and office, and encumbered as it was with educational and legal systems which allowed for little flexibility and innovation, there was not much room for the genuinely able person who had acquired some aspect of the new learning, and who was motivated by patriotism rather than self-interest, to put his skills and commitments at the service of the state. His opportunities for official recognition and advancement depended not so much on the capacity of existing governmental and social structures to absorb him as on the encouragement of individual enlightened officials in high places—mostly provincial viceroys and governors—and on their willingness to make room for fresh talent and skills within their own jurisdictions. Thus, certain provinces, such as Hupei and Hunan, became renowned for the progressive outlook of their governors and for the relative ease and speed with which modern industry and modern schools were established within them, whereas other regions were noted for their conservative ways, and even for backwardness. The political instability of the nation, both internally and in its dealings with the outside world, and the uncertainties attached to the outcome of any new venture—and even, occasionally, to the lives of those involved in it—made it difficult for anyone to behave in a totally exemplary manner. All these difficulties are recorded with fidelity by Li, and if the reader finds it emotionally disappointing to have virtually every emergent hero brought low, he can at least take comfort in the certainty that he is being offered a portrayal of life in China during the final years of the nineteenth century and the first five years of the twentieth century which goes a long way toward explaining the reasons for subsequent upheavals in the country.

But although Li was reluctant to accord any of his characters an unqualified accolade for their contribution to the well-being and progress of the nation, he comes close to doing so in one case, and thereby reveals the kind of person he believed was needed and should be supported in China. The character whose abilities Li holds in such high esteem is a banking expert called Chin who, in some unexplained way, has acquired the rank of intendant of a circuit. Intendant Chin is introduced to the reader in chapter 48 when he visits Shanghai to give an acquaintance who is establishing a bank the benefit of his expertise. The acquaintance, Lu Mu-han, throws a feast in his honor and, during it, the subject of national finance is discussed in some detail. When Intendant Chin gives his opinions he is made to deliver what is probably the longest speech of any in the whole novel. He begins by agreeing with another speaker that nothing can be accomplished without money, but then goes on to assert that all talk of finance and the need for a good banking system is superficial if divorced from the more fundamental issue of trust. He quotes appropriate passages from the Confucian classics which emphasize the need on the part of a ruler to win the trust of his people and then goes on to refer to a recent attempt to raise a public loan. Collecting the money, he says, was relatively easy, but mismanagement of the affair by those responsible for carrying out the scheme had lost them the trust of the contributors and, finally, they had dissipated the confidence of the people of the whole nation. It was because of this, he says, that subsequent attempts to raise money by similar means were doomed to failure. "In China today," he says, "it is not the lack of ways to raise funds which should grieve us, but rather the lack of any way to strengthen the people's trust." "In the situation as it is today," he continues, "it is not the people below, but the men who govern them, who must bear the blame." [22]

Intendant Chin next proceeds to discuss monetary reform and begins by drawing attention to the anomaly of different provinces in the nation minting their own currency. The man in the street always loses when he has to change the currency of one region into that of another, and in some instances he even finds that dollars from one province are not acceptable in another. What is required, says Intendant Chin, is a national currency which would circulate freely throughout the empire and have the same value everywhere. It would have to replace all other currencies, including widely used foreign dollars, and be employed in all government transactions. Intendant Chin next goes on to discuss the advantages of paper currency over silver and copper and ends by insisting that notes issued by banks in foreign settlements and treaty ports should have their circulation limited to those cities.

The other guests at the feast are suitably impressed with Intendant Chin's long discourse, and Lao Hang-chieh, a foreign-trained lawyer who has been practicing in Hong Kong but who is on his way to the province of Anhwei to serve as an advisor on foreign affairs, is made to respond with considerable surprise to the revelation that China really did have men of ability.

VIII *Didactic Role of the Novel*

As we have already seen, Liang Ch'i-ch'ao and other reformists at the turn of the century saw the novel as a major tool for the bringing about of social change, and Wu Chien-jen, in his obituary, stated that Li Po-yuan deliberately wrote this and other novels to help people understand the events that were taking place around them. The didactic role of this novel is played out on a variety of fronts. It sets out to wean its readers from superstition; to undermine the esteem in which the Confucian classics are held; to shed light on the Western world; to inveigh against the evils of foot-binding; to show the impor-tance of modern education for girls as well as for boys and the part that modern journalism can play in disseminating information; and to explain the wonders of modern science and technology.

The reader will recognize all these elements as he makes his way through the novel, and there is no need to dwell on each of them here in greater detail. A few remarks on Li's efforts to undermine people's faith in the classics and on his attempts to provide scientific informa-tion are, however, called for.

It would be wrong to assert that Li was totally opposed to the teachings of Confucius. He was obviously familiar with the books which purport to contain his teachings (as, of course, were all edu-cated Chinese in his day), and, when appropriate, would quote from them. In the speech which he puts into the mouth of Mister Yao in chapter 1, and which, as we have noted, probably reflects Li's own views, the old man is made to say, "all my life I have had the utmost respect for Confucius," and then to go on to quote from the *Analects of Confucius*; and in the discourse of the banking expert, Intendant Chin, there are Confucian quotations which, one would suspect, would not have been included had Li wished to downgrade the classics absolutely. The Confucian classics were the repository of basic moral principles and a compendium of early Chinese wisdom which Li continued to value and hold dear, and as such, it is probably correct to say that he still regarded them as being, in some sense, authoritative.

It is evident, however, that he was very much opposed to the "fundamentalist" attitude, adopted by many conservatives, which invested the Confucian classics with a degree of "sanctity" so great that critical examination of them or the questioning of the assumptions and judgments contained within them, was frowned upon. This comes out clearly in chapter 25 where an intelligent and precocious young lad who has been told to make a careful study of the *Tso Commentary* to the *Spring and Autumn Annals* (one of the five basic classics of Confucianism) begins to question the veracity of the record contained therein. The reactions of his teacher are interesting and were no doubt typical of many a scholar of his day. In answer to the question whether or not the *Tso Commentary* is "totally free from hearsay" the teacher replies: "This book has been handed down to us by sages and worthy men; how can you speak of hearsay in this context?" [23] When pressed to say how the writer could possibly have known the contents of a conversation which he was not present to overhear, but which was recorded as direct speech, the teacher is forced to retreat somewhat and angrily replies: "When you're studying a book you've got to examine its overall approach; whoever came across anyone so determined to test the veracity of every word in every sentence? If you adopt that attitude, no book will stand up to criticism." [24]

On the evidence of this novel one must conclude that Li Po-yuan's knowledge of modern science was extremely shaky. His description of the nature of an eclipse in chapter 59, for example, is somewhat ambiguous, and the account he gives in chapter 53 of the reasons for variations in the hours of daylight in different parts of the world is full of errors. In the following extract we have attempted to provide an accurate translation of the passage in question, but cannot be absolutely sure that we have penetrated its obscurities: "If you went to St. Petersburg, in Russia, in the winter, you'd find it begins to get dark shortly after two o'clock in the afternoon and that it grows light before one o'clock in the middle of the night," said the interpreter. "This is because Russia is below the North Pole. In winter, when the sun emerges and is in direct line with the ecliptic, it gets dark early in the day, but very quickly grows light again. It is not at all like summer time when the sun moves slowly round the equator." [25]

The truth of the matter, of course, is that at this period, when Li was writing his novels, the number of Chinese with reliable knowledge of scientific matters was very small indeed. The importance of Li's efforts to impart this knowledge lay, if one may so put it, not so much in the accuracy of his information as in his enthusiasm for modern knowledge and in the eagerness he was undoubtedly able to awaken in others for similar information.

IX *Identities of Characters*

We must now turn our attention to the question of the identities of the characters which appear in this novel. Like his other novels, *Modern Times* is meant to be a faithful reflection of political and social events of Li's own day and, in consequence, a restatement, albeit in fictional form, of events and issues which were common fare in the newspapers and magazines read by his audience. One would expect, then, that the characters which people *Modern Times* would bear a close resemblance to the persons directly involved with the events he depicts and would be readily recognizable to his readership. Li does not seek to deny this; in fact, quite the contrary. In the final chapter of *Modern Times* Governor P'ing Cheng, the central character at this point, is made to inform a large group of scholars, who have applied to join his entourage as he prepares to go overseas to make a study of constitutional governments, that their "daily activities have all been investigated and enumerated in a book entitled *A Brief History of Enlightenment*" and that "They have been portrayed more clearly than in a photograph taken by a Western camera." [26]

A clue as to the accuracy or otherwise of this claim is provided in the character of Governor P'ing himself. Li describes his public career and his private interests in such detail that should he be modeled on a living official it should not be too difficult to recognize him. Li begins by informing his reader that P'ing is a Manchu and a member of one of the six Boards of Government; that he was appointed to serve as provincial judge and later governor of Shensi; that he was eventually recalled to Peking and, when the question of governmental reform arose, was appointed by the emperor grand minister in charge of an investigation into governmental systems overseas. Li also goes into great detail concerning P'ing's personal interests. The reader is told so meticulously of his passion for antiques, rare books, and old paintings that he must either conclude that Li is showing off his knowledge of such things, or that he is giving him an intimate and reliable picture of a real man concerning whom he had detailed knowledge.

Now it just so happens that there was a Manchu and antiquarian who matches this description in almost, if not every, detail. The official is Tuan-fang who, late in 1898, was appointed "judicial commissioner of Shensi and, in the following year, acting governor." [27] Between 1901 and 1905 Tuan-fang held a number of posts in central China and supported the reform policies of Chang Chih-tung in education and administration. In July 1905 he was selected to be one of five special ministers to visit Western countries to investigate differing systems of government, and, although the party ended up being somewhat depleted, finally left Shanghai with his colleagues on 19 December 1905.[28] During its four months abroad, the party visited the United States as well as Germany, France, Russia, Italy, and England.

But not only was Tuan-fang a leading official of his day, he was also one of the most important collectors of antiques and works of art, some of which were eventually to find their way into Western museums such as the Metropolitan in New York.

The parallels between Governor P'ing Cheng of the novel and Tuan-fang the real-life official are too close to be coincidental, and when we consider the fact that Tuan-fang's return to China must have been at just about the time that Li Po-yuan's life came to an end, it is not surprising that the novel should close in the way it does.

On investigation, other characters in this novel can also be shown to be modeled closely on real people. Chapters 35–37 tell the story of a group of young radicals who decide to go to Japan to further their education but who find, on arrival in Tokyo, that the Japanese authorities refuse to allow them to enter a military academy because they have arrived in Japan without being sponsored by the Chinese government. The episode might have been a fictionalized version of any number of groups of Chinese students seeking to further their educational fortunes in Japan but for the incident in chapter 37 where Nieh Mu-cheng, one of the group, is so overcome with depression that he tries to commit suicide by jumping into the sea. In real life such an incident did in fact occur, although not exactly as related in the novel. The historical incident centered on Wu Chih-hui (1864– 1953) who, interestingly enough, was, like Li Po-yuan, born in Wu-chin in Kiangsu.[29] Successful in the examination for the *chu-jen* degree, he nevertheless failed the *chin-shih* degree examinations despite three attempts. While in North China he came to know the reformers K'ang Yu-wei and Liang Ch'i-ch'ao. Following the Boxer Uprising, however, he became increasingly radical in his thinking and consciously sided with the people against the ruler, with students against their teachers, and with sons against their fathers. Awarded a fellowship for study in Japan, Wu went to Tokyo in 1901. Later in the same year he and his friend Niu Yung-chien were recommended to go to Canton to help the governor-general of Kwangtung and Kwangsi to set up a college and military school. In 1902 the two men were asked to escort twenty-six students to Japan. Wu soon came into conflict with the Chinese minister to Japan, a man by the name of Ts'ai Chun, who refused to recommend a number of students for entry into Japanese military schools. The Japanese authorities decided to deport Wu who, on his way to Kobe under police escort, attempted to commit suicide by jumping into a canal.[30] Ts'ai Yuan-p'ei, who was later to become president of Peking University and who had been a colleague of Wu, happened to be holidaying in Japan at the time. Afraid lest Wu would again try to take his life, he joined him and accompanied him back to Shanghai where the two men, along with other like-minded revolutionaries, formed the China Education Society to promote modern education. They also established a school known as the Patriotic Society with Ts'ai as its principal and Wu as a member of its staff. They contributed anti-Manchu articles to the *Su pao*, and when the government took action against it, Wu escaped from Shanghai and made his way to Edinburgh. In 1904 he moved to London where he joined the revolutionary T'ung-meng Hui, the forerunner of the Kuomintang or Nationalist party.

That there are discrepancies between the story in the novel and the actual events in which Wu Chih-hui was involved is clear. Nieh Mu-cheng is a young man whereas Wu was thirty-eight or thirty-nine; the young men in the novel have no official backing, whereas Wu and Niu were clearly assigned to their task of escorting students by an important governor-general. Parallels between Wu's experiences, both in Japan and, subsequently, in China, and those of Nieh and his fellow students, however, clearly indicate that Wu and his friends served as the model for this episode.

Other characters readily identifiable as contemporary scholars and politicians are Lao Hang-chieh, An Shao-shan, and Yen I-hui in chapters 45–46. Despite certain discrepancies, Lao Hang-chieh seems clearly to be modeled on the lawyer and sometime government advisor and diplomat Wu T'ing-fang.[31] In chapter 45 Lao is said to have begun his legal studies at Waseda University in Japan, but then to have gone to a college in the United States to continue his studies. Following graduation Lao goes to Hong Kong, and our author states that he "could be regarded as the man who opened the way for his fellow Chinese lawyers to practice in Hong Kong." Wu T'ing-fang (1842–1922) achieved rather more than Lao Hang-chieh in his lifetime, but he certainly spent much of his life in Hong Kong, first, as an interpreter in the Hong Kong courts and, later, after reading law in London where he was the first Chinese to be called to the English bar, becoming the first Chinese to practice law in Hong Kong.

In the novel Lao Hang-chieh becomes adviser to the governor of Anhwei province. Wu T'ing-fang's involvement with the Chinese government was at much higher levels: he joined Li Hung-chang's secretariat in 1882 and took part in the negotiations which led to the Sino-French treaty of 1885. In 1897 he was appointed Chinese minister to the United States, Spain, and Peru. Recalled to China, Wu was made vice-president of the Ministry of Foreign Affairs and cochairman with Shen Chia-pen (1840–1913) of the Bureau for the Compilation of the Law. Shen and Wu proposed changes in the Ch'ing legal code in 1905, and it seems highly likely that Li Po-yuan had this event in mind as well as Wu T'ing-fang when, in chapter 29, he recounted how the throne was petitioned to bring about changes to the Chinese law code. Wu, if he is the model the author had in mind, is now, however, described as Ambassador Lu Ch'ao-fen who is said to have returned from England where he was serving as Chinese ambassador. Lu is given the task of reforming the law.

An Shao-shan and Yen I-hui are, of course, K'ang Yu-wei and Liang Ch'i-ch'ao, who, following the abortive reform movement of 1898, spent part of their exile in Hong Kong. As in the case of Wu T'ing-fang, it seems likely that Li Po-yuan also used these men as models for characters whom he placed in other settings. It is probable, for example, that Li had K'ang Yu-wei in mind when he introduced the impatient and arrogant young character, K'ang I-fang, in chapter 41.

That one could go on almost indefinitely equating Li's characters with prominent men of his own day is now obvious; but it is also evident that the manner in which he employed his models must make the reader cautious when he seeks to determine the extent to which Li's characters are accurate reflections of those models. Although he did, as we have seen, draw heavily on real-life individuals to provide him with his raw material, he clearly did not feel bound to stick strictly to the facts. One real person may serve as a model for two or three different characters, and, one can safely assume, one character can be a composite figure created out of several models. It is possible, for example, that Marshal Pai Hu-wan, viceroy of the Kiangnan provinces in chapter 41, is a composite reflection of the two well-known leaders Tseng Kuo-ch'uan (1824–1890) [32] and Liu K'un-i (1830–1902). [33]

Before putting this topic aside it may be worth trying to identify one or two more of Li's characters. Huang Shen in chapter 43 would seem to be modeled on Chang Yin-huan (1837–1900), [34] and the viceroy of Hupei and Hunan in chapters 12–14 can only be the great official, reformer, educator, and modernizer Chang Chih-tung (1837–1909) who was transferred to Wuchang, the viceroy's seat of government for the region, in 1889 and remained there for some eighteen years. Apart from being a celebrated administrator and reformer, Chang was noted for his frugality and honesty in money matters, and when he died, he was a poor man. There may therefore be much truth in the episode in chapters 12–13 in which the viceroy finds himself having to pawn his wife's trousseau to meet expenses.

CHAPTER 5

The Bureaucracy Exposed

W E now come to the novel for which Li Po-yuan is best known
and the work of fiction which, in the eyes of certain Chinese
critics at least, is the most important of that group of novels which Lu
Hsun designated "novels of reproach" (*ch'ien-tse hsiao-shuo*).[1]

Unlike the other novels which we are examining in this book, *The
Bureaucracy Exposed* has been reprinted on a number of occasions
and in a variety of formats. However, it (or part of it, since the work
was incomplete when Li died in 1906) seems first to have appeared in
book form in 1903 in an edition prepared by the Fan-hua Publishing
Company.[2]

According to Chang Yu-ho, in his introduction to the 1957 edition
published in Peking, Li's original plan was to write a novel with ten
p'ien ("sections") and with twelve chapters in each section. He is
believed to have commenced the work in 1901 and to have completed
five sections by the time of his death. A friend then finished the fifth
section, providing the sixty chapters which form the present novel.

I *Aim of the Novel*

As with each of his other novels *The Bureaucracy Exposed* sets out
to deal with a particular topic: in this instance, the Chinese
bureaucracy of Li Po-yuan's day. Li was not content, however,
merely to describe how the bureaucracy was meant to function or
simply to invent a few stories in which the characters would all be
members of China's civil service. His ambition was much greater
than that. He sought, rather, to write an exposé of the whole governmental system which would have the effect of encouraging men of
goodwill to demand and strive for thoroughgoing reform.

To bring this truncated novel to an end in such a manner as to make
it seem complete, Li's friend who undertook the task states, in
chapter 60, that "the first half of this novel is devoted to pointing out

the faults of those who follow an official career, so that, having read it, they will be aware of them and feel bound to change their ways. The latter half of the novel was designed to instruct officials in the techniques of their vocation. But this latter half has been burned and only the first half remains. As to the first half, it is not like a textbook, but is similar to the novels *The Investiture of the Gods* and *Records of a Journey to the West*, full of malicious spirits of every kind." [3]

It is possible, of course, that Li did intend to inject a different mood into the second half of his novel: to employ his last sixty chapters to instruct his readers in the nature of good government and to fill it with men of exemplary character and vision. In all probability, however, these remarks represent a clever ploy on the part of the friend both to bring the novel to a close and to clear Li's name of any suggestion that his hatred of current circumstances represented a totally negative attitude toward government. There is, in fact, little indication in the chapters we have that Li would have altered, or even modified, his method of writing at any stage, and every suggestion that, had he lived to finish the novel, he would have continued it by simply adding more episodes of the kind already included.

Although there appears at first sight to be no introduction to this novel similar to those which Li provided for his other works and which set out to inform the reader of Li's reasons for writing them, in the 1903 edition a preface by a certain Mao-yuan Hsi-ch'iu Sheng ("The Scholar Who has a Fondness for Autumn in the Luxuriant Garden") is already attached to it. [4]

There is little likelihood that Hu Shih is right when he suggests that this is one of Li's several pen names;[5] but in view of the fact that it appears to belong to someone closely associated with Li and a person, moreover, whose comments he was willing to accept as an introduction to his novel, it can be assumed that we have, in this preface, a clear declaration of the author's intention in composing this work. It will therefore pay us to examine it in some detail.

II   *The Introduction*

The first thing to emerge from it is the way in which its author lays stress on the decline of moral standards and, in consequence, of morale within the civil service. Whereas at one time entry into, and advancement within, the civil service had depended almost exclusively on scholarship and talent tested in the examination hall, now, he tells us, other methods of selection and promotion are so flourishing that scholars are neglecting their studies, and men who at one time had been content with their lot as farmers, artisans, and men of commerce are abandoning their vocations to devote all their attention to the business of acquiring those ranks and official posts which can reward the successful with social status and wealth.

The scramble for official positions, the author suggests, has been fostered because officials are able to reap all the benefits which would normally accrue to scholars, farmers, artisans, and businessmen without any of the labor which men in these walks of life have to undergo. A man, he says, has to plan well and to work hard if he is to succeed in any of these professions; but in the world of officialdom what matters is servility, fawning, and dependence on others in positions of power, the wheels of the system being kept oiled, more often than not, with gifts and monetary contributions both secret and legitimate. So serious is the situation, the author claims, that the bureaucracy has lost all order and discipline within its ranks and has become a class in which the most extreme state of anarchy prevails.

The author admits that abuses, such as the sale of offices and titles, can be traced back deep into Chinese history, but he holds that such practices have in his own day been greatly intensified, so much so that men have been led to gamble with their talents and abilities, releasing them on the "market" only at moments which they judge opportune. Years in which there are famine, drought, and floods seem to provide just such moments, since rewards and commendations are forthcoming for those who can claim to have contributed in some way to the relief of distress. These are times when there is an inexhaustible flow of persons eager to offer themselves for public service. There is never a sufficient supply of officials to support the emperor, says the author, but there are more than enough to oppress the common people. He continues: "The maliciousness of a goat and the insatiability of a wolf are not tolerated in other people, but they are in officials; the way flies bustle about after things and dogs scavenge is not what other people care to do, yet officials engage in such activities. . . . They long for carnal pleasures, goods, and profit as if these things were their very life; and they are so steeped in pleasure and wine that they regard them as normal. When we observe their external behavior we find that they violate all the rules, and when we examine into their private lives we discover that they break the moral conventions and engage in licentious conduct. Even if I should exhaust all my supply of paper and ink I would not be able to enumerate their every absurdity and perversity." [6]

It must be clear from the foregoing that the author of this preface regarded the morally unhealthy state of the bureaucracy, and even of society at large, of his day as largely traceable to the increasing commercialization of rank and office. As we shall see when we come to examine the novel in some detail, Li Po-yuan has no hesitation in drawing a parallel between this trend and prostitution.

Having thus surveyed the world of officialdom, and having pinpointed what he believed to be the primary cause of the corruption affecting every corner of it, the author of the preface then proceeds to outline the manner in which Li Po-yuan sought to portray this world and the effects which he hoped would result from the writing of the novel. The Master of the Southern Pavilion (Li Po-yuan), says the writer, has a particular facility for satire and humor, and since he is also well acquainted with the foibles of officials, while, at the same time, being free of any constraint which membership of the world of officialdom might impose upon him, he has sought to provide a humorous, yet absolutely serious, account of the bureaucracy of his day. Nor, we are given to understand, was Li's aim merely to entertain. As with all his works, *The Bureaucracy Exposed* was written with a distinct purpose in view, namely, to "foster honesty and straightforwardness" in the world of the bureaucrats.

III   *Nature of the Bureaucracy*

But what was the nature of this bureaucracy which Li attempted to expose and satirize? What was its structure and what its origins? Historians and social scientists have made close and detailed studies of it in recent years and published their findings in a number of books and articles which are readily available. All that is required here, therefore, is the briefest of accounts.

The bureaucracy in the last days of the Ch'ing dynasty was a direct successor to the governmental structure worked out during the Ch'in (221–206 B.C.) and Han (206 B.C.–220 A.D.) dynasties. At the apex of the bureaucratic pyramid was the emperor whose most important title was "Son of Heaven." As this title suggests, the emperor possessed an aura of sacredness. He ruled by the will of Heaven, thus representing Heaven to his people, and was regarded as the high-priest of his nation, possessing the sole right to offer sacrifices to Heaven, thereby representing man to Heaven. However, despite this exalted view of the role of the ruler, it needs always to be borne in mind that the will of Heaven was usually associated in the Chinese mind with the dictum that "Heaven sees as the people see; Heaven hears as the people hear," and that, in consequence, Chinese rulers were never permitted to lose sight of the possibility of popular rebellion which, if the bulk of the population felt it to be justified, could lead to a change of dynasty.[7]

Until 1729 the main organ of government at the capital was the *Nei-ko* (Grand Secretariat or Inner Cabinet). In 1730, however, it was superseded and power passed to a new organization which, because it put public affairs on a military footing, was called the *Chun-chi ch'u* (Center for Military Strategy), but which is commonly referred to in the West as the Grand or Privy Council. Although a considerable center of power, the Grand Council functioned only in an advisory capacity and its members were appointed—or dismissed—by the emperor at will. Moreover, the emperor was kept directly informed of events and was not bound to inform, or to take the advice of, his grand councillors. To add to their difficulties, grand councillors were subject to constant surveillance by censors.[8]

Despite the importance of the Grand Council central government administration was shared between six Boards or Ministries which the Manchus inherited when they came to power in 1644. The Boards, which were directly subordinate to the emperor and in no way answerable to the Grand Council, were responsible for the civil office, which was concerned with all matters related to rank and office; for state revenue; for rites and ceremony; for war; for punishments; and for public works. Other organs of government also existed, however, to deal with specific tasks. Prior to 1860, for example, relations between China and other nations were handled chiefly by provincial governors, but the central government, when necessary, conducted its diplomacy through the *Li-fan yuan* (Colonial Office) which, as its name implies, was chiefly concerned with the control and affairs of Mongolia and Tibet, but which dealt occasionally with other countries on the assumption that they too occupied a "colonial" or "tributary" status vis-à-vis China. After 1861 and following the peace treaties of that year, foreign relations were carried on through the *Tsung-li ko-kuo shih-wu yamen* (Office of Foreign Affairs). Under the provisions of the Boxer Protocol of 1901 the Office was elevated to the status of a ministry.[9]

To help the emperor in his task of supervising government officials there existed a Censorate (*Tu-ch'a yuan*). Although they had no powers to promote or to demote the men on whose work and characters they could comment, censors were entitled to memorialize the throne and to recommend courses of action. Divided into supervising and inspecting censors, they played a supervisory role in relation to government offices in the capital and regularly inspected the administrations in the provinces. Forced to act as individuals rather than as a body, and expected to show neither fear nor favor in their comments, they were entitled to report on any official within the realm, including the emperor. Since censors were accorded no privileges and ran the constant risk of incurring the displeasure of powerful men, much courage was required to carry out their duties with integrity.[10]

Serving as the hub of government, the emperor not only had oversight and control of governmental administration in the capital, but was the channel through which the Boards directed their instructions to the provinces. Civil strife and the wars with foreign powers which had greatly disturbed the nation in the middle years of the nineteenth century, however, had encouraged the growth of a spirit of regional independence in the provinces and the strengthening of the power of eunuchs and favorites at court. Although the frequent transference of senior officials from one province to another by the court made it virtually impossible for such men to become deeply entrenched in any one locality, the fact that the provinces had their own military forces and systems of taxation meant that they could sometimes adopt policies different from those pursued by the central government when the throne was experiencing a period of weakness. This type of regional independence was especially obvious during the Boxer Uprising when a number of provincial governors denied the central government their active support.[11]

Regional government in China was organized on a provincial basis. Each province had its own governor who had to report to the Boards and to the emperor on the territory under his jurisdiction. Many of the eighteen provinces, however, were also paired. The administrations of these pairs of provinces were presided over by viceroys or governors-general who were initially responsible for overall supervision of the military and of the civilian population, while the governors had the oversight of "educational, financial, judicial, and administrative matters." However, distinctions between these two offices became increasingly blurred in the latter half of the nineteenth century. Governors were aided in their administrative duties by two lieutenant governors responsible, respectively, for finance and judicial matters.[12]

The chief administrative units within a province were the prefecture, presided over by a prefect, and the district and county, administered by magistrates. There were, in all, about 1,300 counties with an average of 70 to 100 to a province. Consisting of a city together with 500 to 1,000 square miles of countryside dotted with villages, the magistrate, who normally administered it for a period of three years, was the most important point of contact between the government and the people.[13] The *fu, chou, hsien*, or prefects and magistrates formed the "general administrative body of the provincial civil service"[14] and as such had the task of maintaining law and order; collecting revenue; holding examinations; and of exercising "all the direct functions of public administration."[15] Commonly referred to as parent-officials (*fu-mu kuan*) they stood *in loco parentis* to the people under their charge.[16]

There is not the space here to comment on the many facets of the Chinese civil service such as its social composition and its examination system, which was so important a technique for the selection of candidates for the service. The following points need to be made, however, if the reader is to understand the circumstances in which the bureaucracy found itself toward the end of the nineteenth and during the early years of the twentieth century. First, in spite of the impression in the West that the Chinese governmental system employed vast numbers of officials, the reality was very different. China's social elite, represented by families whose members usually possessed academic qualifications, never exceeded two percent of the population. Although elite status was usually attained through the "regular" route of the examination system, "irregular" routes were recognized, one of the most common being the military. Another important route was that which involved the purchase of rank. It must be borne in mind, however, that the mere possession of rank, however gained, was no guarantee that a person would receive an official appointment. With an administrative structure which was limited in size, but which at the same time offered great rewards for the successful, it was inevitable that aspirants to office should come greatly to outnumber openings available.[17]

Partially to solve this problem, a candidate for office was placed on a waiting list, his place on the list being determined by his rank. Although senior positions were filled by the emperor himself, most candidates for office were assigned to a post in Peking or the provinces through the casting of lots. Once assigned to a province, lots were again cast in order to place the hopeful candidate on the governor's waiting list. Since one could easily spend a lifetime waiting for a suitable appointment, every avenue possible was usually explored by candidates to have themselves appointed out of turn. "Under these circumstances," says Donald Holoch, "a purchase system developed which greased the upward path and helped the central government finance military campaigns and major relief and public works programs. Like the examination system it was a legitimate path to status controlled by the state; price lists were published by the emperor. For sale were merits, grades, ranks . . . , offices . . . , and the privilege of appointment ahead of turn." [18]

The commercialization of rank and office, although theoretically controlled, was obviously open to abuse and corruption, and, since it involved the highest authority in the land, even that authority was unable to remain immune to its worst effects.

IV *Major Themes*

But to return to the novel. That Li related the episodes in *The Bureaucracy Exposed* to themes should come as no surprise in view of the thematic approach he obviously adopted for each of his major novels, and it is fair to say that without an examination of each theme contained in this and, for that matter, in his other novels, the reader fails to gain the overall view of Chinese society which Li sought to present. Space, however, prevents us from engaging in so detailed an investigation and we must, therefore, content ourselves with a presentation of those elements of the novel which were drawn to the attention of the reader in the preface, and which may therefore be regarded as fundamental to it.

Li Po-yuan begins this novel by placing his first episode in a rural setting and by highlighting those interests which dominated the lives of many a successful peasant: the acquisition of land, the ambition to raise the lot and status of the family, and the provision of education for male members of the family in the hope that they will pass through the examination system and into the bureaucracy. There are the inevitable jealousies between families resulting from the successes and failures of their children. "Thanksgiving" feasts are thrown by the family of a boy successful in the examinations for a family tutor and for a local official who, it is hoped, will be able to help further the career of the lad. Nor are the ancestors forgotten. Consciousness of their presence and of their contribution to their descendant's success leads to concrete expressions of thanks in the form of sacrifices.

The location of this first episode is described as a two-family village some thirty *li* south of Ch'ao-i *hsien* in the province of Shensi. The two families, which bear the names Chao and Fang, set out on the path of competition when a grandson in the Chao family wins his *hsiu-ts'ai* degree. Not to be outdone, the Fang family raises sufficient cash to open a school and hires a holder of the *chu-jen* degree, called Wang Jen, to serve as tutor. Jealousy is intensified, however, when the grandson in the Chao family is successful at the triennal examination held at the provincial capital and is awarded the *chu-jen* degree. Wang Jen, the tutor in the Fang family's school, tells one of his pupils that his father wants him to do as well as the Chao boy. When the boy asks his tutor what good is to be derived from working for a *chu-jen* degree, Wang Jen is made to express both the value currently laid on education in most circles, and the dominant reasons in men's minds for seeking official office. He tells the boy that having won the *chu-jen* degree he can then go on to take the *chin-shih* or doctor's degree; that this could lead to membership in the prestigious Hanlin Academy, and, in turn, to his becoming an official: an achievement which could bring him wealth, power, prestige, and control over others, etc. Being a cheeky young lad, the boy asks his tutor why *he* has not accomplished all these things.

The point of the opening scene is clear. By introducing ambition, competition, jealousy, and greed at this humblest of social levels—the country village—and by putting into the mouth of a lowly tutor current popular philosophies of education and of social advancement, the author has shown how such thinking permeates all levels of society and set the stage for the themes which are to dominate every episode of the novel.

Having been successful in the triennal examination and having gone through the necessary formality of registering himself as a graduate in the provincial capital, Chao Wen, as the grandson in the Chao family is called, begins to be introduced into the world of officialdom, although, of course, at a fairly lowly level. Through his tutor and the local magistrate, Wang Hsiang-shen, he comes to meet a relative of the latter known as Chief-of-Police Ch'ien.

Chief-of-Police Ch'ien is offered to the reader as an example of the kind of man who buys himself into office. Although he has only served one term as chief of police, he has made a lot of money out of the post and built himself a new home which commands the admiration of the magistrate. Praising his achievement, and at the same time revealing where his priorities lie, the magistrate is made to say: "Only when you serve as an official in such a fashion can you be reckoned as not having wasted your time." Ch'ien is said to live by the principle that "one travels a thousand *li* to be an official only for the wealth it brings" and that his formula for success is: "Be selected for a post sufficiently early in life." If one can achieve this, and one has sufficient ability, one is bound, he claims, to make a profit, no matter how hard the post may turn out to be.

The enunciation of philosophies of official life such as these in the first pages of his novel is clearly meant by the author to be a further intimation of the thinking of aspirants to government service, and an additional element within his introduction to the whole work. To launch into a novel which purports to portray the lives and activities of bureaucrats, however, it is necessary to set out from the center of government—the capital. He therefore has Ch'ien accompany Chao Wen to Peking where Chao Wen is to make the necessary preparations to take the metropolitan *chin-shih* degree. The young man fails the examination, however, not because of any academic inadequacy, but because he is not lavish enough with gifts of money in the right quarters. He is about to return home when he receives a letter from his father, together with 2,000 ounces of silver. He is told that if he becomes an official his family will cease to be imposed on by others, and that he should therefore use the remittance to purchase a post.

V   *Bribery and Sale of Rank*

Ch'ien finds Chao Wen a go-between who undertakes to arrange everything successfully provided Chao Wen pays him an additional 500 ounces of silver. When negotiations are complete and Chao Wen has acquired his post, our author puts him to one side. He then informs his readers that Ch'ien, who had lost his first posting because of some unspecified fault, manages to have his unfavorable record altered, and his right to reinstatement as chief of police recognized, through bribery, and then shifts his stage to Kiangsi province by having Ch'ien posted to that region.

When he arrives in Kiangsi Ch'ien finds the situation there rather more complex than he had expected in that the official who had first laid accusations against him has just been appointed to the same province as acting governor. Although the acting governor fails to recognize him, the post Ch'ien was hoping to fill has been given, temporarily, to another man. Faced with the prospect of having to hang about doing nothing for several months, he tries to approach the local prefect, Huang, since Huang is the acting governor's right hand man. However, Ch'ien soon discovers that access to the prefect can only be gained through a certain Tai Sheng, Huang's majordomo. Tai Sheng takes the earliest opportunity to mention Ch'ien's name to Prefect Huang who asks Ch'ien to see him during the night. When Huang finally summons Ch'ien into his presence he informs him that he interviews many people and that Ch'ien will have to increase the value of his "gifts" if he is to succeed.

Ch'ien returns to Tai Sheng with a mournful look on his face, but Tai Sheng tells him he ought to know that a man does not get a job after only one interview and that with his help he is bound to succeed. When, some time later, Ch'ien calls on Tai Sheng, Tai Sheng takes him into an inner room and gives him the good news that he has been appointed to the position of clerk in the Office of Receipts and Disbursements.

Li Po-yuan now (chapter 4) puts Ch'ien to one side; promotes Prefect Huang to the rank of intendant of a circuit, and thereby introduces his readers to a higher level in the world of Chinese officialdom.

It turns out that the acting governor of Kiangsi is in the process of opening up special avenues for the sale of official positions and that his younger brother, San Ho-pao, is acting on his behalf. The reason for this is that the acting governor knows that when a governor is appointed he will lose his status and that he must therefore make as much money as he can while he is a position to do so. Taking advantage of a request from the court for funds to meet the needs of victims of drought in Shansi, and its expressed willingness to confer rank on those whose contributions merit it, San Ho-pao persuades those wishing to obtain a rank in this manner to do so through him. Wanting more from one "customer" than San Ho-pao has negotiated for, and therefore threatening to reduce San Ho-pao's share of the deal, the acting governor and his younger brother get into an argument. The acting governor's wife tries to mediate, but with almost disastrous consequences. She is pregnant and, when accidentally butted in the stomach by San, collapses. Fortunately, there is no miscarriage and she recovers from the fall. The family mediates between the brothers and the acting governor is mollified, his anger evaporating with the opportune arrival of a wealthy customer introduced by San.

With some of the money San Ho-pao makes out of the transactions he persuades a grand councillor to act as his patron and to enter into a master-pupil relationship with him. The grand councillor writes a letter of introduction for him and instructs him to deliver it to the governor of Shantung who promptly posts San Ho-pao to Kiaochow—a region of some importance because of Germany's interest in it and because of the large number of foreigners—mainly Germans—resident there.

VI   *Dealing With Foreigners*

Although foreigners play a smaller part in this novel than in *Modern Times*, the injection of a "foreign dimension" here does much to liven up what, up till this point, has been a rather pedestrian story. Faced with a situation with which he is totally unfamiliar and people with whom he finds it difficult to communicate, San Ho-pao seeks advice from an old crony, Warden Lu, on measures he should take. He purchases clothes and furnishings appropriate to his job and is advised to have a few rooms in his residence decorated in foreign style and therefore made suitable for foreign visitors.

As in *Modern Times* Li takes a malicious delight in highlighting the inadequacies of Chinese officials in their dealings with foreigners. Instructed by his governor to invite German officials to a meal in return for their hospitality, San discusses how to go about it with the governor's translator. The translator gives the impression of being an authority on all things foreign, but quickly reveals he knows nothing. Fortunately, another translator is able to give him details of what to do.

Two pages in this chapter (7) are devoted to a discussion of difficulties encountered by Chinese who set out to entertain Westerners, and descriptions of the way in which officials try to cope with knives and forks, etc., and of the trouble they have trying to communicate in foreign languages provide Li with opportunities to poke fun at them and to show up their inadequacies. This lighthearted interlude, however, is made to serve as a prelude to an important statement regarding the lesson Chinese can learn from the foreigners. Discussing recommendations which he wishes to put before the governor regarding business and industrial developments in the region, an official by the name of T'ao Tzu-yao says the proposals have to be taken seriously because they are all based on foreign experience. When asked how foreigners who have never visited China can appreciate circumstances peculiar to China, T'ao replies: "I am not saying that foreigners understand the situation in China. I am simply providing evidence that foreigners manage their affairs with evident success, and I want us to do things the way they do them."

VII   Emulating the Foreigner in Commerce and Industry

The governor is convinced, as a result of conversations with foreigners, that the development of commerce and industry will contribute to the wealth and power of the nation, and he consequently endorses T'ao's proposals. He tells T'ao that his ideas for extracting oil and making paper are good and will not prove costly, but that machinery necessary for such a project will have to be purchased with foreign currency. When T'ao says that all this can be arranged through foreign firms in Shanghai, his proposals are accepted and he is commissioned to go to Shanghai himself to effect the necessary purchases.

Forewarned of the evils current in Shanghai society, T'ao makes up his mind to concentrate on the task he has been given and to refrain from attending parties and from having anything to do with prostitutes. Circumstances, however, conspire to undermine his resolve. Invited out to a restaurant and introduced to a number of men, he is told that ninety percent of business in Shanghai is done in brothels, and that if he refuses to have anything to do with women or drink, he will get nowhere. Every official does these things, he is told, and so he gives in.

Kiaochow, in Shantung, as an area within the German sphere of influence, allowed Li to introduce the topic of Westerners in China and, in particular, the subject of Western efficiency. His change of backdrop and adoption of Shanghai as the stage for his next little drama gives him the opportunity to portray something of the business world in that city and the corrupt atmosphere in which many Chinese officials and businessmen carried on their business activities.

VIII   Officials Likened to Prostitutes

The Shanghai episode (chapters 8–11) begins in a predictable way with T'ao entering a well-known house of pleasure and being helped to draw up a list of guests, most if not all of whom are unknown to him, for a party, as well as to summon singsong girls. The introduction of prostitutes provides Li with an opportunity to draw a comparison (as he does in *Modern Times*) between prostitutes and officials. The topic is inadvertantly introduced by T'ao himself in a conversation with Hsin, a prostitute and friend of a certain Wei P'ien-jen who has latched on to T'ao as a possible source of easy money. T'ao tells her that officials like himself are never masters of their fate since they rarely know from one day to the next where they are likely to find themselves. Hsin replies that being the objects of commerce, prostitutes too are under the control of others and no longer free to do as they wish. Angry that a parallel should be drawn between the conditions of service current in the Chinese bureaucracy and those of prostitution, T'ao Tzu-yao says: "Our status as officials may be purchased with silver, but we don't sell our bodies as those of you in brothels do. . . . How can you compare us with you prostitutes?"

IX *Failure Due to Frailties of Character and Lack of Official Support*

Having provided the foregoing as an introduction, Li launches his readers into the episode proper by making two of T'ao's new acquaintances, Wei P'ien-jen and Ch'ou Wu-k'o, a compradore for a foreign firm, conspire together to make as much money as they can out of T'ao by drawing up a contract for the sale of machinery. When T'ao learns that a foreigner is involved in the contract any doubts he may have had are dispelled. Taken to this foreigner, he makes a down payment of 11,000 ounces of silver and promises to pay the balance on delivery of the goods.

Having squandered a considerable portion of the funds he had brought with him to Shanghai on the girl Hsin and finding himself with only 3,000 ounces of silver left in his bank account, T'ao telegraphs the governor of Shantung for a further 15,000 ounces. Receiving no reply, he wires his brother-in-law who informs him that the governor has fallen sick and that in the meantime another foreigner has been found who will supply the required machinery very cheaply. T'ao is told to cancel his own order and to return to Shantung. When T'ao takes the matter up with his new friends, however, they tell him he cannot ask for his money back from a Westerner and that once the machinery arrives he will be liable to make full payment for it.

T'ao's misery, caused when he realizes the difficulty of his situation, is compounded (chapter 9) when he receives a telegram from his relative in Shantung telling him he must hand over the 20,000 ounces of silver with which he had originally been issued to a certain Intendant Wang who is on his way from Shantung to Japan on official business and who will shortly pass through Shanghai. Appalled at this fresh turn of events, T'ao turns to Wei P'ien-jen, but receives little comfort. When Intendant Wang arrives in Shanghai to board his steamer he sends a messenger to T'ao to ask for the money. Cornered, T'ao decides to pay the intendant a personal visit the following day. In the meantime Wei tells him not to try to cancel his contract for the machinery, but to make it plain to his superiors that he was deputed by the governor of Shantung to purchase it, and that if he no longer has the money he set out with, it is not his fault. Wei tells T'ao to inform Intendant Wang that the machinery cost 40,000 ounces; that T'ao had had to place an order for it right away and had had to make a downpayment of 20,000 ounces, and that if there was going to be a court case involving the foreigner, it should be handled by the official responsible for such matters and not by T'ao. T'ao is advised by Wei to hire a Western lawyer when he goes to see the intendant.

Meanwhile, Intendant Wang makes his own inquiries and discovers what T'ao has been up to since coming to Shanghai. When he asks T'ao for receipts for payments made, T'ao withdraws and consults his friend once more. Wei and Ch'ou Wu-k'o provide him with forged documents, but also advise him that as a last resort he will have to rely on the power of the foreigner. Ch'ou devises a telegram which the foreign manager of his firm can send to the foreign resident governor in Shantung and which requests that this foreign governor put pressure on the governor of Shantung. The point is then made that foreign officials protect their men of commerce whereas Chinese officials mistreat them. The chapter ends with the acting governor of Shantung receiving a telegram of complaint from the foreign governor of Kiaochow and lamenting over the fact that there is no escape from the foreigner. He is subsequently replaced by a new governor.

With foreign pressure to support him, T'ao's brother-in-law in Shantung advises the new governor to instruct Intendant Wang to try to cancel T'ao's contract for machinery, but if that proves impossible, to purchase it as agreed. T'ao, quite naturally, is delighted with the news when he receives it, but his delight turns to further anxiety when he is informed by his friends that the false documents drawn up by them to help him prove to Intendant Wang that the machinery cost 40,000 ounces of silver must now be treated as valid, and when he is visited by his wife's brother, a Buddhist monk from Shaohsing, who tells T'ao, angrily, that he has made no remittance to his wife for three months. T'ao soon discovers that his wife has also arrived in Shanghai, and when the two meet she complains to him that whereas wives of officials expect to live well, she has experienced nothing but hardship. She also vents her anger on him for acquiring an amour in Shanghai and for no longer having the money he set out with from Shantung. When a messenger informs her that money has been sent to Intendant Wang from Shantung, and that it is to be paid to T'ao so that he can honor his contract, her brother, the monk, calls on Intendant Wang to intercept it on his sister's behalf. Needless to say, the episode ends with T'ao having to meet his marital obligations and having to honor the false and highly inflated contracts with which, due to inept officials in Shantung as well as to his own frailties of character, he finds himself encumbered. So much for the wish, expressed by T'ao at the beginning of this episode, that he and his colleagues should emulate foreign efficiency.

X Ineptitude and Chicanery among Military and Civil Officials

The second half of chapter 11 sets the stage for a long episode which, in location and cast, is in marked contrast to the one just described. In this story, which is drawn to a close in chapter 18, the action takes place in Chekiang province, and the type of official who holds the center of the stage is the military man.

Although the framework for this episode is simply a campaign for the suppression of bandits, it does not lend itself easily to summarization because of the several levels on which the story simultaneously operates. A campaign of sorts certainly takes place, but in almost every scene rivalry, intrigue, corruption, ineptitude, cowardice, cruelty, and self-serving are the real subjects under review.

Occupying the center of the stage throughout most of the episode is a certain Hu Hua-jo who is a military man appointed by the provincial governor of Chekiang to command troops deputed to rid the region of its bandits. The story is launched, however, with the introduction of a character called Tai Ta-li who fails to be appointed to a post on which he has set his heart because a colleague of his, Chou Lao-yeh (the character who serves as a bridge between the former episode and this one), advises the governor temporarily to refrain from promoting Tai. Chou's overt reason for making such a recommendation is the conveniently correct one that Tai is indispensable in his present position. In reality, however, he resents Tai who is his immediate superior and who treats him with disdain.

Angry at having his hopes dashed and embarrassed because he had celebrated the promotion prematurely, Tai plans to take his revenge as soon as he learns that the postponement was made on Chou's advice.

The appointment of Hu, a friend of Tai, to the task of rooting out bandits provides Tai with the opportunity he is looking for. Judging Chou to be the kind of man who enjoys taking the initiative and concluding that he will eventually clash, to his disadvantage, with Hu, Tai advises Hu to ask for Chou to be placed on his staff. Being the governor's right hand man, says Tai, Chou will be given full responsibility for ensuring the success of Hu's expedition, but will also have to carry the blame should anything go wrong. The subtlety of Tai's plan is revealed when Chou indicates his delight at having been selected. His pleasure is due to the fact that victory will probably result in promotion for him. Tai's parting shot to ensure the success of his scheme is to sow the seed of dissention by telling Chou, when he congratulates him on his appointment, that Hu is a coward and that Chou must therefore be decisive, and that if Chou defers to Hu, Hu will have little respect for him.

The campaign begins in a leisurely way when the army sets off up river in a flotilla of small boats to Yenchow, the reported center of bandit activity. Although the trip from Hangchow, his starting point, normally takes only two days, Commander Hu makes it last five or six days—and not surprisingly, since he decided to hire a pleasure craft for himself and he and his subordinates devote much of their time to the girls whose occupation it is to make the journeys of boating customers as enjoyable as they can. Hu has two girls on his boat, but when he wakes from sleep he finds them both gone. Hearing them singing, and finding them in the company of one of his officers, a man called Wen, he gets angry. When the girls hear him in his fury throwing the furniture about they rush back to molify him. Jealous, Commander Hu spends much of the night interrogating one of his girls about Wen and tries to find out how long she has known him. The mistrust thus created between Hu and Wen becomes another thread in this complicated episode.

When the flotilla finally reaches Yenchow Commander Hu is told by the people there that there are no bandits in the vicinity. However, two robberies, at a pawnshop and at a moneychanger's, result in the closing of the city gates and the spreading of rumors, and when the stories grow to the point that the robberies are said to have been committed by a "king" fomenting rebellion, Commander Hu sets out at the head of his troops to deal with the enemy. Aware that if there are bandits in the region they must be very few in number, Hu is advised not to enlighten his superiors, but to paint as serious a picture for them as he can, since a resounding victory will guarantee him good treatment when he returns to base.

The expedition sets out, and when villagers see the troops advancing they scuttle away out of fear. Concluding that if people flee they must be bandits, Hu puts their houses to the torch and any women and children found are arrested and interrogated. As is common in such circumstances, the troops also pillage the homes of the villagers and rape the women.

Since he meets no opposition Hu considers he has won a great victory; his troops are rewarded and a victory feast is given aboard the boats. Amid all the feasting, however, a messenger arrives from the magistracy and informs Hu that many wounded men and women have entered the city from the surrounding villages and that they are demanding redress for hurt done to them. Their wounds, they claim, were not inflicted by bandits but by the troops led by Commander Hu.

When the magistrate of Yenchow, who is at the feast, returns to his magistracy he finds a large crowd waiting for him. The villagers kneel beside his palanquin and plead for justice the moment he passes through the gates of the magistracy. Affecting concern, the magistrate tells them the troops are hateful, that he has reported them to their commander, and that the commander will deal with each according to his crime. Having lit the lanterns and torches in his courthouse, he examines the villagers and informs them that they do indeed present a pitiable sight. Moved by his apparent concern, the villagers heap praise on the magistrate and call him their "father and mother." Knowing he has got them in the right mood, the magistrate tells the villagers to draw up a detailed report of the crimes committed against them. Reporting first to his prefect and then to Commander Hu, the magistrate informs them that he has a solution to the problem the villagers have posed which will keep the villagers from pursuing the matter further and which will not neccessitate the punishment of the commander's troops.

The magistrate returns to the magistracy where he asks the villagers for their statement and promises them monetary redress. He doles out some money but says that the women who claim to have been raped must identify the culprits and must provide evidence of the violence done against them. Since the women do not wish to be inspected the villagers find themselves in a quandry. When the village leaders are invited to speak to the magistrate they are over-awed as they are forced to walk past ranks of troops and attendants drawn up for the occasion. However, the magistrate continues to give the impression that he is on their side. He curses the evil soldiery and deplores their behavior so that the deputation soon feels he has taken the words out of their mouths and said everything they would have wished to say. Their dilemma grows when he urges them to hurry and identify the culprits. Soon the magistrate's apparent indignation against the troops turns to anger against the villagers. "You have made accusations which have been passed on to the commander and he is now calling for evidence," he says. "Where is it? If there is no evidence you have committed perjury and must return the money I gave you."

This segment of the episode ends, as one would expect, with the temporary defeat of the villagers and the joy and gratitude of Commander Hu when he is informed that no serious charges are to be laid against him and his men. As a reward the magistrate seeks only commendation in the commander's report to his superiors and the bestowal of official ranks upon his sons.

Other subplots within this major episode include the suicide of a prostitute wrongly accused of stealing, the ill-treatment of her "foster-mother," and a short detective story in which the real thief is apprehended. Here again we are brought face to face with the immoral and self-serving attitudes of officials.

The man whose goods are stolen is the young and wealthy Wen Hsi-shan whose relations with Commander Hu turned decidedly chilly following the visit of the latter's girl friend, Lung Chu, to Wen's boat. Wen Hsi-shan is sharing his boat with Commander Hu's poor assistant Chao Pu-liao. Chao falls in love with Lan Hsien, the girl who has been summoned to keep him company, and boasts to her of his "riches." Eager to give the girl a present he borrows fifty dollars from Wen. Later, Wen throws a party during which the men become thoroughly drunk and fall asleep. When he wakes up Wen finds that his money and goods have been stolen. He lays an accusation against the crew of his boat with Commander Hu, and the commander promptly hands captain and crew over to the magistrate of Yenchow. When a search of the boat is made, however, Chao Pu-liao's gift to Lan Hsien is found among her belongings and she is immediately arrested as the most likely suspect. Delivered to the wardress, Lan Hsien's hair adornments and jewelry are removed—ostensibly to be offered as evidence at the trial. Knowing that she has nothing to look forward to except injustice and suffering, Lan Hsien determines to end her life.

When the wardress finds the girl dead the following morning a report is made to the magistrate who holds a hearing. The magistrate scolds the wardress for allowing her charge to take her life and orders her to be given a beating. He then tells the wardress that her life is in the hands of the dead girl's "foster-mother." The wardress pleads with the old woman for her life and the old woman, not knowing to what extent the wardress was in fact responsible for the girl's death, and fearful of what the ghost of the dead wardress might do to her, tells the magistrate that the wardress did not kill her. The magistrate therefore pardons the wardress. When the old woman has signed a declaration freeing the wardress of all responsibility the magistrate passes his final judgment. Lan Hsien, he says, stole Wen's money and committed suicide out of a sense of guilt.

Needless to say, Lan Hsien was not the real villain, and the persistent detective work of a policeman results in the true culprit being found. The thief is a man called Lu, captain of Commander Hu's flotilla. Because of his official status and his willingness to "recompense" those of his official colleagues involved in the case, the findings of the detective are kept secret and no further action is taken against Lu.

Learning the name of the real thief, Wen Hsi-shan states that he regrets the death of the prostitute, Lan Hsien, and says that he did not know of the charge brought against her until it was too late. The magistrate dismisses the tragedy, however, by saying that they must worry about the living rather than the dead.

As the larger episode, dealing with Commander Hu's and his subordinates' exploits, draws to a close the two men Tai Ta-li and Chou Lao-yeh again come to the fore. Inevitable friction between Hu and his outspoken adviser, Chou Lao-yeh, has cooled their relationship, and when Hu, at the instigation of Tai, comes to suspect Chou of seeking to enhance his own prestige through a report on the campaign submitted to the governor, Hu puts the blame for everything that went wrong on Chou—just as Tai had expected, and much to his satisfaction.

The episode is given a fresh lease on life with the arrival of what appears to be a threatening letter from a member of the Yenchow gentry called Wei Chu-kang which states that there had not been any bandits in the region and which tells Commander Hu of some of the unpleasant things being said of him. This is clearly a letter of reproof which, Hu knows, could well herald the laying of complaints before his superiors. Hu therefore considers ways to silence the letter writer. After consulting Chou, on whom he still finds himself having to rely, Chou goes to Yenchow to see an assistant district magistrate called Shan, and together they plan to extort money from Hu, as well as to gain promotion. Chou advises Hu to pay Wei 30,000 ounces of silver to keep him quiet; but Hu, to Chou's surprise, turns stubborn and refuses to pay. Chou now decides to play for high stakes and suggests to his fellow conspirator that they draw the senior official and censor Chang Ch'ang-yen, a cousin of Wei, into the picture. Shan goes to see Wei, who is angry that Hu has so far refused to respond to his letter, and says he will take the matter up with the provincial governor. Shan says that the governor will back Hu and tells Wei that he would do better to approach his relative in Peking. Wei responds by saying that all officials at the capital act as if they were in business and that trying to get action from his cousin will cost him 500 ounces of silver. Shan therefore goes to Chou and tells him the operation will cost 1,000 ounces; Chou gives Shan 600 ounces, and Shan hands Wei 300 ounces. Wei finally sends his cousin fifty ounces with an accompanying letter.

XI   *Corruption Bolstered by Hypocrisy*

A whole new set of circumstances now emerges, and the stage is set for a radical purge of the Chekiang bureaucracy when the provincial governor receives a telegram informing him that two imperial emissaries are on their way to Fukien via Chekiang and, three days later, that he has been impeached by three censors. Although the names of the censors are not given one cannot help but conclude that Wei's letter to the capital has had something to do with this sudden portent of doom. News of the impending arrival of the emissaries spreads alarm through all members of the bureaucracy in Chekiang. Civil and military officials are deputed to greet them as they arrive by steamer. On their arrival all movement in and around Hangchow is checked, and on the second day the emissaries order new instruments of torture and punishment such as chains, sticks, clubs, manacles, cages, etc., to be prepared. Officials in the region are terrified as they wait for information as to what it all means. They are not kept in suspense for very long, however. Suddenly, a public notice is issued and the governor is ordered to remove certain officials from office, among them Commander Hu. Altogether, 150 officials are named, but the governor is kept in ignorance as to the nature of their crimes.

If the reader thinks that at last a degree of probity is being introduced and that the officials from Peking are about to cleanse the province of Chekiang of its incompetent and immoral officials in order to introduce good, clean government into the region, he is quickly disappointed. These senior officials from Peking soon reveal themselves to be more than equal to their provincial colleagues in venality. Despite all the activity occasioned by their presence and the busyness of their assistants as they seek to carry out their commands, the emissaries themselves spend their time smoking opium and enjoying the fruits of the uncertainty they have created in people's minds. There is method in the way they keep silent regarding the reasons for the dismissal of certain officials; it encourages intrigue and, inevitably, bribery—a lucrative source of income for themselves. Whispers reach the governor, who is anxious to clear his name, that the emissaries want two million ounces of silver to bring the whole affair to an end. A queue soon forms at the door of an intermediary, and those who can pay what is demanded of them have the charges against them—whatever they are—dropped. Those unable to pay, however, are eventually summoned to face certain charges and are beaten and thrown into prison.

When the emissaries are about to return to the capital the governor is again impeached. He is dismissed from his post and the assistant emissary is made acting governor. Having acquired his seal of office, this acting governor issues a proclamation which asserts that the evils found among officials in Chekiang are due to corruption and to their failure to study the Confucian classics. All officials who have purchased their offices, it goes on, must therefore sit for an examination within three months, and those who fail will be dismissed.[19] "Not," he says, "that I despise those who have purchased rank; it's just that there is a principle here which I find thoroughly despicable. Any Tom, Dick, or Harry can have a whore if he's willing to pay for her, and it's the same with official rank. Ever since the court made it possible for rank to be purchased it has been available to anyone with sufficient cash; and doesn't that put it on the same level as the prostitute?"[20] It is quite otherwise with the man who goes through the examination system and who proves himself worthy of rank and office, he says.

The acting governor dresses simply and lets it be known that he will accept no presents. He emphasizes Confucian teaching on frugality and asserts that those who are lacking in virtue cannot practice it. Those who insist on living well, he says, have gained their wealth by robbing the common people.

Such are the principles he claims to maintain; but our author will not even allow this man to match his deeds to his words. When officials later discuss the acting governor among themselves, one says that although he gives the impression of being incorruptible he is not averse to acquiring money, and that he made 500,000 ounces of silver out of the recent investigations into malpractice in Chekiang. He does everything through others in order to preserve his good image, says the speaker, so that one can usually achieve one's end by sending gifts to his concubine and to his son.

The intricacies of corruption in government circles are pursued and unraveled in bewildering, and often fascinating, detail throughout this novel and, unfortunately, mere summaries of the numerous episodes included within it cannot do justice to the flavor and atmosphere conjured up by Li Po-yuan in the original text. Two segments of the novel (chapters 24–29 and chapters 43–45) should, however, be mentioned because they have merited special notice on account of the contrasting levels of the bureaucracy which they purport to describe, and because of the degree of artistry Li achieved in them.

XII   *Crown and Grand Council Implicated*

Chapters 24–29 claim to describe circumstances in high official circles in Peking. The springboard to this section is found in chapter 23 in the attempt by a certain Prefect Chia in Chekiang to obtain a post for his son for whom he purchased a rank when the young man was a mere boy. Serious flooding in Chingchow seems to provide him with the opportunity he has been looking for since he knows that to be successful in controlling the rivers of China is to be certain of wealth and fame. When the governor summons Chia and other officials to inform them of the calamity, Chia telegraphs an influential official in Peking—a certain Grand Councillor Chou—and asks for a job for his son. The official replies that he is not in a position to do anything and that, in any case, the task is too great for so young a person. Undismayed, Chia's son takes matters into his own hands by forging a few letters, going to the work site, and bullying the official in charge into believing he is a protégé of Grand Councillor Chou. He consequently gets the job of supervising workmen on the lower reaches of the river. Once in his post he sacks staff and fills their positions with his own men in order to make as much money as he can and to pave the way toward even higher rank.

When the work is completed Chia's son is summoned to Peking where he visits Grand Councillor Chou. Chou, however, receives him with less than warmth. He then looks up a man called Huang, who is a banker and well known in Peking as a "fixer," and is told by him that Grand Councillor Chou is behind the times and that he should not waste his time on him. Chou is out of favor, says Fatty Huang (the name by which Huang is popularly known), because he championed a reformer and thereby gave the impression that he espoused the reformists' cause. Chia informs Fatty Huang that he knows of a woman—a Buddhist nun—through whom it is possible to gain access to high places. Fatty Huang, however, concerned lest he be bypassed and lose Chia's custom, tells him that nuns, and Taoist priests whom he has also mentioned as useful contacts, are all "minor avenues" and that his best policy is to make a direct approach to the grand councillors.

At a party Fatty Huang introduces Chia to a number of his friends who are skilled in smoothing the paths for aspirants to rank and office; he also provides him with a male entertainer. When Chia gets drunk and begins to exude unpleasant body odors the male entertainer tries to avoid his company by suggesting that he return home. Enraged, the young Chia picks a quarrel with the entertainer and begins to hurl things about. The following day he is informed by Huang that a censor, who is particularly fond of the entertainer, had witnessed the scene he had made at the party and that the consequences could be serious. He intimates, however, that he is willing to act as a mediator and to bribe the censor to keep silent. He next advises Chia that if he wishes to get in touch with the grand councillors he should do so through Hei Ta-shou, a majordomo at the palace and the uncle of a certain Hei Pa-ko whom he had met at the party. He also tells him that the grand secretary, Hua, whom he should try to meet, refuses cash gifts but is always willing to accept fine antiques. The right kind of antique, he points out, can be purchased from Liu Hou-shou who was also at the party.

Arrangements are made for the young Chia to have interviews with Grand Secretary Hua and with Grand Councillor Hsu, among others, and suitable presents for them cost him 30,000 ounces of silver; but nothing concrete emerges from these efforts. Fatty Huang informs him, however, that his name has been put down for an interview with the emperor. When Chia asks how much the position of intendant of the Shanghai circuit would cost him he is told 500,000 ounces of silver. The emperor, says Fatty Huang, has a garden which he wants completed and he is short of cash.

Realizing that the intendancy lies beyond his means, young Chia nonetheless visits a moneylender to raise some cash and earmarks the loan for various councillors, etc. He is granted an audience with the emperor and is finally appointed an expectant official in the province of Chihli. On hearing of young Chia's audience and appointment, Grand Councillor Chou is angry for, although the young man could be regarded as his protégé because of his former connections with the Chia family, he had paid him no more than the one visit. He invites Chia to a meal with the intention of getting some money out of him, but the young man, unhappy with his first audience with the grand councillor, replies that he is having a party of his own and cannot accept his invitation.

Young Chia's arrogance leads him to treat a tutor by the name of Wang with disdain. Tutor Wang, consequently, enlists the support of his fellow townsman, Wang Po-kao, and together they decide to lodge a complaint with Grand Councillor Hsu. Too timid at first to interfere, Hsu is finally goaded into action when Wang Po-kao suggests that Chia favors other councillors above Hsu. Wang then rehearses the manner in which Chia has won his way to office and tells Hsu of the money Chia made as a supervisor of works during the floods. Hsu quarrels with Grand Secretary Hua over Chia and Wang Po-kao is asked to collect evidence of Chia's shortcomings. During his quarrel with Hua, Hsu asserts that Chia is a slippery character whom he would never recommend for office. Hua replies: "Where will you find a genuinely good person in this world? All you and I can do is to be a little magnanimous."

Wang now sees Fatty Huang in private and shows him a notice of impeachment directed against Chia, but which implicates Huang as well. When Wang departs Huang sends for Chia and tells him everything. He suggests Chia spend a further 3,000 ounces of silver on Grand Councillor Hsu to mollify him and that he also send something to Wang Po-kao and the censor to still their tongues. But Chia now finds himself in difficult financial straits as his creditors begin to close in on him.

XIII *In Search of Dignity*

Whatever may be said of the authenticity of the picture presented to the reader by Li Po-yuan of the behavior of bureaucrats at the capital—and Chinese disagree among themselves on this—there is little argument over the accuracy with which officials are portrayed in chapters 43–45. These chapters represent, possibly, the finest part of the novel for it is here that the full flavor of life in a provincial magistracy can be savored, and the author exhibits his artistry at its best. As with other episodes in this novel incident dominates over plot, so that what we are given is a series of small acts or cameos placed against the backdrop of the larger, bureaucratic scene.

The first act takes place at the door of the Grand Hall—the court-house—located in the prefectural residence in Wuchang *fu*, a prefectural capital. It is the place where minor officials and those hopeful of a posting stand in attendance on the prefect, and on the day in question the prefect summons one of these officials—a head constable and warden of the jail—into his presence to talk with him. Suffused with glory at the honor paid to him, and regarded with interest and envy by his colleagues, he is surrounded by twenty or thirty of them as he emerges from his audience. There then follows a passage which represents Li's writing at its best.

It was the depth of winter. Some wore unlined outer garments, and some, believe it or not, were still dressed in sheer cotton. Each garment had been patched with yellow thread, and in some cases the yellow thead had come loose. The tips of their boots had, in the majority of cases, grown pairs of "eyes." Two of these officials, however, were wearing "pawing tigers," and these still appeared to be in good condition. As to their hats, some were made of woolen cloth and some of felt, but all were old and tattered and beyond repair. Among them were one or two made of fur, but the fur was no longer in evidence and all that was left was the worn hide.

The men stood huddled together in the spacious grounds below the Grand Hall, their eyes bloodshot and their noses red with cold. Tears and mucus from their noses hung from the beards of the bewhiskered who sought to wipe them away with grey-colored handkerchiefs. Having now heard that the chief prefect had summoned Sui Feng-chan to ask him to recommend a person for a post and to act as that person's guarantor, they drew the conclusion that Sui Feng-chan was certain to have a great future. They all closed in upon him asking him his name and his courtesy title. Among them was one who appeared a little more elegant than the rest. He made his way to the back of the private apartments to the rear of the Grand Hall where he espied the frame of a "ceremonial umbrella." He moved it out and placed it against a wall and then invited Sui to sit down and to have a chat.[21]

Below the umbrella sit several minor officials—Sui Feng-chan, Shen Shou-yao, and Ch'in Mei-shih among them—and they engage in a profound discussion. Later, an old female servant of Shen Shou-yao's household comes to pick up Shen Shou-yao's clothes and unintentionally lets it be known that the family is so badly off financially that it has not even sufficient rice for the next meal. Embarrassed, Shen Shou-yao strikes the old woman across the face in anger. The old servant refuses to retract her statement and throws herself to the ground where she begins to wail. Her behavior quickly causes a crowd to gather. Shen Shou-yao feels both shame and anxiety but is unable to drag the woman to her feet. Later, she so annoys the majordomo that he comes out and curses her and threatens to take her to the chief district magistrate. At this she stops crying and stands up.

Shen Shou-yao now felt inexpressible gratitude and wanted to go to the majordomo to say a few words of appreciation. He had just stepped over to him and was about to speak when, unexpectedly, the majordomo gave him a look of disdain, turned on his heel, and went back inside. Shen Shou-yao felt even more embarrassed and did not know where to put himself. He decided to go home and thought to take advantage of the situation to give the old servant a scolding; but he found that she had long since scuttled away. His boots, hat, and bundled-up clothes lay scattered on the ground with not a soul to pick them up.[22]

Fortunately, Sui's companion, Ch'in Mei-shih, shouts for his son "Doggie" to come and lend a hand: "Doggie drew a small cloth bundle from inside his jacket, took out some shoes, and waited for his father to change into them. The old man divested himself of his gown and folded it up, placing it alongside his boots; he then handed Shen Shou-yao's bundle, boots, and hatbox to his son as well. . . . Alas! Doggie's hands were unable to hang on to so many objects. Fortunately, however, the other men had their wits about them and were able to find a stick under the Grand Hall which would serve as a carrying pole." [23]

So ends the first act. The second takes place in Shen Shou-yao's home. Shen returns home with Doggie where he finds the old female servant sobbing and cursing in one of the rooms. Shen wants to drive her away, but she is determined to obtain all the wages due to her before she will leave; she also demands to be given a gratuity. Shen has no money and the female servant therefore continues to wail and curse, repeating over and over, "My master refuses to pay me my wages and my gratuity!"

The lady of the household just happened to be upstairs catching fleas and therefore did not come down. But after a while, when the din became unbearable, she had no alternative but to appear, with her hair in disarray, in order to pacify the woman. Doggie had still not left. . . . Restraining Shen with his hand, he said: "Uncle Shen, take no notice of the bitch. If you want to send presents to anyone when she's gone, I'll do it for you, and should you wish to go to the magistracy I'll carry your clothes and hat for you. . . ." Shen Shou-yao said: "Brother, you're the son of my friend Elder Brother Ch'in; how can I constantly trouble you to deliver presents and to carry my clothes and hats for me?" Doggie replied: "I'm used to doing this kind of thing; furthermore, delivering presents is one way in which you can help me earn some money. For every ten coppers I shall only demand four." [24]

Even when the lady of the house has calmed the old servant down, Ch'in's son refuses to leave.

Shen asked him if there were something he wished to tell him, and he said: "I'd like to ask you, Uncle Shen, for eight coppers to buy some T'ang-shou tea."

Poor Shen Shou-yao. . . . He had no alternative but to step into the inner apartment to discuss the matter with his wife. His wife said: "I've twenty-three coppers left over from the things I pawned the day before yesterday. They're under the mattress; but they're not sufficient to buy even half a pint of rice. Either way, we shall have to pawn something else since there's no rice for the stove today. Give him eight and save the rest for me." A moment later Shen Shou-yao had brought out the money. Doggie groveled on the ground and kowtowed before his Uncle Shen before taking the money; then he left, counting the coins as he made off. Ch'in's secret as to how to be an official was: In a contest of wills, never give way. It was a secret which had been well learned by his son! [25]

The third act takes place in the guestroom of the governor-general's residence, but the prelude to it is the arrival of a friend at Shen Shou-yao's home just when Shen's wife is lamenting her lot.

"When I first married you," [she said], "I had no thoughts of wealth or rank and was quite satisfied provided our rice bowls were kept full. Later, you became an official and my parents said: 'Now everything'll be fine. There's no need to worry any more once someone becomes an official.' When people become officials they gain promotion and grow wealthy; but with us it's different. Since we became officials we've grown steadily poorer, and now we don't even have anything more to pawn! What am I to do if this daily decline continues?'"

Shen Shou-yao's face was suffused with embarrassment and shame and he said: "Ever since I became an official I've made every effort to win advancement, and I've never been absent when bulletins have appeared on the official bulletin board. I've been unlucky and can't think of a way out." When he had finished speaking he sighed repeatedly and his wife wept until the tears rolled down her face like rain and she was unable to continue eating her meal.

Seeing the state she was in, Shen Shou-yao could eat no more than half a bowl of rice himself. Then, fortunately, a friend came looking for him.[26]

Although Shen Shou-yao normally stayed out till midnight following his midday meal, the news his friend had brought him had him rushing home a mere two hours later to inform his wife, with uncontrollable excitement, that all their problems had been resolved. The governor, he said, had indicated that at future audiences assistants, such as himself, would be provided with chairs and would no longer be expected to stand. The governor had stated, he went on, that "We are all officials of the royal household, whether senior or junior, and if I treat a colleague with disdain I am abusing a commissioned officer of the court. If they are seated I shall be able to chat with them about anything they have on their minds."

Shen's wife doubts that this change of attitude on the part of the governor will have any effect on her husband's fortunes, and ends a long conversation in which she seeks to curb his excitement by saying "I don't care whether you stand, sit, or kneel when you see the governor so long as I have sufficient money to meet expenses . . . and can stop pawning things."

Eager to take full advantage of the governor's declared willingness to listen sympathetically to the problems of his subordinates, Shen Shou-yao hurries over to the governor's residence early the following morning hoping he might be granted an audience after the governor has finished seeing his senior officials.

The officials arrived at the governor's residence at seven o'clock in the morning, but it was twelve before the governor finished interviewing each one of them. Afterward, a policeman appeared holding a number of calling cards. He announced that the governor had indicated his willingness to receive thirty assistants in audience. He then called out their names, and as he did so, they entered the chamber in strict order like a row of fish, one behind the other. Although each of these officials was overjoyed, none could help trembling or prevent his teeth from chattering on this his first experience of official protocol.

Several, whose names appeared at the bottom of the list, jumped the queue for fear of being overlooked. Those ahead of them refused to let them get away with this manoever and stepped forward to pull them back. The men from the rear refused to comply and began to quarrel with the men in front. Impatient, the policeman repeatedly urged them forward saying: "Hurry along there! . . . If you've got something to say, leave it till later when the audience is over. What am I going to do with you gentlemen!" Having been thus reproved by the policeman, the officials were afraid to utter another word. They simply let down the sleeves of their gowns, which were provided with flaps to protect the hands which held the reins of a horse when they were on horseback, and followed each other inside.

When they arrived in the reception room they found the governor already standing in the center. They were instructed not to kneel or to strike their foreheads on the ground in front of him. They therefore all went down on one knee together in a kind of curtsey. The governor spread out his hands toward them and said: "Sit"; whereupon they all sat down in groups. Some of the men simply fixed their eyes on the governor and paid no attention to anything behind them; others sat on the small tea tables, while one tried unsuccessfully to sit on a seat which was already occupied before hurrying, in a grand circular movement, to the opposite side of the room. There was considerable turmoil before everyone was finally seated.

With the utmost respect, and with bated breath, they listened to the commands of their master. All that could be heard was Governor Chia saying: "The etiquette in each center of officialdom today requires assistants in most instances to stand to attention when they are being interviewed by chief prefects, let alone governors and governors-general. I have now done away with this practice and hope you will all take note of the fact and act accordingly. I shall be busy for the next couple of days, but in a few days time I shall be sending for you . . . and will then test you personally and individually. Have I made myself clear?"

At first, when the gathering heard the governor say that he was going to examine them, they simply looked at each other speechless. It was not until he asked, "Have you all heard me?" that a couple managed to reply that they had. When the governor saw that the men had said all they would, and that there was nothing further for him to say, he raised his teacup and dismissed them.

When Sui Feng-chan had entered the reception room he had been prepared to talk to the governor about a great many things; but when he actually found himself in the presence of the governor, the governor, unaccountably, seemed to put a damper on his courage, and he could not get a word out. When everyone else said "yes" he found that he, too, could do no more than say "yes," and when the others raised their teacups he had to raise his also.

He had just lifted up his teacup when he heard a crashing sound. Someone or other had dropped his cup and it had smashed to pieces. When he looked in the direction of the sound Sui found that in some unaccountable way one of the last two officials on his right had dropped his cup on the floor and that it had broken into small pieces, splashing tea all over the floor. Even the governor's gown was spattered by it.

The governor stood to his feet and, shaking the liquid from his clothes, said: "What's all this! What's all this!" The official was so overcome with anxiety that he fell to his knees and began to gather up the broken pieces of porcelain into his long riding sleeves until they, too, were soaking wet. Mumbling he said: "This lowly official deserves to die! I've broken a teacup but this lowly official will make up the loss." The governor ignored him.

After he had spent some time gathering the fragments together the man could not think what he should do next and therefore decided to get to his feet. Only at this point were the other officials able to tell who exactly had dropped and broken the cup; it was none other than Shen Shou-yao.

Originally, when he had been granted permission by the governor to sit down, he had regarded it as a favor beyond compare, and for a moment his hands and feet had danced for joy and his heart had brimmed with happiness. When he saw the teacups raised signaling the end of the interview he could hardly wait to get outside in order to boast to his colleagues. But what he had failed to realize was that the tea tray on which his cup stood had no coasters; that his tea had been made with freshly boiled water and that, in consequence, even the tin tray was burning hot. . . . He wanted to put them down but did not dare to, and then, in a moment of carelessness, he inadvertently stuck a finger beneath the tray; tipped it up, and sent the cup crashing to the floor.

When everyone saw that it was Shen Shou-yao he blushed to the roots of his hair and did not know where to put himself. The governor glared at him and wanted to give him a good telling off, but there was nothing he could usefully say. He simply stood up and, turning to a policeman, said: "I think that in future we had better revert to our old practice. These men don't know how to attend an audience. They're not people you can do a favor." So saying he went straight inside without bothering to see his guests on their way.[27]

Not surprisingly, these poor, minor officials withdraw from the governor's presence dejected and angry with their colleague who, it seems, has deprived them of their one hope of being treated with dignity. Two further acts follow but space does not permit us to include them.

XIV A Dream

We commenced this chapter by drawing attention to the fact that both the introduction to *The Bureaucracy Exposed* by Mao-yuan Hsi-ch'iu Sheng and the novel itself maintain the thesis that the sorry state in which the Chinese bureaucracy found itself in the final years of Manchu rule was due mainly to the increasing commercialization of rank and office. The final chapter of the novel underlines this view in its first two sentences when a businessman is made to say that after surveying all the various kinds of commerce a person might engage in, he finds that being an official is the most lucrative. The problem, he concludes, is how to accumulate sufficient funds to make the initial investment—the purchase of rank and office.

This last chapter, however, also employs the device of a dream in order to provide an overall view of the state of government in China. The dream is in four sections and begins with a man hiding from wild beasts in a wood on a hillside. The animals include wolves, tigers, and leopards, but also dogs, cats, rats, monkeys, and weasels, and, finally, pigs, goats, and oxen. The larger animals are obvious predators and much to be feared; the smaller wild animals, however, also do their share of harm by burrowing everywhere into the hillside. Faced with the menace of the larger animals, they employ every means at their disposal—from wagging their tails to aping the more powerful beasts—to preserve their lives. The domesticated farm animals in the dream are good for nothing, the ox being impressive merely for its size. The dreamer wishes to escape this world of animals but finds there is no place to which he can flee.

It is clear that we have here a symbolic representation of the bureaucracy with each type of animal finding its counterpart among the human species. That the dreamer wishes to escape but cannot, suggests that he is hemmed in by the all-pervading presence of the bureaucracy.

The second part of the dream begins when the dreamer believes himself to be on a major highway full of people and traffic. The highway, he says when recounting the dream, is like a road in Shanghai. He walks along it and comes eventually to a tall building with eighteen steps. Tired, he sits on a foreign-style chair in a hallway and falls asleep. He is rudely awakened when someone nudges him and tells him to move on. The building, he is told, is full of gentlemen who are sitting quietly, engaged in serious, official business, and they can do without ill-mannered yokels such as himself. When the dreamer asks if these men in official garb do not themselves engage in unmannerly conduct at times, he is threatened with violence. Unwilling to submit, the dreamer fights back, but desists when men emerge and inform him that serious business is being carried on within and that he is to cease creating a disturbance.

The symbolism in this and the subsequent parts of the dream are very much more difficult to interpret. We may take it, however, that the building with its eighteen steps represents China and her eighteen provinces, and that the grave men engaged on a serious task are the country's bureaucrats. The fact that the building stands on a busy commercial thoroughfare similar to those in Shanghai, and that it is modern and furnished with foreign-style chairs, however, suggests a China, not of the past, but of a period when her life is directly related to the modern world. It is not traditional China but China as a modern state—the China of the reformists. The men at work in the building should not, then, be regarded as the "old guard" bureaucrats, but rather as the reformists who governed China during the Hundred Days of Reform in 1898.

At the end of this second part of the dream the dreamer is asked where he comes from. He cannot remember and his mind grows confused. Suddenly, however, he asks his interrogator what he and his colleagues in the building are doing. The interrogator's reply introduces the third section of the dream. He says: "We are editing a book." When the dreamer asks what kind of book it is the man answers:

God (the Sovereign-on-High) pities China because she is now so poor and weak and wishes, with all his heart, to save her. However, because China has more than four hundred million inhabitants he cannot save them all at once. He has therefore devised a method to deal with the most outstanding problem. He says: "From birth the common people seem to fear officials and therefore do whatever the officials themselves do, those below following the example of those above. Consequently, I have decided to educate and fashion all those who wish to become officials up to a certain standard so that when they go out into society they will be upright in person and set a good example, thus saving the nation and the people." He also thought to himself: "There are hundreds of thousands of officials in China, both great and small, yet it's almost as if their faults were taught them by a single teacher. I have therefore thought up a new method [for instructing them]. Using the way teachers instruct pupils in schools as a model, I shall have a number of textbooks prepared which can be used for their instruction. Moreover, employing the pedagogical methods in common use in every country in the world, [prospective officials] will begin at the kindergarten level of study and advance, step by step, through elementary school to middle school, and then to high school. Only after they have completed their studies at high school will they be allowed out to become officials, and at that stage they'll naturally be good officials. Will anyone continue to grieve over a lack of peace twenty years after such a scheme has been put into operation?" [28]

If, as we have suggested, the author has in mind the Reform movement during the period when it seemed to be experiencing its greatest success, then this "divine plan" must be regarded as signifying the attitude of the reformists to bureaucratic reform during the period they were in power. The Sovereign-on-High (the traditional Chinese term for God) undoubtedly refers to the ruler under whose auspices the movement was launched, and the proposed educational reforms designed to transform the bureaucracy are, therefore, attributed directly to him. The book that the men in official garb are working on with such seriousness in the building is, we are told, a textbook which is to be used in the new educational program for the bureaucracy.

The man who is recounting the divine plan to the dreamer is suddenly approached by someone from inside the building who tells him to hurry back inside and to get on with his work of editing the book. With his return to this task the dream moves into its final sequence.

A few moments after the man has entered the building the dreamer hears cries of "Fire!" People rush out carrying the book which has been partially destroyed. When the flames reach the roof of the building a Western fire appliance arrives which eventually extinguishes the fire. Oddly enough, when the dreamer eventually looks over the building he sees no sign of any damage either from the conflagration or from the dousing the building has received from the fire appliance. All is back to normal. At this point the dreamer hears the men who had been working in the building return to their table to examine the damage done to the book. They discover that only half of it has been lost. The dreamer learns that this textbook was meant to have been in two parts, the first pointing out the faults of officials so that, becoming aware of them, they will wish to reform, and the second, providing specific information on the conduct of government. The loss of this second part of the book, the dreamer is told, reduces the book from a textbook proper to something resembling novels such as *Records of a Journey to the West* and *The Investiture of the Gods* which are peopled with every kind of malicious spirit imaginable.

The editors decide that the missing part of the book should be rewritten, but one among them insists that the task would be so great and take so long (about two years) that it would be best to publish the first half on its own since, although it may not serve a positive role and induce its readers to do good, it should at least restrain them from doing evil. If, in ancient times, men had been able to govern the world with only half the *Confucian Analects*, says the man, why should not this truncated work also suffice? The editors accept this argument and advice and then disperse. The dreamer wakes up, finds he has recovered from the illness which had confined him to bed, and lives to a ripe old age. The title of the mysterious textbook is, of course, *The Bureaucracy Exposed*, part 1.

We have already noted that the description of a fire is a clever device used by the author of this final chapter to bring his book to an abrupt end; but it is, of course, more than that. In the context of the dream it probably refers to the calamities which were to befall the state and the reformers when the Hundred Days of Reform were brought to an untimely end. The backlash of reaction which swept the reformists from power and which even resulted in the deaths of some of them might well be symbolized by fire, and if the conservative reaction is extended to include the Boxer Uprising of 1900 the symbolism becomes even more appropriate. It would certainly make sense of the Western fire appliance which is brought in to quench the fire. The loss of the second half of the textbook with its specific instructions on how government should be conducted clearly refers to the cancellation of the reform program and the legislation introduced during the time the reformists were in power; nevertheless, the author does not believe that all is lost. He seems to be hinting at the more moderate reform program, introduced after the failure of the Boxer Uprising, when it is suggested that the rewriting of the second part of the textbook will take time and that the book, as it stood, could at least contribute to an awakening to what was bad in government and thereby serve to restrain the forces of evil. The dreamer is himself an example of the new spirit which can imbue the bureaucracy. A representative of the old type of bureaucrat, he is sick and about to expire when his dream begins. When the dream is over and he has gained through it an understanding of the nature of

China's current bureaucracy, however, he wakes up cured and lives on to a great age.[29]

XV *Identification of Characters*

Concerned as it is with officials at every level of the bureaucratic system *The Bureaucracy Exposed*, like *Modern Times*, has a number of characters who can be readily identified with eminent personages active in Li Po-yuan's own lifetime. Hu Shih, in his preface to this novel, identified Grand Secretary Hua and Hei Ta-shou, two of the high officials we met in our survey of chapters 24–29, as Jung-lu and Li Lien-ying respectively. Jung-lu was an important official at the Chinese court during the years immediately before and following the Boxer Uprising and was at the center of much controversy. Li Lien-ying, as we have already noted, was the empress dowager's favorite eunuch.

In an article entitled "Kuan-ch'ang hsien-hsing chi suo-yin" ("Exposition of the Obscure in *The Bureaucracy Exposed*") Chou I-po reveals the identities of a number of additional characters of which the following are the most important: Grand Councillor Hsu, who appears in chapter 26 and to whom we have already referred, is Wang Wen-shao (styled K'uei-shih, posthumous name Wen-chin, 1830–1908) whose home was in Jen-ho in Chekiang province. Wang served as an assistant secretary and then as senior secretary in the Board of Revenue and Population. Following service as an intendant and then as governor in the provinces, and after holding various positions at the capital, he was made a member of the Grand Council.

Shu Chun-men in chapter 28 is Su Yuan-ch'un (styled Tzu-hsi, d. 1908). Su came from Yung-an in Kwangsi province and followed a military career. In 1885, during clashes between France and China, he shared a command with Li Ping-heng in Kwangsi. His career later took him to Kwangchow Wan and Sinkiang, but he was also censured by the censors Chou Shu-mo and Li Cho-hua toward the end of his life.

In chapters 42–43 several incidents are described involving a governor-general by the name of Chia. This person, says Chou I-po, is the famous official and reformer Chang Chih-tung who, as we have seen, also served as a model for a character in *Modern Times*.

In chapter 46 there is a character called T'ung Tzu-liang who is a high official and who has a hatred of all things foreign. Chou I-po equates this person with Grand Secretary Hsu T'ung (styled Yü-ju, 1819–1900) who was a conservative and friend and associate of Associate Grand Secretary Kang-i, another conservative. Chou equates Kang-i (styled Tzu-liang, d. 1900) with the character Shih Pu-t'ung in chapter 47.[30]

CHAPTER 6

Conclusion

T HAT it is difficult accurately to evaluate Li Po-yuan's achieve-
ments in the field of fiction is confirmed by the diverse reactions
to his writings found among Chinese critics. Li's work invites a
variety of responses because of the purpose to which he dedicated it.
By deliberately turning the novel into a weapon with which to attack
social evils and into a vehicle for heaping abuse on certain segments
of society, he was bound to stir up both admiration and animosity
among his contemporaries. But he has also had both detractors and
admirers in more recent times. Critics since the overthrow of the
monarchy in 1911 agree that Li, with few exceptions, selected the
right targets for his attacks, but disagree over the solutions he offered
and over the quality and value of his artistic creations. It will be our
aim in this final chapter, therefore, to examine certain features of the
novels we have surveyed in order to draw some conclusions of our
own.

I   *Sources Employed by Li Po-yuan*
in the Composition of his Novels

Since Li's declared aim in writing novels was to draw his readers'
attention to the social and political issues of the day, he had to relate
his writing to topics and personalities of concern to the press and its
readership, which consisted chiefly of students, teachers, and merchants.

A clue to the technique he employed in selecting his material has
already been referred to in the chapter in which we looked at the
ballad which recounts the events of the Boxer Uprising. It will be
remembered that in a footnote to that work Li stated that he had
based it on both press reports and news which had reached him by
word of mouth, and that the material which he had contributed out of
his own imagination amounted to between ten and fifteen percent.

Since Li was clearly aiming, in this instance, to produce as accurate an account as possible of the Boxer Uprising—albeit in an artistic form—he had, of course, to use the correct names of the officials involved in the story and to exploit his sources as judiciously as possible; but since he was also opposed to the Boxers and to those in official circles who had supported them, he allowed the narrator in the ballad to pass judgment whenever he thought it appropriate, and no doubt also intended the imaginary conversations between officials and others to influence his readers' attitudes toward them.

Although, as we have already noted, we would probably have little difficulty in identifying the major characters, and perhaps many of the minor ones too, in his other novels if it were possible to compare them with persons who appear in the daily press, magazines, and tabloids of his times, Li did not feel himself bound, as he was in the *Ballad*, to a similar degree of factual accuracy. Since these other novels were not designed to be histories, he felt free, among other things, to invent names, and many that he assigned to his characters he intended as puns to illustrate the peculiar characteristics of his protagonists rather than as unequivocal pointers to the persons he had in mind. Of course, the fact that so many of the characters in *Modern Times* and in *The Bureaucracy Exposed* are recognizable is sufficient indication that Li wanted the reader to know which personages he was writing about; but since many of the stories in these novels have to do with the private rather than the strictly public lives of the characters within them, they are of the nature of rumor and gossip, and therefore probably had their origin among household servants and in the convivial gatherings of minor officials, teachers, students, and merchants rather than in official press reports. Obviously, there would be increased scope for the use of the creative imagination.

Two episodes, one of which appears in *Modern Times* and the other in Wu Chien-jen's *Vignettes from the Late Ch'ing*,[1] resemble each other sufficiently to suggest that they had a common origin. The manner in which the original material was handled by these two authors undoubtedly throws considerable light on their attitude to their sources as well as on the nature of them. In *Modern Times*[2] the episode, which is recounted in chapter 58, begins with the governor-general (the viceroy) resident in Nanking telling his subordinates that he is old and unwell. An official who has been waiting for a post seizes the opportunity and informs the governor-general that his wife is a skilled masseuse and that she might cure his ailments through manipulative therapy. After a show of reluctance the governor-general accepts the services of the wife who, after making herself presentable, goes to the governor-general and remains with him considerably longer than her husband had bargained for. In mental agony over the possible implications of this the husband takes to his bed. The wife finally returns, smilingly comforts her husband who is in tears, and presents him with a letter from the governor-general ordering him to take charge of the copper mint. Not surprisingly, other officials remark on the bad form of using a wife to win preferment.

In *Vignettes from the Late Ch'ing* the author is given to greater elaboration and is very much more explicit. He tells us that the viceroy of Nanking was sexually insatiable, and that even at an advanced age he had six or seven concubines of seventeen or eighteen. So noted was he for his sexual appetite that some people sought to win his favor by pandering to his taste for women. One day, when the viceroy was sick, a young expectant intendant who claimed to have some knowledge of medicine said he personally could do nothing to help him, but that his wife might be able to deal with his sickness. The next day the official's wife visits the viceroy and pronounces that medication is not required, only massage. She says her kind of massage is of such a nature that it must be administered in private with the accompaniment of spells and the burning of incense. All the servants and concubines are consequently dismissed. However, two concubines whose curiosity gets the better of them peep through a partition and discover that the massage is of an erotic nature. They become hysterical, burst into the room, and beat up the woman. The woman seeks the viceroy's protection and is escorted to the gates of his residence. Although she is again beaten and disgraced, within ten days her husband receives two appointments and is further promoted at a later date. He therefore takes pride in his achievement.

In Li's version of this story his reticence (he never says what actually took place in the governor-general's residence), his portrayal of the husband as a man who regrets the rashness of his action and awakens to the fondness he has for his wife, and his description of the wife's return and the manner in which she comforts her husband, all exhibit a sensitivity to human frailty, and artistic skill, beside which Wu's account appears crude and harsh. Wu's comment, however, that "Word of this incident soon spread throughout Nanking," is instructive. Though put into the mouth of the narrator and therefore strictly part of the story, there can be no doubt that we have here a clear reflection of the type of source of which both Li and Wu made much, and probably most, use.

Most of the stories in *Modern Times* and in *The Bureaucracy Exposed*, we would suggest, are of this kind, and we would therefore agree with Hu Shih when, in his criticism of *The Bureaucracy Exposed*, he says that it is probable that the author's descriptions of Peking society in that novel, and, in particular, of the life of the most senior officials in the capital, are based entirely on current gossip and leave the reader with the feeling that Li is indulging in exaggeration bordering on caricature.[3] The situation is otherwise, however, when we turn to those parts of Li's novels which seek to open up the world of the local magistracy and to describe its clerks and minor officials. The undoubted authenticity of Li's descriptions of officials and official life at this level would suggest that Li possessed personal and intimate knowledge of this milieu.

We may conclude, then, that the sources available to Li were the press, gossip concerning the highest circles of officialdom, and personal observation, and that he blended this raw material together as best he could in accordance with the aims he had set himself in his several novels. The question which is of greatest importance, however, is concerned not with sources but with the success or otherwise of his finished novels. To gauge this we must examine, first, the form of these novels and, second, how his novels measured up to the norms writers of this period had set forth as standards of achievement.

II *The Form of Li Po-yuan's Novels*

It is now fairly common knowledge that traditional Chinese fiction owes many of its features to the professional storyteller of the Sung dynasty (960–1279 A.D.). Depending on this "trade" for his living, the storyteller of those times had, first, to spread his tale over a number of sessions, and, second, to ensure that his audience would patronize him until it was completed. The outcome of these constraints on his art when his stories came to be written down was the creation of chapters of fairly regular length, which corresponded to the sessions, and the tendency to end a chapter, like the original storyteller, at a critical point in the story, drawing it to a close with some such formula as "If you wish to know what happened to . . . please read the next chapter."

Although Chinese novelists at the end of the nineteenth and the beginning of the twentieth centuries were becoming increasingly aware of the Western novel through the many translations which were appearing in both Japanese and Chinese, they tended, on the whole, to retain the structure of the traditional Chinese novel. The reasons for this are twofold. First, they wished to cater for a readership which, most likely, would have shunned books that were unfamiliar in appearance and style, and second, the traditional form of the novel was more suited to serialization in the press. Appearing, as most of these novels at first did, as serials in newspapers and magazines, regular length of text and stimuli to purchase succeeding episodes were important to the publishers for economic reasons.

In the traditional novel each chapter was usually prefaced with a brief summary of its contents. To heighten the reader's sense of anticipation these prefatory passages were usually rhythmic in structure and often cryptic in content. Li continued this practice in his novels, though in its most economical form. His summaries consist of no more than two parallel lines of either seven or eight characters in length. Each line tends to summarize an episode or subepisode, and the impression is therefore given of a chapter made up of two acts. In practice, however, these summaries can be regarded as no more than rough indications of the contents of a chapter, since an act thus summarized may be cut short midway and carried over into the succeeding chapter.

Since Li Po-yuan also adheres to the traditional practice of ending a chapter at a critical juncture in a story, it follows that his chapters cannot be taken as indicators of the beginning or ending of episodes. Some, we find, may be no more than a page in length, but others as many as several chapters.[4]

This adherence to tradition in the matter of structure must not, however, be allowed to obscure the fact that in the Chinese novel of the last decade of imperial rule a considerable revolution has taken place. Whereas traditional fiction had on the whole sought to weave stories around heroes of ancient times or to create highly fanciful accounts of the activities of supernatural beings, the novel of late Ch'ing times concerned itself with the society of its own day, emphasizing patriotism in the face of foreign encroachment; the need for probity in place of corruption; and constitutional reform, and the importance of accepting science and technology so that China might become a powerful and respected nation in the modern world.

We have already noted the special features of Li's two works *Ballad of the Rebellion of the Year Keng-tzu* and *Living Hell* in the chapters devoted to these creations, so we will concentrate here on his two major novels. In both *Modern Times* and *The Bureaucracy Exposed* the reader is presented, not with neat plots which run the length of the novels and in which the personalities of a small group of protagonists are explored through the interplay of their lives and by techniques now common to the European novel, but with something more akin to a medieval tapestry or a painting by Brueghel in which a location comes to life through the great variety of activities and incident depicted in every part of it.[5] It has been pointed out that in *The Bureaucracy Exposed* even the episode is sometimes denied a "consecutive narrative," and that "in many cases episodes interrupt each other so that as many as four plot lines are in progress at one time." [6]

If, then, the reader is presented with episodes—and even clusters of episodes—rather than with a sustained plot, it is clear that some other technique must be employed to provide these novels with a feeling of cohesion. At the superficial level this is achieved either through the employment of a single narrator or storyteller who, after bringing one episode to a close, may say that he must now turn the reader's attention to another location or another person, or by making one or two characters serve as links between one episode and the next. The most common examples of this latter technique are those in which a character is assigned to a new post in a different part of China and finds himself in a new milieu, having to cope with a fresh set of circumstances and with a new range of individuals. Having served their function as links, however, such characters are usually shunted to one side and ignored, attention being focused on the new story and the new cast. The novel with which *The Bureaucracy Exposed* has been most frequently compared, and which employs similar techniques to link its episodes, is *The Scholars*, composed about 150 years earlier.[7]

At a deeper level, of course, the unity of each novel is maintained through its underlying theme: reform and modernization; the venality of the men in government service; and, in the *Ballad* and *Living Hell*, the futility of the Boxer Uprising and the iniquities within the penal system. The question arises, however, as to whether there is a single element which binds all Li Po-yuan's novels into a unity? Whether there is a theme by which all the other themes are subsumed? The answer to this question must surely be yes. The fundamental theme which can be discerned in all Li's novels is: the restoration of China to the status of a genuinely independent, wealthy, and well-run nation.

III *Characters and Characterization*

The episodic nature of Li Po-yuan's novels and the consequent creation of clusters of minor plots subordinate to an overriding theme rather than a single sustained plot, means that they are peopled by a bewildering array of characters. Because of the themes of the novels the majority of these characters are drawn from the world of the bureaucracy. Interest is sustained, however, by ensuring that every level and every compartment of government is represented. Thus, in one episode the setting may be a local, county magistracy, and in the next the residence of a viceroy or even a grand councillor in Peking.

Important as the bureaucracy is as a source for Li's *dramatis personae*, it must be admitted that it is often those drawn from other spheres and other walks of life—the booksellers, the students, the gentry, the peasantry, and the foreigners—who give Li's novels the necessary variety and vitality without which they would cease to hold the reader's interest. It is undoubtedly true that the foreigner in Li's novels functions as a catalyst and that in *The Bureaucracy Exposed* he tends to remain external to the action he precipitates.[8] This is less true, however, of *Ballad of the Rebellion of the Year Keng-tzu* and *Modern Times*. In the *Ballad* the foreigner creates a crisis for the nation, but he is also an integral part of the story. It can be argued, of course, that since the *Ballad* purports to be an account of an historical event the author could hardly do otherwise than allow the foreigner to play out his proper role in it. In *Modern Times*, however, where Li was no longer under the same constraint to conform to events or to adhere to facts, the foreigner still occasionally serves a function beyond that of a mere catalyst. In chapters 6–14, for example, there is an intermittent episode in which a group of young students run foul of their local prefect and end up by being absorbed into the administration of the enlightened viceroy of Hupei and Hunan. Their release from the clutches of their prefect and their eventual arrival in Wuchang is engineered by a missionary whose part in the story is so vital, and the descriptions of whom are so interesting, that without him the narrative would lose much of its flavor. He is introduced as a man with an excellent knowledge of the Chinese language and a keen, if somewhat eccentric, interest in Chinese scholarship. He is a person with a profound dislike of Buddhism, yet is a kind man who comes to the aid of a young scholar when he is sick and in trouble. He is a man of principle who expresses indignation over the injustices people are forced to endure at the hands of officials. He behaves high-handedly, though with justification, in order to bring about the release of young students who have been wrongfully detained by the authorities. He persuades the students to broaden their horizons by furthering their studies in Shanghai, accompanies them on their journey as far as Wuchang, and encourages them when their spirits are low and some are tempted to return to their homes. A catalyst this character may be, but in this particular instance he participates fully in events and is integral to the story.

As is common in traditional Chinese fiction, devices akin to those employed in drama (to which fiction was, of course, closely related in its origins) are made use of to indicate to the reader the type of person he is reading about. The successful and the unsuccessful, the venal and the ambitious, the opium smoker and the self-styled reformist, etc., all tend to be described, when they are described, in language tailored to their roles. Names are frequently puns designed to sum up the character or appearance of a person, and dress, complexion, and family background are also used to apprise the reader of the natures of characters. It has to be admitted, however, that Li uses these devices sparingly. Even locations, with a few interesting exceptions, receive scant attention. Instead, the atmosphere of an episode and of each novel as a whole is conjured up through action and dialogue. Introspective passages which can do much to throw light on inner conflicts of conscience and problems of choice cannot be said to exist. The only approximations to such reflective narrative are the silent remark, usually prefaced with the words "He said to himself . . ." and an occasional comment by the narrator, who invariably dismisses his aside at the moment when the Western reader, at least, suspects him of being on the verge of saying something significant.[9]

The character of a protagonist, then, is generally conveyed by direct means: through external appearance (though descriptions tend to be brief and somewhat formalized), but chiefly through speech and action. For this type of presentation to be completely successful, the author must, of course, be able to assume that his readership shares the same experience of society and people as himself.

Economy of description, which in many instances actually amounts to no more than the provision of nomenclature, and the briefness of so many of the episodes in *Modern Times, The*

Bureaucracy Exposed, and *Living Hell,* means there is little opportunity for characters to develop, and, on those occasions when some development seems to be taking place—usually through the incorporation of a character in a fresh episode—the development is frequently erratic and even illogical. The attention of the reader is held through the variety of situations presented to him rather than through a developing fascination with a protagonist as a result of the gradual unfolding of his character. Having assumed that his readership shares his jaundiced view of the bureaucracy and that it has an equally cynical attitude to officialdom at work, all that is necessary is to recount, for the amusement of all, numerous and varied instances in which their faults and weaknesses result in ludicrous failure. It is as if Li Po-yuan is saying to his audience: "We all know what civil and military officials are like. Here are some anecdotes of what happens when they are let loose on the important issues of the day." Knowing what they are like there is little need for author and reader to dwell on them as persons; but the "issues of the day"—governmental reform, modernization, the penal system, the social evils of opium smoking and foot binding, etc., and international relations—are important and the concern of the nation as a whole. How these matters are handled is vital to China's future; but so far, the efforts of those responsible for them rarely deserve more than to be joked about.[10]

IV   *Final Assessment*

Lu Hsun in his assessment of *The Bureaucracy Exposed* (and we can assume that he felt much the same about Li's other novels), asserted that it consisted of nothing but gossip, and that whereas it resembled *The Scholars* structurally, it lacked that novel's refinement. Branding it a collection of casual records of real people by an author who cared little for facts, Lu Hsun held that its popularity was due to its timeliness rather than to any intrinsic artistic qualities.[11]

Agreeing substantially with Lu Hsun's judgments, Hu Shih states that it is a great misfortune in the history of literature when what promises to be a satirical novel ends up by being merely a piece of abusive writing. "The reader," says Hu, "sees only a pack of famished dogs barking their way in and out of the novel." There is not a single good official, or even good person, in the whole novel, he continues, and the author is so bent on vilification that he lacks any trace of compassion and sympathy. It is because the novel aims at spreading gossip rather than at the delineation of characters, he goes on, that hardly any of the persons have any individuality to speak of. Further, says Hu, there is little genuine satire, and Li Po-yuan therefore not only alienates his reader but fails to raise even a smile. Such writing, he concludes, represents literature at its worst. Hu attributes what he regards as Li's failure to the times in which he lived. The pressure of earning a living and the demands of a shallow society, he says, forced Li to sacrifice his art and to accommodate himself to the mood of the times. But the novel has, says Hu, one redeeming feature. It reflects an awakening on the part of Chinese to the evils and short-comings in Chinese life and society and a willingness to attribute China's political ills to corruption and weakness at home instead of simply putting the blame for all that was wrong on the shoulders of others.[12]

That Lu Hsun and Hu Shih should see little but unrelieved un-pleasantness in *The Bureaucracy Exposed* is not altogether surpris-ing given the purpose of this novel which, as we have seen, was to look squarely at the corruption prevalent in official circles and to lift the lid off the system. The commercialization of rank and office, which Li asserts over and over again amounted to nothing short of a kind of prostitution, was, in his view, poisoning the bureaucracy at its roots and destroying the character it was designed to have. Instead of being a servant of the people it had turned into a tyrant. Any humor in a novel such as this is bound to be bitter.

When we take all the novels under review into consideration, however, and judge his writings by the norms which the best and most influential writers of his time had established for themselves, and which appear to have been adopted by him, we must conclude that Li Po-yuan was successful. Fiction was popular among the masses, so it was held, because its appeal was to the emotions; and surely nothing appeals more to the emotions than gossip and rumor about people in the public eye. Fiction should aim to educate and inform the people of a nation, it was maintained; and Li's novels, in their treatment of themes of importance to the nation, as well as in the many smaller pieces of information which they incorporate, do just that.

Li's novels, we may conclude, fulfill the social role assigned to them, and must, in consequence, be judged successful on that score. But what of their literary merit? Can Li's novels be rated significant literature? No unqualified answer is possible since they are qualita-tively patently uneven. We have noted that their strength does not lie in characterization, although, and particularly when persons at the humbler levels of the social scale are being portrayed, there are passages in which types of person are cleverly sketched and their characters skillfully evoked.[13]

In what, then, does Li's artistry lie? It lies, we would suggest, in his unfolding of the setting—in the skill with which he evokes a "spirit of place," to borrow an expression used by Laurence Durrell. In our examination of *Modern Times* we made the point that the reader is like an eavesdropper who is privileged to listen in on the whole nation as it debates the issues which are of overriding importance to its existence. It is not so much the lives of individuals that are supremely important here but the life of China. "Character," says Donald Holoch writing of *The Bureaucracy Exposed*, "is subordinate to plot and the great number of plots serve to illustrate the specific social setting, late Ch'ing China."[14] Taken together, the conversations and actions of the characters in Li's novels reflect the attitude of self-criticism current in his day. Li's artistic achievement, however, rests in the fact that in his novels, and particularly in *Modern Times* and *The Bureaucracy Exposed*, he successfully captured the mood of his period and continues to convey it to the modern reader.

Notes and References

Chapter One

1. A number of monographs which elaborate on the origins and development of reform and modernization in nineteenth- and early twentieth-century China have appeared in recent years. The following are particularly worthy of mention: M. E. Cameron, *The Reform Movement in China, 1898–1912* (Stanford: Stanford University Press, 1931); M. C. Wright, *The Last Stand of Chinese Conservatism: The T'ung Chih Restoration, 1861–74* (Stanford: Stanford University Press, 1957); and A. Feuerwerker, *China's Early Industrialization* (Cambridge: Harvard University Press, 1958). Especially valuable, both as a survey of recent scholarship in this field and as a stimulus to further investigation into a great variety of aspects of this most important period in Chinese history, is the work *Reform in Nineteenth-Century China* ed. Paul A. Cohen and John E. Schrecker (Cambridge: Harvard University Press, 1976).

2. For details concerning the lives of these reformers see Cameron, passim, and appropriate biographies in A. W. Hummel, *Eminent Chinese of the Ch'ing Period*, 2 vols. (Washington, D.C.: U.S. Government Printing Office, 1943–1944), and H. L. Boorman and R. C. Howard, eds., *Biographical Dictionary of Republican China*, 4 vols. (New York: Columbia University Press, 1967–1971).

3. See, for example, Feuerwerker, pp. 2–8.

4. For a survey of the history of the Chinese press see R. S. Britton, *The Chinese Periodical Press, 1800–1912* (Shanghai: Kelly & Walsh, 1933); S. I. Woodbridge, "Newspapers, Chinese," in *Encyclopaedia Sinica*, ed. S. Couling (Shanghai: Kelly & Walsh, 1917), p. 297. Important Chinese works on the press are Ko Kung-chen, *Chung-kuo pao-hsueh shih* (Shanghai: Shang-wu yin-shu kuan, 1931); Chang Ching-lu, *Chung-kuo chin-tai ch'u-pan shih-liao* (Peking: Chung-hua shu-chu, 1957); and Chu Ch'uan-yü, *Chung-kuo min-i yü hsin-wen tzu-yu* (Taipei: Cheng-chung shu-chu, 1974).

5. For a biography of Wu T'ing-fang see Boorman, III, 453–56.

6. Ko Kung-chen, (1931 ed.), p. 76; Britton, pp. 39–40; and Hummel, p. 838. There appears to be some disagreement among these authorities concerning the facts. Britton (pp. 45–46) doubts whether Wu T'ing-fang could have had anything to do with the first newspaper.

7. Britton, pp. 41–47; and Hummel, pp. 836–39. See also H. McAleavy,

Wang T'ao—The Life and Writings of a Displaced Person (London: Chinese Society, 1953).

8. Britton, pp. 63–69.

9. Ibid., p. 51.

10. Couling, p. 397.

11. See especially Timothy C. Wong's study on satire in the *Ju-lin wai-shih* in his book *Wu Ching-tzu* (Boston: Twayne Publishers, 1978). See also Lu Hsun, *A Brief History of Chinese Fiction* (Peking: Foreign Languages Press, 1959), chap. 23, and Wu Ching-tzu, *The Scholars*, trans. Yang Hsien-yi and Gladys Yang (Peking: Foreign Languages Press, 1957), pp. 9–10.

12. It needs to be borne in mind that the Western type "short story" was not experimented with until the Literary Revolution of 1917. C. T. Hsia asserts in "Yen Fu and Liang Ch'i-ch'ao as advocates of New Fiction" (in *Chinese Approaches to Literature from Confucius to Liang Ch'i-ch'ao*, ed. A. A. Rickett [Princeton: Princeton University Press, 1978], p. 224) that "the short stories featured in late-Ch'ing fiction journals are of little or no interest. . . ."

13. Britton, p. 91; and Boorman, II, 347. The Chinese name of the Association was *Ch'iang-hsueh hui* which has been variously translated Society for the Study of National Strengthening, Strength Study Society, Society for the Study of National Rejuvenation, and Society for the Diffusion of Enlightenment. The concept of "self-strengthening" (*tzu-ch'iang*) originated some years earlier as certain Chinese officials came to realize that China had to adopt Western technology in order to strengthen her defenses. See William Ayres, *Chang Chih-tung and Educational Reform in China* (Cambridge: Harvard University Press, 1971), pp. 138, 98.

14. These details are taken from Ko Kung-chen, p. 170. The attitude of Chinese authority to the press is also described in Britton, pp. 102–10.

15. V. Purcell, *The Boxer Uprising* (Cambridge: Cambridge University Press, 1963), pp. 90–92; and Cameron, p. 29.

16. Purcell, p. 104.

17. For a detailed account of the "Hundred Days of Reform" see Cameron, pp. 23–25; but see also Sue Fawn Chung's article "The Image of the Empress Dowager Ts'u-Hsi," in *Reform in Nineteenth-Century China*, pp. 101–10, in which she questions commonly held views concerning Tz'u-hsi's attitude to reform.

18. Ko Kung-chen, p. 170, and Chu Ch'uan-yü, p. 104. See also Britton, pp. 105–8.

19. Chu Ch'uan-yü, p. 104.

20. Ko Kung-chen, p. 171.

21. Ibid., pp. 169–70.

22. A list of these publications is provided in Ko Kung-chen, p. 171. See also Chu Ch'uan-yü, p. 406. Tsou Jung's *The Revolutionary Army* has been translated into English under this title by John Lust (The Hague: Mouton, 1968).

23. Chu Ch'uan-yü, p. 407.

24. Ibid. See also Britton, p. 94.

25. For accounts of the case involving the *Su pao* see Britton, pp. 94, 113, 116; Chu Ch'uan-yü, pp. 407–8; Hummel, p. 769; and Boorman, I, 94.

26. Yen Fu and Hsia Sui-ch'ing (Tseng-yu)'s article is reproduced in *A Ying's Wan-Ch'ing wen-hsueh ts'ung-ch'ao—hsiao-shuo hsi-ch'u yen-chiu chuan* (Shanghai: Chung-hua shu-chu, 1960), pp. 1–13 (hereafter cited as *HHYC*), and has been summarized by Donald Holoch in "A Bourgeois View of the State: Li Po-yuan's Novel *The Bureaucrats*", (Ph.D. diss., Cornell University, 1975), p. 138. C. T. Hsia examines this and other articles related to the emergence of late Ch'ing fiction in his article in Rickett, pp. 221–57. See also Tsau Shu-ying, "The Emergence of Modern China in Fiction" (Ph.D. diss., University of Toronto, 1971), pp. 29–33. Other valuable surveys of the steps which led to the development of the "novel of enlightenment" in the first years of the twentieth century are to be found in Milena Doleželová-Velingerová's "The Origins of Modern Chinese Literature," pp. 30–33 and in Ching-mao Cheng's "The Impact of Japanese Literary Trends on Modern Chinese Writers," pp. 63–69, both in *Modern Chinese Literature in the May Fourth Era*, ed. Merle Goldman (Cambridge: Harvard University Press, 1977).

27. Holoch, p. 141.

28. Ibid., p. 142.

29. Quoted in ibid. pp. 138–39.

30. Holoch, p. 136; *HHYC*, pp. 13–14.

31. Holoch, pp. 135–36; *HHYC*, p. 13.

32. *HHYC*, p. 14. See also Rickett, pp. 222–23. I regret that C. T. Hsia's article came into my possession too late for me to make full use of it.

33. *HHYC*, pp. 14ff.

34. Pen name of the critic Wang Wu-sheng. See Rickett, p. 247, n.

35. A Ying, *Wan-Ch'ing hsiao-shuo shih*, rev. ed. (Hong Kong: T'ai-p'ing shu-chu, 1966), p. 3; hereafter cited as *WCHS*.

36. Holoch, pp. 137–38; *HHYC*, pp. 100–101; and Rickett, p. 247.

37. A case can be made out for regarding a magazine entitled *Hai-shang ch'i-shu* which was published in 1892 as the first magazine to be devoted to fiction. Liang's magazine, however, was the first really influential journal of its kind. See A Ying, *Wan-Ch'ing wen-i pao-k'an shu-lueh* (Shanghai: Ku-tien wen-hsueh ch'u-pan she, 1958), pp. 12–13.

38. *WCHS*, p. 2.

39. Holoch, p. 129.

40. *WCHS*, passim.

41. Ibid., p. 7.

42. Ibid.

43. The *All-Story Monthly* was the successor to Liang Ch'i-ch'ao's *Hsin hsiao-shuo* (*New Fiction*) and Li Po-yuan's *Hsiu-hsiang hsiao-shuo* (*Illustrated Stories*). It ran to twenty-four monthly issues.

44. Hu Shih, *Hu Shih wen-ts'un*, 4 vols. (Taipei: Yuan-tung t'u-shu kung-szu, 1953), III, 514–15. The title of the article, dated 12 October 1927, is "Kuan-ch'ang hsien-hsing chi hsü" ("Preface to *The Bureaucracy Exposed*"). See also pp. 7–8 of A Ying's preface to the 1935 edition of the novel *Keng-tzu kuo-pien t'an-tz'u*, (Shanghai: Liang-yu t'u-shu kung-szu, 1935); hereafter cited as *KTKP*.

45. Ibid., p. 514.

46. Ibid.

47. Ibid., pp. 514–15.

48. Ibid., p. 515.

49. A Ying, *Hsiao-shuo hsien-t'an*, rev. ed. (Shanghai, 1958) pp. 13–19.

Chapter Two

1. For a detailed examination of the causes of friction between Chinese and foreigners see Purcell, pp. 121–38. See also P. Fleming, *The Siege at Peking*, (London: Hart-Davis, 1959), chap. 3 passim.

2. Fleming, p. 37.

3. The Roman Catholic view of the Church's legal obligations to its Chinese members is summed up in Purcell, p. 137. The Protestant view, which reveals a disinclination to interfere in law suits involving Chinese Christians but which recognized the difficulty facing missionaries when they saw "their converts suffering from the grossest injustice . . ." appears in a "Statement of Protestant Missionary Societies" published in the *Times* (London) of 24 August 1900. It is quoted in part by Purcell, pp. 136–37.

4. Fleming, pp. 41–42.

5. Quoted in ibid.

6. Quoted in ibid., p. 43.

7. Ibid.

8. Ibid., p. 44.

9. Purcell points out that the leaders of both the late eighteenth- and late nineteenth-century Boxers bear the name Li Wen-ch'ing (p. 160). The name "Plum Blossom Fists" appears in a report to the throne made by Chang Ju-mei, governor of Shantung, in June 1898 (p. 198). It should also be noted that there was "a close connection between the White Lotus and the Boxers . . ." (p. 145).

10. For a detailed examination of this complex issue see Purcell, chaps. 9–10.

11. Fleming, p. 49.

12. The religious beliefs of the Boxers are outlined in Purcell, chap. 11; and Fleming, pp. 49–51.

13. Purcell, p. 119.

14. Ibid.

15. The events of the summer of 1900 are described in Purcell, chap. 12; and in Fleming, passim.

16. Purcell, pp. 255–56; Fleming, pp. 54, 55, 59.

17. Fleming, pp. 241–44.

18. The foregoing information is found in A Ying's preface to the 1935 edition of the *Ballad*.

19. *KTKP*, author's preface, pp. 1–2.

20. Despite discrepancies the foregoing account is clearly related to events reported by Governor Chang Ju-mei on 20 April 1898 and summarized in Purcell, pp. 191–92, and to the so-called P'ingyuan affair of 1899 described by Purcell, pp. 198–208.

21. Cf. ibid. chap. 11.

22. *KTKP*, p. 21.

23. As Purcell points out, gods worshipped by the Boxers were all drawn from popular novels (p. 225).

24. The leader of the Boxers in Tientsin.

25. The sentence beginning "What was ludicrous . . ." is meant, of course, to be a comment by the narrator on the silliness of taking seriously a sect which peoples its shrines with such a medley of deities.

26. *KTKP*, pp. 23–26.

27. For biographical information on Yü-lu see Hummel, p. 407.

28. *KTKP*, p. 27.

29. Cf. Purcell, pp. 165, 233, 235, 238.

30. The killing of the chancellor of the Japanese legation and the German minister are described in Purcell, pp. 250–52, and in Fleming, pp. 91–92, 106–9.

31. General Nieh Shih-ch'eng's military actions are referred to in Purcell, pp. 29, 248–50, 256, and in Fleming, pp. 75–76, 78. See also Hummel, p. 406.

32. *KTKP*, pp. 77–79. In a "dramatic" presentation of the events of the uprising based on published reports by George Lynch, H. K. Thomson, and Roland Allen, entitled *With the Allies in Peking*, G. A. Henty says that "The effect of the lyddite shells from the heavy guns had been terrible; indeed, the Chinese looked upon lyddite as a sort of death-dealing magic" (p. 264).

33. *KTKP*, pp. 99–100.

34. Ibid. pp. 101–7.

35. H. B. Morse, *The International Relations of the Chinese Empire*, 3 vols. (Shanghai: Kelly & Walsh, 1918), III, 243. For other accounts see A. Malozemoff, *Russian Far Eastern Policy 1881–1904* (Berkeley: University of California Press, 1958), pp. 138–39, and L. Deutsch, *Sixteen Years in Siberia* (London: John Murray, 1905), pp. 327–43.

36. Li probably considered that the Russians had the danger of Boxer attacks on the railway in mind. This would justify his inclusion of this episode.

37. There can be little doubt, of course, that whatever Li's personal views, the empress dowager had seized power and did, to all intents and purposes, hold the emperor prisoner. On the other hand, Sue Fawn Chung's views referred to in footnote 17 of the last chapter should also be borne in mind.

The fact that Li seems to be willing to involve the emperor in the business of selling rank and office in *The Bureaucracy Exposed* suggests that by about the year 1903 his faith in the monarchy had been eroded.

38. The following remarks are based on Cheng Chen-to's *Chung-kuo su wen-hsueh shih*, (Peking: Wen-hsueh ku-chi k'an-hsing she, 1959), pp. 348ff; but see also A Ying, *T'an-tz'u hsiao-shuo p'ing-k'ao*, (Shanghai: Chung-hua shu-chu, 1937).

Chapter Three

1. *Huo-ti-yü* (Shanghai: Wen-hua ch'u-pan she, 1956), pp. 1–3; hereafter cited as *HTY*.

2. This information is culled from Chao Ching-shen's preface to the 1956 edition of the novel. A Ying's argument that Mao-yuan Hsi-ch'iu Sheng is Ou-yang Chu-yuan is contained in his *Hsiao-shuo hsien-t'an* (Shanghai: Ku-tien wen-hsueh ch'u-pan she, 1958), pp. 20–23. Hu Shih had earlier taken the view that Mao-yuan Hsi-ch'iu Sheng was one of Li Po-yuan's pen names, see Hu Shih, p. 515.

3. Ibid., pp. 14–15.

4. Ibid., pp. 33–38.

5. Ibid., p. 56.

6. The episode in question is related to events described in the last chapter of *Modern Times* and is summed up in Tuan-fang's biography in Hummel, pp. 780–82.

7. *HTY*, pp. 206–9.

8. Ibid., preface, pp. 2–3.

9. Ibid.

10. Ibid., p. 3. The characters which make up Hsin Kuo-min are among the first in Liang Ch'i-ch'ao's article on the function of the novel in society where the word *hsin* is used to mean "to renew" and the words *kuo* and *min* mean "nation" and "people" respectively. See ibid., p. 16. There is little doubt that the author of this story had these words of the reformer in mind when he devised this name.

11. Ibid.

Chapter Four

1. *Wen-ming hsiao-shih* (Hong Kong: Chin-tai t'u-shu kung-szu, 1958), introduction, p. 2; hereafter cited as *WMHS*.

2. Ibid., pp. 67–74. The episode begins with the suspension of a public examination when news reaches the presiding prefect that an Italian mining engineer has reacted angrily to the breaking of a teacup by an innkeeper! A

man with good intentions, but indecisive, the prefect fails to maintain order among angry students and the populace and is replaced by Prefect Fu. Cyril Birch has summarized this episode and commented on Li Po-yuan's portrayal of Prefect Fu in "Change and Continuity in Chinese Fiction" in Merle Goldman, pp. 386–90.

3. *WMHS*, p. 70.

4. Ibid., p. 72.

5. Ibid., pp. 73–74.

6. I am indebted to Professor Cyril Birch for drawing my attention to the fact that recent editions of this novel have had this speech removed from the text. The speech is based, almost verbatim, on one made in chap. 11 of Liu E's *The Travels of Lao Ts'an*.

7. *WMHS*, p. 2.

8. Ibid., pp. 148–49. *La Dame aux Camelias* was translated into Chinese by the famous translator Lin Shu in 1897. It gained great popularity among the young as instanced here and elsewhere in this novel.

9. Ibid., pp. 271–72.

10. Ibid., pp. 273–74.

11. Ibid., pp. 274–75.

12. Ibid., p. 186.

13. Ibid., p. 194.

14. Ibid., p. 193.

15. Chu Hsi's dates are 1130–1200 A.D. He was one of the leading early exponents of neo-Confucianism. Wing-tsit Chan has published a translation of *Reflections on Things at Hand* under this title (New York: Columbia University Press, 1967).

16. *WMHS*, p. 204.

17. 1850–1864.

18. *WMHS*, pp. 103–4.

19. Ibid., pp. 119–20.

20. Ibid., pp. 120–21.

21. Ibid., pp. 126–27.

22. Ibid., pp. 311, 312.

23. Ibid., p. 158.

24. Ibid.

25. Ibid., p. 339.

26. Ibid., p. 384.

27. Hummel, pp. 780–82.

28. Cf. the final story in *Living Hell*.

29. See Boorman, III, 416–19.

30. Ibid., pp. 195–99.

31. See chap. 1, n. 5.

32. Hummel, pp. 749–51.

33. Ibid., pp. 523–24.

34. Ibid., pp. 60–63.

Chapter Five

1. C. T. Hsia translates *ch'ien-tse* as "castigatory"; see "The Travels of Lao Ts'an: An Exploration of Its Art and Meaning," *Tsing Hua Journal of Chinese Studies*, n.s. 7, no. 2 (August 1969), 40–66.

2. According to Hu Shih in his "Preface to *The Bureaucracy Exposed*," pp. 514–5, Mao-yuan Hsi-ch'iu Sheng wrote a preface for the book in 1903 when only three sections had been completed. Hu maintains that one further section was completed in the two years 1904–1905 and that since Li Po-yuan died early in 1906 the last section (i.e., most if not all of the last twelve chapters) was probably completed by a friend. A Ying states (*WCHS*, p. 129) that Li completed three sections in the years 1902–1904 and that in the following two years he wrote two further sections, but died before the book reached its final form. A friend, he says, completed the fifth section and it was published by the Fan-hua Publishing Company with a preface by Mao-yuan Hsi-ch'iu Sheng. However, Chao T'iao-k'uang in his "Kuan-ch'ang hsien-hsing chi k'ao" ("A Study of *The Bureaucracy Exposed*") which appears on pp. 3–9 of the Taipei edition of the novel argues that the whole novel, as we have it, was completed by Li. He states that Li may have planned a 120 chapter novel, but that having written sixty chapters he probably felt he had said all he could say and cleverly rounded the novel off with the dream. A Ying (*WCHS*, p. 129) asserts that the novel was pirated and issued in Japan in 1903 by the Nippon Chishinsha as the work of a Japanese writer called Yoshida Tarō.

3. *Kuan-ch'ang hsien-hsing chi* (Peking: Jen-min wen-hsueh ch'u-pan she, 1957), p. 1050; (Taipei: Wen-yuan shu-chu, 1977), p. 892; hereafter cited as *KCHC*.

4. See n. 2.

5. See chap. 3, n. 1.

6. *KCHC*, Taipei ed., p. 12.

7. Purcell, pp. 3–4. Purcell provides an excellent summary of the nature and structure of Chinese imperial government in chapter 1 of his book. For works providing more detailed information see Bibliography.

8. Purcell, p. 5.

9. Ibid., pp. 5–6.

10. Ibid., pp. 6–7.

11. Ibid., pp. 13–14.

12. Ibid., pp. 14–15.

13. Ibid.

14. W. F. Mayers, *The Chinese Government* (Shanghai: Kelly & Walsh, 1897; reprint ed., Taipei: Ch'eng-wen, 1966), p. 40.

15. Ibid.

16. Ibid.

17. Holoch, pp. 35–36.

18. Ibid., p. 39.

19. *KCHC*, Peking ed., 305–6; Taipei ed., p. 256.

20. *KCHC*, Peking ed., pp. 307–8; Taipei ed., p. 258.

21. *KCHC*, Peking ed., pp. 727–28; Taipei ed., pp. 613–14.

22. *KCHC*, Peking ed., p. 735; Taipei ed., p. 620.

23. *KCHC*, Peking ed., p. 736; Taipei ed., p. 621.

24. *KCHC*, Peking ed., p. 738; Taipei ed., pp. 622–23.

25. *KCHC*, Peking ed., pp. 738–39; Taipei ed., p. 623.

26. *KCHC*, Peking ed., p. 739; Taipei ed., pp. 623–24.

27. *KCHC*, Peking ed., pp. 741–43; Taipei ed., pp. 725–27.

28. *KCHC*, Peking ed., pp. 1049–50; Taipei ed., p. 892.

29. Holoch offers somewhat different interpretations of the last three parts of the dream. The Western elements in part 2 he sees as signifying "an indeterminate foreign influence on the state" and the placing of the building on a highway similar to those found in Shanghai rather than Peking as indicating that Shanghai is "*the* center of such influence." Because he seems to regard the events of the dream as taking place at about the time of writing Holoch believes that the empress dowager is being satirized in the third part of the dream in which we have the "divine plan." The term "Shangti" ("Lord-on-High"), he thinks, refers to her. He also believes, however, that since Protestant missionaries had adopted this term for "God," that its use here is also meant to emphasize the presence of foreign influences. Holoch suggests that the author of the final chapter of the novel wished to draw attention to the bankruptcy of reformist policy. He therefore states toward the end of his analysis of the dream that "The view that there can be no reformist conclusion to this exposé of officials is flaunted: the spectacular fire has no apparent cause and leaves no trace, it simply eliminates the second reformist half of the book produced in response to the divine proposal. . . . In brief, the fourth section of the dream sets up a straw man, the possibility that the book might aid reform, and then mocks such a view of the book as well as the very idea of reform." For the whole of Holoch's argument see Holoch, pp. 199–201. The optimistic note on which the dream sequence ends would seem to be justified if Tsau Shu-ying is right when she asserts that the empress dowager read this novel and, in consequence, had a number of senior officials punished (ibid., p. 99).

30. Chou I-po, "Kuan-ch'ang hsien-hsing chi so-yin," *Wen-shih tsa-chih*, 6, no. 2 (May 1948), 56–63.

Chapter Six

1. Wu Wo-yao, *Vignettes from the Late Ch'ing*, trans. Shih Shun Liu (Hong Kong: Chinese University of Hong Kong, 1975), pp. 8–9.

2. *WMHS*, pp. 372–75.

3. Hu Shih, pp. 519–20.

4. Holoch, pp. 150–52.

5. An even more appropriate comparison would be with the traditional long Chinese handscroll depicting city life or life at Court.

6. Holoch, p. 152.

7. See chap. 1, n. 11.

8. Holoch, p. 158.

9. Ibid., p. 161.

10. In that part (pp. 386–90) of his article "Change and Continuity in Chinese Fiction" in which he examines the Prefect Fu episode, Cyril Birch points out that Prefect Fu is a caricature of a bureaucrat, and that the man he followed, though honest and humane, is depicted as "indecisive and incompetent."

11. Lu Hsun, pp. 373–75.

12. Hu Shih, pp. 526–28.

13. See Cyril Birch, pp. 388–89, for a description of the manner in which Prefect Fu and his colleagues are depicted and of the way the author's narrative technique contributes to character portrayal. It needs to be borne in mind, however, that some of the looseness of structure and ambiguities in the narrative may well be due to the circumstances in which the author wrote rather than to any design on his part. It would seem that Li never found time to correct and improve his texts before publication, a fact which Chinese critics all claim to have lowered the quality of his writing.

14. Holoch, p. 174. Cyril Birch, p. 388, speaks of a lack of any "consistent center of vision" and of a "shifting focus" when commenting on the narrative technique used in *A Brief History of Enlightenment (Modern Times)*. This is certainly true if we consider only the multitude of characters and events in the novel and the manner in which they are paraded before the reader. As he proceeds through this and Li's other major novel, *The Bureaucracy Exposed*, however, the reader is made increasingly conscious of the backcloth to the personages and events brought before his eyes, namely, China in a state of transition. It is this on which the author is seeking to focus the reader's attention.

Selected Bibliography

PRIMARY SOURCES

Regretably it has not been possible to locate and read all the works attributed at one time or another to Li Po-yuan. In part 2, therefore, I cite only those of which I have been able to make use.

In part 1 works attributed to Li Po-yuan are cited, with dates of publication where available.

1. Attributed works

A. Full-length novels
Keng-Tzu kuo-pien t'an-tz'u (*Ballad of the Rebellion of the Year Keng-tzu*) 44 chapters. 1901–1902.
Kuan-ch'ang hsien-hsing chi (*The Bureaucracy Exposed*) 60 chapters. 1901–1906.
Hai-t'ien hung-hsueh chi (*Boundless Snow*) 30 chapters. 1903–1904.
Wen-ming hsiao-shih (*A Brief History of Enlightenment or Modern Times*) 60 chapters. 1903–1905.
Huo ti-yü (*Living Hell*) 43 chapters. 1903–1906.
Ping-shan hsueh-hai (*Icy Wastes*). Translator and compilor. 12 chapters. 1906.
Chung-kuo hsien-tsai-chi (*China Today*).
Li Lien-ying.
Fan-hua meng (*Extravagant Dreams*).
Hsing-shih yuan t'an-tz'u (*A Call to Wakefulness*).

B. Collections of short comments
I-yuan ts'ung-hua (*Comments on the Arts*).
Hua-chi ts'ung-hua (*Humorous Comments*).
Ch'en-hai miao-p'in (*Masterpieces of the World*).
Ch'i-shu K'uai-tu (*Glimpses of Unusual Writings*).

C. Jottings
Nan-t'ing pi-chi (*Jottings from the Southern Pavilion*) 16 *chuan*.
Nan-t'ing ssu-hua (*Four Kinds of Comment from the Southern Pavilion*) 10 *chuan*.

D. Miscellaneous

Yü-hsiang yin-p'u (*A Treatise on Seals*). The foregoing has been drawn up by Lin Jui-ming in his "Wan-Ch'ing ch'ien-tse hsiao-shuo te li-shih i-i" ("The Historical Significance of the Late Ch'ing Novel of Reproof") (M.A. thesis, Taiwan University, 1976). Lin states in a footnote (pp. 114–15) that he has based his information on Wei Ju-hui's "Ch'ing-mo ssu ta hsiao-shuo-chia" ("Four Great Writers of Late Ch'ing Times"), *Hsiao-shuo yueh-pao* (*The Story Monthly*), 1 October 1941, Anniversary Issue, and on information contained in an edition of the *Kuan-ch'ang hsien-hsing chi* (Taipei: Shih-chieh shu-chu, 1974) (see "The Biography of Li Pao-chia," p. 8). Lin further provides a list (pp. 109–11) of twenty-seven novels published between 1905 and 1911 which emulate Li Po-yuan's *The Bureaucracy Exposed* in form and style.

2. Works published under the name Li Pao-chia or one of Li's known pseudonyms.

Huo ti-yü (*Living Hell*). Shanghai: Wen-hua ch'u-pan she, 1956.

Keng-tzu kuo-pien t'an-tz'u (*Ballad of the Rebellion of the Year Keng Tzu*). Shanghai: Liang-yu t'u-shu kung-szu, 1935.

Kuan-ch'ang hsien-hsing chi (*The Bureaucracy Exposed*). 2 vols. Peking: Jen-min wen-hsueh ch'u-pan she, 1957.

Kuan-ch'ang hsien-hsing chi. Taipei: Wen-yuan shu-chu, 1977.

Nan-t'ing ssu-hua (*Four Kinds of Comment from the Southern Pavilion*). Taipei: Kuang-wen shu-chu, 1971.

Wen-ming hsiao-shih (*A Brief History of Enlightenment or Modern Times*). Hong Kong: Chin-tai t'u-shu kung-szu, 1958.

Hsiu-hsiang hsiao-shuo (*Illustrated Stories*). 72 issues. Editor. Shanghai: Shang-wu yin-shu-kuan (Commercial Press), 1903–1906.

SECONDARY SOURCES

AYRES, WILLIAM. *Chang Chih-tung and Educational Reform in China*. Cambridge: Harvard University Press, 1971.

A YING. *Hsiao-shuo hsien-t'an* (*Chats on Literature*). Shanghai: Ku-tien wen-hsueh ch'u-pan she, 1958.

————. *T'an-tz'u hsiao-shuo p'ing-k'ao* (*An Examination of Fiction in Ballad Form*). Shanghai: Chung-hua shu-chu, 1937.

————. *Wan-Ch'ing hsiao-shuo shih* (*History of Late Ch'ing Fiction*). rev. ed. Hong Kong: T'ai-p'ing shu-chu, 1966.

————. *Wan-Ch'ing wen-hsueh ts'ung-ch'ao: hsiao-shuo hsi-ch'u yen-chiu chuan* (*Material Related to Research into Late Ch'ing Fiction and Drama*). Shanghai: Chung-hua shu-chu, 1960.

————. *Wan-Ch'ing wen-i pao-k'an shu-lueh* (*An Account of Late Ch'ing*

Periodicals Devoted to Literature). Shanghai: Ku-tien wen-hsueh ch'u-pan she, 1958.

BETTIN, WERNER. "Die Darstellung der Gentry in Li Boyuans Roman 'Die Beamten.'" *Wissenschaftliche Zeitschrift der Humboldt-Universität zu Berlin*, 40 (1962), 425–28.

BIRCH, CYRIL. "Change and Continuity in Chinese Fiction." In *Modern Chinese Literature in the May Fourth Era*, edited by Merle Goldman, pp. 385–404. Cambridge: Harvard University Press, 1977.

BRITTON, ROSSWELL S. *The Chinese Periodical Press, 1800–1912*. Shanghai: Kelly & Walsh, 1933.

BOORMAN, H. L., and HOWARD, R. C. eds. *Biographical Dictionary of Republican China*. 4 vols. New York: Columbia University Press, 1967–1971.

CAMERON, MERIBETH E. *The Reform Movement in China, 1898–1912*. Stanford: Stanford University Press, 1931.

CHANG CHING-LU. *Chung-kuo chin-tai ch'u-pan shih-liao* (*Material Related to the History of Modern Publishing in China*). Shanghai: Chung-hua shu-chu, 1957.

CHENG CHEN-TO. *Chung-kuo su wen-hsueh shih* (*History of Folk Literature in China*). Peking: Wen-hsueh ku-chi k'an-hsing she, 1959.

CHOU I-PO. "Kuan-ch'ang hsien-hsing chi so-yin" ("An Explication of *The Bureaucracy Exposed*"). *Wen-shih tsa-chih* (*History and Literature*), 6, no. 2 (May 1948), 56–63.

CHU CH'UAN-YÜ. *Chung-kuo min-i yü hsin-wen tzu-yu* (*Popular Opinion in China and the Freedom of the Press*). Taipei: Cheng-chung shu-chu, 1974.

CHU HSI. *Reflections on Things at Hand*. Translated by Wing-tsit Chan. New York: Columbia University Press, 1967.

COHEN, PAUL A., and SCHRECKER, JOHN E., eds. *Reform in Nineteenth-Century China*. Cambridge: Harvard University Press, 1976.

COULING, SAMUEL, ed. *Encyclopaedia Sinica*. Shanghai: Kelly & Walsh, 1917.

DEUTSCH, L. *Sixteen Years in Siberia*. London: John Murray, 1905.

FEUERWERKER, ALBERT. *China's Early Industrialization*. Cambridge: Harvard University Press, 1958.

FLEMING, PETER. *The Siege at Peking*. London: Hart-Davis, 1959.

FRANKE, WOLFGANG. *The Reform and Abolition of the Traditional Examination System*. Cambridge: Harvard University Press, 1960.

GOLDMAN, MERLE, ed. *Modern Chinese Literature in the May Fourth Era*. Cambridge: Harvard University Press, 1977.

HAO YEN-P'ING. *The Comprador in Nineteenth Century China*. Cambridge: Harvard University Press, 1970.

HO P'ING-TI. *The Ladder of Success in Imperial China: Aspects of Social Mobility, 1368–1911*. New York: Columbia University Press, 1962.

HOLOCH, DONALD. "A Bourgeois View of the State: Li Poyuan's Novel *The Bureaucrats.*" Ph.D. dissertation, Cornell University, 1975.

HOWARD, RICHARD C. "K'ang Yu-wei (1858–1927): His Intellectual Background and Early Thought." In *Confucian Personalities*, edited by A. Wright and D. Twitchett, pp. 294–316. Stanford: Stanford University Press, 1962.

HSIA, C. T. *The Classic Chinese Novel*. New York: Columbia University Press, 1968.

————. "The Travels of Lao Ts'an: An Exploration of its Art and Meaning." *Tsing Hua Journal of Chinese Studies*, n.s. 7, no. 2 (August 1969), 40–66.

————. "Yen Fu and Liang Ch'i-ch'ao as advocates of New Fiction." In *Chinese Approaches to Literature from Confucius to Liang Ch'i-ch'ao*, edited by A. A. Rickett, pp. 221–57. Princeton: Princeton University Press, 1978.

HSIAO KUNG-CHUAN. *Rural China: Imperial Control in the Nineteenth Century*. Seattle: University of Washington Press, 1960.

HSIEH PAO-CHAO. *The Government of China (1644–1911)*. Baltimore: Johns Hopkins Press, 1925.

HU SHIH. *Hu Shih wen-ts'un (The Collected Writings of Hu Shih)*. 4 vols. Taipei: Yuan-tung t'u-shu kung-szu, 1953.

HUMMEL, ARTHUR W., ed. *Eminent Chinese of the Ch'ing Period (1644–1912)*. 2 vols. Washington, D.C.: U.S. Government Printing Office, 1943–1944.

KING, FRANK H. H. *Money and Monetary Policy in China 1845–1895*. Cambridge: Harvard University Press, 1965.

KO KUNG-CHEN. *Chung-kuo pao-hsüeh shih (History of Chinese Journalism)*. Shanghai: Shang-wu yin-shu kuan, 1931.

KRACKE, E. A., JR. "Region, Family and Individual in the Chinese Examination System." In *Chinese Thought and Institutions*, edited by J. K. Fairbank, 251–58. Chicago; University of Chicago Press, 1957.

KU CHIEH-KANG. "Kuan-ch'ang hsien-hsing chi chih tso-che" ("The Author of *The Bureaucracy Exposed*"). *Hsiao-shuo yueh-pao (The Story Monthly)*, 15, no. 6 (June 1924), 14.

LEVENSON, JOSEPH. *Liang Ch'i-ch'ao and the Mind of Modern China*. Cambridge: Harvard University Press, 1953.

LEWIS, CHARLTON M. "The Reform Movement in Hunan (1896–1898)." In *Papers on China*, vol. 15. Cambridge: Harvard University Press, 1961.

LI PAO-CHIA. "Modern Times" (chapters 1–5). Translated by D. Lancashire. *Renditions*, 2 (Spring 1974), 126–64.

LIANG CH'I-CH'AO. "I-yin cheng-chih hsiao-shuo hsu" ("On the Translation and Printing of Political Novels"). In *Wan-Ch'ing wen-hsueh ts'ung-ch'ao: hsiao-shuo hsi-ch'u yen-chiu chuan*, edited by A Ying, pp. 13–14. Shanghai: Chung-hua shu-chu, 1960.

———. "Lun hsiao-shuo yü ch'un-chih chih kuan-hsi" ("Fiction and the Government of the Masses"). In *Wan-Ch'ing wen-hsueh ts'ung-ch'ao: hsiao-shuo hsi-ch'u yen-chiu chuan,* edited by A Ying, pp. 14–19.

LIN JUI-MING. "Wan-Ch'ing ch'ien-tse hsiao-shuo te li-shih i-i" ("The Historical Significance of the Late-Ch'ing Novel of Reproof"). M.A. thesis, Taiwan University, 1976.

LIU E. *The Travels of Lao Ts'an.* Translated by Harold Shadick. Ithaca: Cornell University Press, 1952.

LU HSUN. *A Brief History of Chinese Fiction.* Translated by Yang Hsien-yi and Gladys Yang. 2d ed. Peking: Foreign Languages Press, 1964. The Chinese version of this work is entitled *Chung-kuo hsiao-shuo shih-lueh* (revised ed., 1930).

LU YAO. "Lun Kuan-ch'ang hsien-hsing chi te ssu-hsiang-hsing" ("Discussion on the Thought behind *The Bureaucracy Exposed"*). *Wen-shih-che (Literature, History and Philosophy),* 8 (August 1958), 38–47.

MALOZEMOFF, A. *Russian Far Eastern Policy, 1881–1904.* Berkeley: University of California Press, 1958.

MAYERS, W. F. *The Chinese Government, A Manual of Chinese Titles, Categorically Arranged and Explained.* 3d ed. Revised by G. M. H. Playfair. Shanghai: Kelly & Walsh, 1897; reprint ed., Taipei: Ch'eng-wen, 1966.

MCALEAVY, HENRY. *Wang T'ao—The Life and Writings of a Displaced Person.* London: Chinese Society, 1953.

MORSE, H. B. *The International Relations of the Chinese Empire.* 3 vols. Shanghai: Kelly & Walsh, 1918.

PRŮŠEK, JAROSLAV. *Chinese History and Literature.* Dordrecht: Reidel, 1970.

PURCELL, VICTOR. *The Boxer Uprising, A Background Study.* Cambridge: Cambridge University Press, 1963; reprint ed., Hamden, Connecticut, Archon Books, 1974.

RANKIN, MARY B. *Early Chinese Revolutionaries: Radical Intellectuals in Shanghai and Chekiang 1902–1911.* Cambridge: Harvard University Press, 1971.

RICKETT, ADELE A., ed. *Chinese Approaches to Literature from Confucius to Liang Ch'i-ch'ao.* Princeton: Princeton University Press, 1978.

RUH, CHRISTEL. *Das Kuan-ch'ang Hsien-hsing Chi—Ein Beispiel für den 'Politischen Roman' der ausgehenden Ch'ing-Zeit.* Bern: H&P Lang, 1974.

SCHRECKER, JOHN E. *Imperialism and Chinese Nationalism: Germany in Shantung.* Cambridge: Harvard University Press, 1971.

SCHWARTZ, BENJAMIN. *In Search of Wealth and Power: Yen Fu and the West.* Cambridge: Harvard University Press, 1971.

SMITH, ARTHUR H. *China in Convulsion.* 2 vols. New York: F. H. Revell, 1901.

STANLEY, JOHN C. *Late Ch'ing Finance: Hu Kuang-yung as an Innovator*. Cambridge: Harvard University Press, 1961.

TAN, CHESTER C. *The Boxer Catastrophe*. New York: Columbia University Press, 1955.

TARUMOTO, TERUO. "Shūzō shōsetsu sō mokuroku" ("Index to *Illustrated Stories*"). *Ōsaka keidai ronshū*, 93 (May 1973), 75–131.

————. "Getsu getsu shōsetsu sō mokuroku" ("Index to *The All-Story Monthly*"). Part 1. *Ōsaka keidai ronshū*, 100 (July 1974), 181–202.

————. "Getsu getsu shōsetsu sō mokuroku" ("Index to *The All-Story Monthly*"). Part 2. *Ōsaka keidai ronshū*, 105 (May 1975), 133–61.

TSAU SHU-YING. "The Emergence of Modern China in Fiction," Ph.D. dissertation, University of Toronto, 1971.

TSOU JUNG. *The Revolutionary Army*. Translated by John Lust. The Hague: Mouton, 1968.

WONG, TIMOTHY C. *Wu Ching-tzu*. Boston: Twayne Publishers, 1978.

WRIGHT, A., and TWITCHETT, D., eds. *Confucian Personalities*. Stanford: Stanford University Press, 1962.

WRIGHT, MARY C. *The Last Stand of Chinese Conservatism: The T'ung Chih Restoration, 1861–74*. Stanford: Stanford University Press, 1957.

WU CHING-TZU. *The Scholars*. Translated by Yang Hsien-yi and Gladys Yang. Peking: Foreign Languages Press, 1957.

WU WO-YAO. *Vignettes from the Late Ch'ing: Bizarre happenings eyewitnessed over two decades*. Translated by Shih Shun Liu. Hong Kong: Chinese University of Hong Kong and St. John's University Press, 1975.

————, ed. *Yueh-yueh hsiao-shuo (The All-Story Monthly)*. 24 issues. Shanghai: Ch'un-hsueh she, 1906–1908.

YEN FU, and HSIA TSENG-YU. "Kuo-wen pao fu-yin shuo-pu yuan-ch'i" ("Our Reasons for Printing Fiction"). In *Wan-Ch'ing wen-hsueh ts'ung-ch'ao: hsiao-shuo hsi-ch'u yen-chiu chuan*, edited by A Ying, pp. 1–13. Shanghai: Chung-hua shu-chu, 1960.

Index